Brother Blood and

The Appalachian Trail:

Thru- and Through

By Alec Kohut

For all the wonderful people who were part of my journey

...and of course, Lois

## Table of Contents

Figure 1 - The Appalachian Trail was completed in 1937 and starts at Springer Mt. Georgia, ending at Mt. Katahdin, Maine. In 2016 its total distance was 2,189.1 miles.

The bottle of Pinot Noir didn't stand a chance. We destroyed it, then headed to the train's Cafe Car for more. There, I bought the first half bottle of Chardonnay, and as the wine flowed, we shared our excitement about the journey we were about to embark on as we rode the midnight train to Georgia, and the Southern Terminus of the Appalachian Trail. Before taking our first step to Maine, we already felt like Thru-Hikers.

I first saw Taylor when my wife and I were waiting at the Amtrak gate; as I boarded, Taylor was hoisting her pack next to mine on the luggage rack and confirmed that she too was thru-hiking. As the train started south, I sat alone realizing that this was it - I was really heading to Georgia to begin my journey thru-hiking north to Katahdin. I had bought a pasta dinner at Sbarro's and a bottle of Pinot Noir before leaving Union Station in DC to enjoy on the train.

Returning from the Cafe Car with two plastic glasses, I stopped where Taylor was seated and said, "I brought a bottle of wine, would you like a glass?" Her eyes lit up, "I love wine! I'd love a glass." I retrieved the bottle, we sat down, made our introductions, and let the wine flow. Before long, we were in the Club Car sharing our story with fellow passengers, that we'd be putting backpacks on in Georgia, and hiking to Maine.

We were set to arrive in Gainesville, Georgia at 6:58 a.m., where my friends, "The Lawyers" Silver Fox and Maverick, along with Maverick's sister Sheryl, who were hiking the first four days with me, would be waiting. We planned to stop for breakfast, then on to Amicalola State Park, where the 8.8-mile Approach Trail to the Appalachian Trail begins. Taylor had no ride, so I texted Silver Fox, who was driving, and asked if we had room for "a young lady hiker," to join us the next morning to Amicalola. To my surprise, I received a text back, "sadly no. I really wish we could. We have a small hatchback and we may have one of our backpacks on our laps."

Unacceptable. Taylor and I went to work devising a plan. Using both shame and sympathy. I would guilt them as hikers to find room for her in the car; while she would employ her sad, stranded, young hiker face. With our plan in place, and both feeling the effect of the wine, Taylor quickly fell asleep, I did not. Maybe it was the excitement of the journey, maybe I was unable to get comfortable in the seat, probably both. I did manage to nod off briefly, but woke up almost immediately, and by the time we were within an hour of our arrival, I figured I had slept only 30 minutes.

We got off the train in Gainesville. The Lawyers and Sheryl were already there. My fears that Taylor would be left to find her own ride melted away, as she was greeted with hugs, before we all jammed into Silver Fox's electric Lexus hatchback and headed off to breakfast.

Our first stop in the state of Georgia seemed harmless enough, a breakfast spot named the Long Street Café. A café located on Long St., I thought. But no, this was the "Longstreet" Café named after Confederate General James Longstreet. So, with 30 minutes of sleep, I sat drinking coffee from a Styrofoam cup with the Southern General's stern face welcoming me to Georgia. I turned the cup to escape the general's stare, only to be greeted on the other side by the Ten Commandments.

Quite the Southern welcome for this Yankee Atheist.

*Figure 2 - Amicalola State Park, the start of the Approach Trail. From left to right: Taylor "Mama Bear," Brother Blood, Maverick, Sheryl, and Silver Fox.*

## CHAPTER 1: IT'S REALLY HAPPENING

I'd been planning my hike since May 2015, the 19th to be exact. That evening, while sitting on our deck enjoying a glass of wine, my wife tearfully agreed to support my dream of thru-hiking the Appalachian Trail (A.T.). We had gone back and forth about it, until her close friend Donna convinced her not to stand in the way of this dream of mine.

It also helped when I explained that we would spend a fair amount of time together as I hiked through Virginia, Maryland, and Pennsylvania. She had originally believed that seeing me on the trail would consist of giving me some resupply, hanging out for a few minutes, then watching me disappear back in the woods. And through the wonders of technology and the cell phone, I'd be able to talk to her almost every day.

Explaining why I wanted to leave for six months and walk from Georgia to Maine wasn't easy. Popular culture celebrates stories of people turning their lives around on the A.T. and "finding themselves." My story is not as glamorous. I wanted to thru-hike to *live* in the woods, not just visit for a week or two. To immerse myself in trail culture, leaving the Rat Race for a journey with the singular purpose of simply living.

Backpacking had changed my life in many ways before embarking on this journey. I had reconnected with nature, and found a certain solace in the woods that made everyday life more tolerable. In a way, the journey was not to change myself, but celebrate the changes I had made in myself.

After two years of "section hiking" small stretches of the A.T., and working at REI, an outdoor store for over a year, I had all the gear I needed. A lot of my planning would be just waiting. It wasn't until the calendar hit 2016 that I started really preparing. Most of the work went into food: marinating and dehydrating homemade beef jerky, and cooking then dehydrating homemade dinners of red beans and rice, Cajun pasta with shrimp and sausage, jambalaya, and chili.

I had joined The Lawyers for a week hiking part of the A.T. in Pennsylvania and took some hikes in Shenandoah National Park, but I mostly just waited for my departure date of March 28th. As it approached I attempted to get into decent shape. I started running, but my right knee began hurting, so jogging was out. I wasn't about to push myself to injury while training for the hike. I did some day hiking with my full pack on, but it was on mostly flat ground, nothing like the Appalachian Trail.

My friend, "Maps," who thru-hiked in 2013, gave me three pieces of advice as my start date neared: 1) don't worry about getting in shape, you'll hike yourself into shape on the trail; 2) don't have a schedule or a plan, just hike; and 3) when you're tired take a day off; don't push it - Katahdin will still be there when you get to Maine. So on Easter Sunday, out of shape, and with no schedule or plan, I boarded that midnight train to Georgia.

### 

I am not a morning person, but the young lady at Amicalola Falls State Park certainly was. She was signing in hikers and giving us the standard "leave-no-trace" advice. I approached to sign in, introducing myself with an outstretch hand to shake. She immediately pulled her hand away and in a bubbly voice exclaimed, "No, no, no, this is how we do it on the A.T.," and gave me a fist bump. Wonderful. It's 7:30 a.m., I've had a half hour of sleep, and now a lady half my age refuses to shake my hand, telling me I'm doing it all wrong.

In her defense, she refused to buy into the *culture of fear*, the idea that A.T. is filled with danger, and noroviruses, and Lyme Disease, and bad people around every corner. She did caution us about the risk of norovirus, but added that she knew of very few cases and we shouldn't be that concerned.

Amicalola Falls State Park is 8.8 miles from the first 2"x 6" painted white blaze that marks the official start of the Appalachian Trail. Behind the park's visitor center is an archway that serves as the entrance to the Approach Trail, one of the most argued about sections of the entire journey. The Approach Trail is not an official part of the A.T., and opinions vary, quite passionately, about whether to start the hike by climbing 604 steps leading to the top of the Amicalola Falls, or start at Springer Mountain, the actual Southern Terminus of the A.T.

I was a bit surprised at the vehemence with which some hikers urged me not to do the Approach Trail, but I had long decided that the nearly nine miles to Springer Mountain would be part of my journey. And what a fantastic start it was. The Falls were gorgeous, and within a quarter mile of starting, people I met were already asking if I was going all the way to Maine. It almost seemed unreal, yet natural, to answer "Yes, I am a Thru-Hiker."

When I reached the first white blaze at the summit of Springer Mountain there was a small crowd at the summit, many of whom I would see throughout my journey. Frisbee (who carried a frisbee that doubled as a plate) his wife Stubbs, Wok-Man, Crazy Moose, Crank, and others.

I introduced myself as "Brother Blood," a trail name I had acquired over the years. Trail names are nicknames that Thru-Hikers acquire one way or another before or during their journey. Some hikers find it morally reprehensible to give yourself a trail name, believing that one must be given to you during your hike. I had arrived in Georgia with mine. It derived from a time working at a bar, where a French-Vietnamese bartender named Liembo, whose native language was one that puts the adjective after the noun, referred to people as his "Brother Blood," rather than his "Blood Brother." Of course, we all were soon calling each other Brother Blood. When I joined REI, the habit stuck, and I continued calling everyone Brother Blood. Naturally, I was soon universally known in the store as Brother Blood.

The Appalachian Trail is marked by white blazes from Springer Mountain, all the way to Katahdin. Almost all are painted on trees, some on rocks, and where the trail cuts through a town, on telephone poles and street signs. There are an estimated 165,000 white blazes over the entire A.T. Standing atop Springer Mountain, I had only 164,999 to go.

We trekked another 2.8 miles to the Stover Creek Shelter for my first night as an Appalachian Trail Thru-Hiker. The shelter was packed, with close to 50 hikers, each one determined to make it to Maine, no one was going to drop out. But someone already had. An unknown hiker had dumped their load of cheap, lousy, Wal-Mart quality gear right on the side of the Approach Trail. I had heard, but never really believed the stories of people dropping everything and saying "fuck it," before their first sunset on the trail, but here was proof.

Feeling the effects of no sleep, and the first few miles of the 2189.1 to Katahdin, I was in my hammock by 7:30, asleep by 7:31. I didn't budge until 7:00 a.m. when Silver Fox came to wake me, and with a gentle nudge he snapped me from a dream, and I sprung up like I was shot from a cannon, scaring him half to death. I came to my senses and realized he would be making the coffee this morning. Silver Fox always made the coffee.

We are coffee lovers, but not coffee snobs. Simple instant coffee and non-dairy powered creamer is all we need. And in the morning, evening, and at least one break during the day, Silver Fox would light up his camp stove and make us coffee. It was Silver Fox who had introduced me to how wonderful an evening cup is after finishing a day's hike. Having a person always ready to make a cup of coffee is an unmatched luxury. Life on the A.T. helps you appreciate the small, wonderful pleasures in life.

After coffee, and still very early, we were getting ready to hike when Maverick let us know he was getting impatient to get going. I understood, but it also reminded me why I love being a solo hiker.

I also began to notice how often Maverick and Silver Fox would visit the privy. For the first few days of the hike it was an Appalachian Trail shit-a-thon. If they had only gotten pledged donations for each turd, they could have raised enough money to rebuild every privy in Georgia. Given the importance our society pays to being "regular," and the marketing dollars spent on probiotics, yogurts, and every other poop-prodding product out there, these guys have achieved astronomical gastrological success.

Doing 13 miles on day two had me realizing that it would take some time to get into hiking shape. Maverick and I were spent by the time we hit the shelter. The only difference between us was that he had an excuse. He had been feeling fatigued and had been coughing most of the night. After returning home he learned he had mono.

### 

Shelters line the A.T., usually spaced about 6-9 miles apart. Some are right on the trail, while most are 0.1 to 0.4 miles off trail. They are three-sided structures, usually made of wood, but sometimes stone, rectangular in shape, with a roof and wooden sleeping platforms. Many have two levels of sleeping areas, and can fit anywhere from 4 to 20+ hikers for a night. Early in the journey, hikers worked hard to arrive at the shelters early enough to secure a sleeping spot inside. Tent sites are almost always nearby, as well as a water source, and privy.

### 

Day Three we hit Woody Gap, 20 miles from Springer Mountain. For the first time in my journey I received "trail magic." Trail magic is an all-encompassing term for any gift a hiker receives on the trail. Mainly food and beverages, but it sometimes takes the form of gear, or even cash.

My first trail magic came from the "Peace Bus," operated by the Twelve Tribes Spiritual Community. I was greeted with a handshake, guessing they didn't get the "fist-bump" memo, and a cup of hot yerba mate, a cloudy greenish tea that looked like a liquid version of Mattel's *Slime* product of my childhood. However, after the first sip, I began looking for a place to dump the tea without offending my gracious hosts.

The bus was beautiful, and the group was really, really friendly, and a little groovy. Initially I was told they were a group of "Deadheads," fans of the Grateful Dead that now enjoyed getting out and doing nice things for people, including hikers. I didn't know then that the Twelve Tribes would become one of the interesting stories of my thru-hiking journey.

Maverick had wondered if he would actually witness a hiker calling it quits. And at the bus we did. A young man hiked in, and within minutes of meeting the Twelve Tribes folks, he decided to get on the bus and head to North Carolina with them. He set his pack on a table and welcomed hikers to take whatever they wanted, but it wasn't exactly the best gear for a thru-hike. He laid out his food at another spot for all comers, and with that, *he was done.*

With Maverick still under the weather, he and Sheryl took a shuttle to the Hiker Hostel located near the city of Dahlonega. After about a two-hour break, Silver Fox and I hiked on to the Lance Creek Campsite, hoping it would not be overcrowded. It wasn't; only two people had set up camp, Hot Rod and Slow Poke, brothers around age 60, hiking the trail together. Two of the nicest guys I met on the entire trail. They both had a great sense of humor, and the willingness to help a hiker if needed.

We found a nice spot for our hammocks, and Silver Fox immediately found a good place for digging a cat-hole, with a small tree to hold on to for balance when doing his business. The wind was starting to pick up when we were joined by Josh, who asked if he could join us. We gladly agreed. I liked the fact the he wanted to join us and share conversation, unlike day-to-day society, where people tend to keep their distance. Silver Fox soon had the evening coffee started. The wind died down a bit and we called it a night. Tomorrow we would face what we were told was the first real rocky and steep test of A.T., Blood Mountain.

It was going to be a wet day; the only question was when the rain would come. We were told that descending Blood Mountain would be rocky, and if wet, slick as well. The ascent didn't prove to be the test we were promised; it was a gradual, not too difficult hike. We were joined by a self-described "big-city liberal" from Germany, who explained that the hot sun of day one had burned him and given him a "real Southern redneck." Of course, I immediately gave him the trail name, "Redneck." We stopped at Woods Hole

Shelter for coffee before making the final portion of the climb. Silver Fox was debating when to put on his rain gear. He decided against it, for now.

It was just over a mile to the summit, and the rain held off until we made it to the Blood Mountain Shelter at the peak. Thru-Hikers don't often sleep at this shelter because of the rule requiring the use of a bear canister, a hard-plastic bear-proof cylinder that weighs over two pounds, rather than simply hanging your food bag out of reach. It was the first of far too many ridiculous rules on the A.T.

It was going to be a wet descent, and for the first time in years of section hiking the A.T., Silver Fox was going to hike through the rain, but he was prepared. He had borrowed a full rain suit, pants and all. It was bright yellow, and after putting it on he looked more like he was hiking in to the reactor at Three Mile Island than the Georgia forest. He mentioned he was a little concerned about falling if the rocks were slippery, prompting Redneck to observe, "Don't worry, with that suit on, Mountain Rescue will find you!"

*Figure 3 - Silver Fox at the Blood Mountain Shelter in his yellow rain suit.*

But our fears of a slippery, dangerous descent never materialized. It was wet and windy, but the rocks provided good grip for our boots. The rain and winds began to subside as we approached the first iconic landmark of the Appalachian Trail, Mountain Crossing at Neel Gap.

### ###

She was very young, very bored, and very sad. Not a look you like to see in a Thru-Hiker. My first thought was that like many, hiking wasn't what she thought it would be, and she was ready to call it quits. It was cold, rainy and we still had 2,159.1 miles to go. I said "hi," and soon realized that she didn't want to quit, she wanted to backpack to Maine.

"I'm hiking with a friend, and her Mom, and..."

It's one form of trail drama. The realization that your hiking partners and their styles are just not compatible with yours. She told me of how they had only made 30 miles in over a week on the trail, and she feared there was no way they would even get close to Maine.

She was a bit worried about hiking alone. I thought the best thing I could do was to introduce her to the hikers I had met over the past four days, and reassure her that we would all look out for her if she decided to hike without her friends. She liked the idea and soon was smiling, ready to continue her hike, at her own pace.

Her hair was a beautiful black, and she wore it with a short pony tail right on top, which earned her the trail name, Pebbles, after the Flintstone's character.

### ###

The building that houses Mountain Crossing Outfitters escaped demolition in the 1970's by earning registration as a national landmark. First erected as a log structure, serving as a "tearoom and entertainment area," it was rebuilt by FDR's Civilian Conservation Corps (CCC) in the 1930's, and served as an inn and restaurant until 1965. An artists' group rented it for a while, but by the 1970's it was empty, and slated for demolition. After escaping destruction, it had been a small store, before becoming Mountain Outfitters.

After introducing Pebbles to the other Thru-Hikers, we all agreed that we would look out for her and keep her safe. With so many hikers on the trail this early in the journey, she would not be alone in the woods. The Hiker Hostel shuttle arrived after Silver Fox and I had dried off from the day's rain, and we were off for my first night off trail. We met Maverick and Sheryl, and after a needed shower, the four of us jumped in a cab for a 15-minute ride to a small Vermont town for dinner.

Dahlonega, Georgia is a charming town of just over 5,000 people, and home to the University of North Georgia. It destroys the stereotype put forth by people like Bill Bryson who took delight in comparing small-town Georgia to the movie *Deliverance*. In fact, it was pleasant enough for a TV crew to have transformed it into a small Vermont town to film a pilot episode of a show called *"Hail Mary."* I later learned the show was not picked up by any network, and Dahlonega is, once again, a charming Georgia town.

On our return to the hostel, I learned that even those who hadn't yet started their hike were already accepting the concept of "hiker midnight." When the sun goes down, it's called hiker midnight, and for many, bedtime. I've always been a night owl, so I stayed up and watched as the owner of the hostel, a former Thru-Hiker, helped a new hiker reduce their pack weight. The hiker was tall and large, and admitted he weighed over 400 pounds. Most hikers like to keep their full pack weight at less than 40 pounds. Some are much lighter, in the 25-pound range. Although he had an ultralight pack, he had over-packed it to almost 60 pounds. A good portion of it was food.

Although he wasn't trying to be funny, the hostel owned looked at the food and made the oft repeated comment that as backpackers, "we pack our fears," then added, "and it looks like you fear going hungry." By the time the exercise was completed, the pack was down to 47 pounds. Given that I was carrying a week's worth of food myself, my pack was actually a pound heavier than his!

He'd made the trip to Georgia with a friend, who truly wanted to see him succeed on his hike, but they didn't have a clue. Their goal was to make Dicks Creek Gap, 70 miles north of Springer Mountain, before she headed back home. She said they had 10 days to make it by next Friday. I corrected her - it was only eight days until next Friday. She replied "We'll make it anyway."

When out of shape and overweight, it's not a good idea to push miles at the start of hike. I feared he wouldn't make it a week before heading home. I later found out I was right. After all, backpacking the A.T. through North Georgia is no walk in the woods.

After breakfast, I said a rainy goodbye to Maverick, Silver Fox, and Sheryl, and boarded a shuttle back to Neel Gap. At Mountain Crossings, hikers were either waiting out the rain or preparing to hike through it, by putting on waterproof jackets and rain pants. I tossed on my rain jacket, and wondered how anyone could hike with rain pants. Even on cold, windy, and rainy days, I have never gotten cold enough to need rain pants. I'd rather be wet with a chilly rain, than have my legs overheated and sweating.

The only section of the entire A.T. under a roof is on the side of the Mountain Crossings where the roof connects the building's two sections. I walked through, then headed north, into the rain, a solo hiker. I thought to myself: *this is really happening.*

## CHAPTER 2: A SOLO HIKER

I'm a solo hiker. I don't like adjusting my schedule to what someone else is doing. If I want to stop early, or push on well into the night, I do it, without consulting another hiker. Many hikers are not like me. The vast majority fall in, very early in the journey, with a "trail family" or maybe just a hiking partner. Some hike separately during the day, then meet at a designated spot for the night, while some actually hike together all day, every day.

I started each day with a tentative plan of how far I might go, and depending on how I felt, I might do more or less miles. Few things can ruin a thru-hike faster than constantly pushing more miles to the point that you forget that you're supposed to be having fun.

*Figure 4 - At the GA/NC Border*

Seven miles into the day, the rain had stopped. I met Norway and Rock City, ladies in their thirties, thoroughly enjoying their journey. Norway hiked with a small Norwegian flag and was going as far as she could before heading back home; her goal was New York. Rock City left a job in Detroit and seemed in no hurry to "figure out" the rest of her life. Pebbles was with them. Gone was the sad young girl I had met just the day before. Pebbles was happy to be stretching out her young legs, and making good miles. After 11.5 miles, we all set up camp at Low Gap

Shelter, where we joined Frisbee and Stubbs, who were hoping to catch up to Wok Man, one of the more interesting characters on the trail. It was well after dark when two people hiking by headlamp arrived at the shelter. They turned out to be Pebbles' friend, Princess, and her mom, Viking.

I slept in the next morning and started the habit of alternating long and short days to let my body adjust to hiking every day. I was one of the last to leave the shelter, something that would be common throughout my journey. I hiked 7.3 miles, and was in camp at the Blue Mountain Shelter before 3:30 p.m. Located on a ridgeline, it was the windiest, and coldest night yet. Temperatures were in the high 20's, but the leafless trees provided no break from the wind.

It was Day Eight, and I was starting to feel the fatigue that comes with being 50 years-old and hiking myself into shape. Uphill climbs of over a thousand feet were now commonplace. It was on one such climb that the statement "misery loves company" proved correct when I met 007, from England (of course). As I ascended the hill following Dick's Creek Gap I saw him ahead of me, leaning over his trekking poles as he yelled back to me (in the King's English), "these hills are kicking my butt!" We inched forward using mutual encouragement to push and pull each other to the top. We would do it again a few miles ahead climbing Buzzard Knob. I was realizing it was going to take some time before I'd be in shape, and have what are known as "hiker legs."

Throughout the day, I leapfrogged with a group of younger hikers, including Shadow Chef, who thought it was good idea to carry a few bottles of booze from their last resupply. I stopped to chat as they were taking a break. Shadow Chef offered me a sip from his bottle of Jägermeister. After taking a swig, and handing him back the bottle, he offered me the rest of the bottle to keep. I politely declined his generous offer, then realized he was just hoping to shed weight, as he pleaded, "Take it, for the Love of God, please take it!" I again declined, but lightened the bottle by another swallow.

Eight days was already the longest I had ever spent hiking, and I had completed just over 3% of the entire Appalachian Trail. But tomorrow I would hit the first really big milestone - I'd cross state lines.

It was a beautiful day, sunny and warm, just after noon, when I saw a small group gathered near a tree, I knew exactly what that meant. Nailed to the tree was a small worn wooden sign, reading GA/NC. We laughed and took pictures. It felt wonderful. The first real evidence that we were indeed on our way to Maine. I had only hiked 78.5 miles, and had over 2,100 to go, but

I was in North Carolina! Goodbye North Georgia. One state down, thirteen to go.

### 

Day 10 was another milestone, the 100-mile mark. But to get there, I had to go up and over Albert Mountain. For the first time on my journey, I had to do some actual rock climbing. And for the first time I saw a blue-blazed "bypass" trail for those not able, or not willing to take on a steep climb. I was not going to skip a single white blaze of the A.T., so up the steep rocks I went. I'm not much of a rock climber, and with over 40 pounds on my back, I couldn't help but think that one bad move, one slip, could easily end my adventure. But it was a great feeling when I reached the summit and stood at the Albert Mountain Fire Tower. When I hit Long Branch Shelter that evening, my confidence was soaring.

Other than the climb up Albert Mountain, most of the day wasn't difficult hiking. As I clicked off miles, I was looking forward to taking a couple days off in Franklin. I had only one small mishap during the day, when I had to stop to clean up a bit. I thought it'd be just a fart.

The next morning the Long Branch Shelter was buzzing with hikers excited about getting to town. Like clockwork, they were up with the sun, making enough noise to let everyone know they were up, and preparing to go. Even on the trail I felt a decided bias against late sleepers like me. Every morning, the diligent, dedicated hikers I called "martyrs" would wake with sun and begin making a racket by banging their tent stakes together to knock off the dirt. It was annoying, and seemed to me their way of announcing to the rest of us that they were up, they were go-getters, they were serious about hiking. To me it seemed they had brought the worn-out ideas of the social order to the A.T. That somehow sleeping until 8:00 a.m., or, God-forbid, even later, was somehow a character flaw.

As I would fall back asleep in my hammock, I dreamed of one day jumping from my hammock and shoving one of their tent pegs through their temple. But every day I had that thought, it was just too early, and was too damn tired.

One of the first lessons I learned in Georgia was to ignore the sort of silent peer pressure that exists around shelter areas: the idea that I should be getting up earlier, or comparing miles with other hikers and thinking to myself that I should be doing more miles. It's common to hear people bragging about the big miles they are planning to hike.

But with a light rain falling, I decided to stay nice and dry in my hammock as long as I could. No one was going to mistake me for a go-getter. With just 7.3 miles to Hwy 64, where I would catch a ride into Franklin, I was in no hurry. I headed to the shelter to make coffee, where I had the chance to talk to Pumba and Timon, named after the *Lion King* characters. Young men, both 22 years old, I liked them immediately when they said they were on the trail after getting sick of all the external pressure to make something of themselves.

Timon even had the crazy idea of physically touching every white blaze to Maine. *Whatever gets you up the next mountain.*

*Figure 5 - Misty morning just before Franklin, N*

## CHAPTER 3: FRANKLIN AND FRENCH WHITE BURGANDY

*"And so we had a little holiday in Franklin, which was small, dull, and cautiously unattractive, but mostly dull."*

Bill Bryson
*A Walk In The Woods*

Poor Bill Bryson just got there 20 years too early.

As localities in North Carolina and throughout the South began to shed the shackles of religiously inspired blue laws and failed prohibition policies, towns like Franklin evolved into vibrant, fun places to visit. And in the process, they became wonderful places for tired Thru-Hikers.

Like so many small towns in America, Franklin is divided into two parts. One part is the older downtown area, made up of small shops and local restaurants that give these towns their own unique personalities. While the other side of town, the highway side, is a cookie cutter assemblage of fast food chains, gas stations, and budget motels. They look the same everywhere in America. The Microtel Inn and Suites where I stayed, was on the highway side of town.

I was looking forward to just relaxing with a beer, and enjoying the fact my body could just rest, for two whole days. I had been on the trail just 11 days, but it sure felt longer. I walked to the Lazy Hiker Brewery where I saw Stefon, later to be known as Hollywood, a quiet hiker who kept to himself, but not in an unfriendly way. We talked about the hike and what we did before, and were likely to do after our journey.

The bartender at the Lazy Hiker was a woman named Kim who was an art teacher by day, and worked at the brewpub at night. She quickly dispelled Bryson's view of Franklin of a backwoods town where there is not much to do but watch men working at the lumberyard. She was kind and enjoyed hearing about our journey. She was one of the many people along the trail that helped restore my faith in humanity.

*Figure 6 - Brother Blood with Kim in 2018*

It was a quiet Thursday night in Franklin, and after a couple of beers I headed back to the motel, and enjoyed a midnight snack of an entire Pizza Hut Supreme pizza.

### ###

Taylor started the trail two days after me, and had a pretty tough first week, which is not uncommon for hikers whose first backpacking trip is an attempted hike from Georgia to Maine. Her body was beat, and her knees were in need of some rest. I had rented a car, shockingly cheap on the weekend, and picked her up at the trail to come to town and rest up.

I gathered up our laundry and headed out to do laundry and errands and give her a couple hours of alone time in the motel room. That night, we had dinner downtown at the Bowery (now called the Root and Barrel Restaurant). It's tough to make it with a somewhat upscale restaurant in a small town, there simply isn't enough "upscale clientele" in a town of 5,000 people. But the Bowery did a great job drawing a balance between the well-to-do and people who earn their paycheck by the hour.

After dinner, we headed to the Rathskeller, a coffee house complete with a guy playing acoustic guitar and a shelf of board games, that also served draft beer! We were joined by Chia Pet and Pebbles, who, that day, turned 16. Chia Pet got her trail name because she grew alfalfa sprouts on the outside pocket of her backpack. She was a very caring person whose goal that night was to make sure that Pebbles enjoyed her sixteenth birthday. So, we sat at a table for four and played Pictionary. We didn't keep score; we didn't roll dice; we just took turns picking categories and drawing funny images. We laughed as if the outside world didn't exist; we felt like Thru-Hikers. We were happy.

Taylor was itching to get back on the trail the next morning, the hiking bug had bit her hard, and she wanted do miles. I got her back to the trail, and I headed back to Franklin. It was still fairly early for me, and since now I could eat whatever I wanted and not gain a pound, donuts sounded good. So, it was off to Happy Daze Donuts.

In college at San Luis Obispo, California, I worked the graveyard shift at Sunshine Donuts. It was a decent gig: serve coffee and donuts to the bar crowd after midnight, then study and do a little cleaning till about 5:00 a.m., when the working folks started coming in. I knew them all, the construction guys, the truck drivers, all the people who truly earned their living.

Where I live now, those places are gone - replaced by Starbucks, where coffee is served in to-go cups, even if you are eating in. No one talks work, or baseball, or politics; in fact they don't talk at all. And no one comes by with a coffee pot for a "warm up," I miss that. But in Franklin they did talk. I was the only customer, so we talked about my hike, we talked about their town, and they made me feel at home.

That night was part Franklin's annual hiker-fest. If there's one thing Southern trail towns have gotten really good at, it's taking advantage of the economic benefits that hikers provide. Almost every town south of Virginia holds some type of trail festival to attract hikers, and their wallets, to their town. These events are scheduled to coincide with the greatest numbers of Thru-Hikers passing through the area.

The Franklin Appalachian Trail Community Council did a survey and estimated that hikers spent $470,000 in Franklin in 2016 alone. The success that small towns in the South have had in getting hikers to spend money actually prevents some hikers from reaching Maine. Limited budgets are hard to stick to in these trail towns.

At every road crossing that leads to a town, hikers hitch in to get resupply, maintaining that they will be back on the trail in a couple of hours. But when they find themselves near a bar, or a store with beer, what's the harm in having a couple? And soon they are splitting the cost of a motel room, buying a pizza, and so on. It's easy to set a budget before the hike, when you're well fed, and sleeping in a warm bed. But after even just a day or two since the last town stop, pizza and beer are almost irresistible. For that reason, many hikers' finances become another of the many obstacles to completing their thru-hike.

I decided to check out the Hiker-Fest in the Yard, where bands were scheduled to play outside of the Lazy Hiker Brewery. The night was much colder than expected, so the music was moved indoors. The music was described as "progressive funk rock," and was meant for outdoors, or a much larger venue. The brewery was crammed with a combination of hikers and locals. Inside was crowded and loud, and the outside patio was too cold. So, I headed back to the Bowery.

The bar was quiet, so I asked if there was time for a glass of wine. There was, so I sat chatting with Heather, the same bartender as last night. Soon a few younger couples had joined us at the bar. I was on my second glass of wine, and got up to use to restroom, when I saw a man who I thought was the manager, he told me he was. I told him how Heather had been so nice both evenings, which seems to have made his day. He said he loved hearing that, and asked if he could buy me a glass of wine. I thought about it, and thought, "yes."

I was talking to a couple at the bar about my hike, when the manager, Robbie, joined us. Soon he asked if I wanted a bottle of wine, to go, for $10. Again, I thought about it, and sure enough, I again thought, "yes." He picked out a French White Burgundy that I would brown bag out. By the time I left the Bowery, I was full of wine, and on the walk back to the Microtel, I knew there was no way I was opening that bottle tonight.

The next morning my backpack was at its full resupply weight, plus the bottle of wine. I returned the rental car and headed to Ron Haven's Budget Inn for their 11:00 a.m. shuttle back to Winding Stair Gap.

### 

There is a Ron Haven in almost every trail town: someone who caters to hikers and makes a decent living doing so. That is not to say they take advantage of hikers; the opposite is true. They work within the budgetary restraints of most Thru-Hikers. At Haven's Budget Inn, a single room is $40, with each addition person adding $5 to the bill. Two hikers can sleep in a clean room, with a shower, for about $25 each after tax. That includes a shuttle to and from the trail head, as well as a shuttle around town for resupply and errands.

A staunch conservative, Haven is known for lecturing shuttle riders on why Ronald Reagan was the greatest thing to ever happen to America. He himself was elected to the Macon County Board of Supervisors in 2010. He lost that seat in 2014, after he was challenged about using his Budget Inn's address as his primary residence, in order to run for office in that district. He claimed that he did not live in the country club home that his wife and kids occupied. The Macon County Board of Elections trusted Haven's testimony and ruled against the challenge, allowing him to keep using the motel as his official residence. Haven testified that he spends about 160 nights a year at the motel, and another 100 nights a year promoting, and participating in gun shows.

Who knows if that played any part in his defeat, or maybe places like Franklin are just becoming less conservative, as Haven, in that 2014 election for two commissioners, was defeated by both a more moderate Republican and a Democrat. Whatever the reason was, it was confirmed in 2016, when he lost a bid to regain a seat on the County Commission, again to a moderate Republican.

### 

I caught the 11:00 a.m. Haven shuttle to the trail, and the ex-Commissioner himself was driving. He has a great personality and tells wonderful stories. Today he was joking about the bewildered look on the faces of tourists looking for something to do on a Sunday in a small Bible Belt town. I felt fortunate that on this Sunday he was not preaching the gospel of St. Ronnie.

After exiting the shuttle, I crossed State Rt. 64, and was again headed north with a full resupply, including a bottle of French wine.

I spent the day hiking with Wild Horse, an awesome, young lady I'd met along with 007 a few days earlier. She was a wine lover as well, so that night I would not have to drink my French wine alone. At lunchtime, she insisted that we hike a side trail up to Silers Bald, as Baltimore Jack had told her in Franklin that it was one of the five best views on the entire A.T.

Baltimore Jack was a trail legend, an eight-time thru-hiker known for his generosity to hikers and people in general. He lived as a trail vagabond, picking up work at hostels and outfitters to have just enough money to get by. He was loved and respected in the trail community. Despite our shared love of the trail, Bruce Springsteen, and Jim Beam, we never had the joy of meeting.

Unfortunately, his passion for the trail was matched only by his passion for liquor, and at the age of 57, in Franklin, from heart complications, on May 3, 2016, Leonard Adam "Baltimore Jack" Tarlin died. So it goes.

We mistakenly took the longest of the side trails to the summit of Silers Bald, but it was worth it. Baltimore Jack was right, it was the most beautiful vista yet. It provided 360-degree views of mountains as far as the eye could see. Balds are mountains whose summits are devoid of trees. They are not above the treeline, and reasons vary about why they are bald. The most popular hypothesis is that the land was cleared for grazing, and before trees could reclaim the summit, the areas were designated as balds and were maintained as to stay treeless.

The base of the hills were showing signs of spring's arrival, while the trees higher up had not yet woke from their winter hibernation. I ate a small lunch of mini-bagels with salami and cheese, and enjoyed just hanging out with Wild Horse, Norway, and Sunshine. A little while later we met up with Pebbles and headed up Wayah Bald. At the summit was the John Byrne Memorial Tower, built in 1935 by the CCC, and named for the first Supervisor of the Nantahala National Forest. It was getting chilly and windy when Wild Horse suggested we avoid the crowd at the shelter, and stop at a primitive campsite 0.3 miles closer. Sounded perfect to me.

We got into camp before dark, got a fire going, and found the spring. Everyone filled their water and claimed their spot for the evening, and began setting up their tents, while I found suitable trees to hang my hammock. I rehydrated and heated some homemade chicken marsala and rice, and found a stick suitable for opening the wine by pushing the cork into the bottle. I poured a sample into my stainless-steel coffee cup, swirled it, smelled it, and then took a sip. Maybe it was the fact I was in the woods, on the Appalachian Trail, maybe because I carried it up and down the balds all day, but it was the greatest wine I ever tasted.

The trail has that effect. Simple pleasures almost taken for granted in everyday life became sheer ecstasy on the A.T. On a section hike the year before, in Shenandoah National Park, I met up with a couple hikers; one had apples, and I had pancake mix and syrup. We made the best apple pancakes any human being has ever feasted on!

Pebbles and Sunshine passed on the wine, so Wild Horse and I enjoyed the bottle by the fire with dinner. The next day I found out how much heavier an empty wine bottle seems than a full one. Now it's just trash, not lightened by the anticipation of enjoying wine by a fire with friends. An empty bottle of wine is indeed far heavier than a full one.

It was another somewhat short day, with only one real hill to climb, and thankfully I was joined again by 007, as the hills were still winning the battles. Going uphill with 007 again made it much easier and almost fun. At one point 007 elicited laughter when he turned a corner, looked up and exclaimed, "Oh *Piss Pots*! another hill?" Later he told me I was "good bloke," and that he wasn't just "blowing smoke up my ass." Then asked me if that was a saying here. "Blowing smoke up your ass? It sure is," I told him. In my view, 007 is a pretty damn good bloke as well

# CHAPTER 4: LANDMARKS, BOOKS, AND PURISM

The A.T. has landmarks iconic to Thru-Hikers. I'd read and heard about them, but now I was *experiencing* them. The Nantahala Outdoor Center, or NOC, is one such place. The first site that sells beer right on the A.T. is where the trail crosses the Nantahala River. Sitting next to the beautiful river, drinking beer with hikers and river people, you feel the joy of being a Thru-Hiker. At places like this, the world just seems right. The NOC is also the first place where people with different outdoor passions converge: river people, kayakers, and hikers. I didn't know that kayaking was an Olympic sport, but it turns out that the NOC has been responsible for 23 U.S. Olympians in the sport of Whitewater Canoe Slalom. The NOC has a large outfitter, as well as a restaurant, overlooking the river, and known for its "Wesser Burger."

We drank beer, ate burgers, while some were worried about where we would spend the night. I wasn't. Wherever the A.T. crosses a river, there's always places to set up camp. And before long, Scout, a 22-year old, with the strong opinions of someone that age, came to tell us he found a great campsite about a quarter mile down the river. It was the kind of night you dream about before starting a thru-hike. A roaring fire, next to a rolling river, with good company. I forgot to throw the empty bottle of wine away at the NOC, and I was tired of carrying it. So, I laid it in the fire to melt the bottle. I can't remember a time in my life when I didn't love putting metal or glass into a fire just to lift it out later and see it almost molten, glowing red.

I laid the bottle down with the cork still inside, close to the neck. As the heat built up, it forced the cork into the neck, and before long, with a fairly loud pop, the heat expelled the cork, and scored a direct hit to Scout's leg. Not realizing that it was just the cork, Scout let out a yell as if shrapnel had been buried deep into his muscle tissue. He quickly realized he was OK and joined our laughter.

Before long, Pebbles and I were only ones left by the fire. It was hard to believe this smart, witty, independent young lady had just turned 16.

*Figure 7 - Morning at our camp on the Nantahala River*

### # #

Like almost all hikers, I have read at least a dozen books about the A.T. From those that simply rehash the day-to-day events of a thru-hike, to embellished, mostly fictional tales of hiking the A.T., as well as the personal memoirs of the life-changing experience. So now it was fun experiencing the places I'd read about. Too many books I'd read focus too much on sketchy, undesirable people, rather than the great people one encounters both on and off the trail every day.

In one book about the A.T. the author rarely passed up an opportunity to bad-mouth fellow hikers. At one point putting down all weekend and section-hikers, she went on to refer to those of us of different political and religious beliefs as "left-wing antifundamentalist... squirrels."[i] I even read one trail book in which the author takes several pages to rant about the injustice of taxes. Complaining about taxes while hiking on Federally protected forest land!

It seemed that far too much focus was given to the presumed bad people, at the expense of the wonderful people hikers encounter both on and off the trail. I didn't want to complain or find faults in people on my journey. I wanted to see the best in people, and I did. Does that mean I liked everyone I met? Or course not, but at times I can be pretty unlikable as well. But throughout my journey, I met people both on and off the trail that restored my faith in humanity.

### # #

The next day, at 9:00 a.m., I started at an elevation of 1,732 feet. Eight miles later I was at 5,062 feet atop Cheoah Bald, where the views rivaled those of Silers Bald. I expected to advance at about a mile an hour given the climb, but the first 3,000 feet weren't bad at all. I was starting to realize that it wasn't the big climbs killing me, but the smaller ones right after the big one that got me. In this case it was the 500+ foot climb after Sassafras Gap. That scenario would repeat itself throughout my hike. I was always mentally prepared for the big mountains, but for whatever reason the smaller ones that followed destroyed me.

It was a slow descent to Locust Cove Gap campsite, where at least a dozen other hikers were setting up. Pebbles, Scout, 007, Hatchet, Frisbee, Stubbs, and others. Right before dark Wok-Man came running down the hill and literally fell and slid into camp. Wok Man was tall and slender with deep black hair and beard. He had the look of a true mountain man. Funny, smart, sarcastic and irreverent, the mood always improved when Wok Man arrived.

The trail cut right through the campsite, forming two distinct sides, each with its own fire ring, about 40 feet off trail. Pebbles, Scout, and I had a fire on one side. About six hikers were on the other, with 007 resting in his hammock between us.

It was then that 007 set an Appalachian Trail record that may never be broken. It's true that are no "official" records on the A.T., but everyone there that night can confirm this one. As camp was quieting down, with little daylight remaining, the sound of beans emanating from 007's hammock surprised everyone, including himself. Everyone stopped, as if waiting for the echo his fart would produce from the Nantahala Gorge. No one was more surprised than 007, in his hammock wearing a look of sheer surprise, coupled with the pride that comes only with great achievement.

### 

It was now Day 18, and a few of us had stopped at a clearing at Stecoah Gap, along North Carolina Hwy. 143 for lunch. As I finished and put my pack on, I headed out as the other hikers looked at me as if to say, "does he know he's going South?" I then put one foot down precisely where I had left the trail, turned around and headed north prompting Wok Man to exclaim, "we have ourselves a *PURIST!*" He was right, I am indeed a purist.

There are many definitions for hikers tossed around on the trail. Purist, supported, un-supported, solo, yellow-blazer, slack-packer, and more. Most have very fluid meanings; after all, is it a "solo" hike if after three days you are hiking on and off with a group? Did hiking with the Lawyers for four days mean I'm not a solo hiker? The answer is a very simple: "who cares?"

A few years ago, a 14-year-old girl broke the record for being the youngest "solo" thru-hiker. Her definition of a "solo" hike was being followed by her mother in a trailer, waiting for her at every road crossing, and sleeping in the trailer nearly every night.

As a purist, I simply wanted to hike every inch, every foot, every yard, and every mile of the Appalachian Trail. I always got back on the trail at exactly the same point where I got off. I also always carried my full pack. Many hikers "slack-pack" sections of the trail, which is leaving your full pack with someone for the day, and carrying only a small day pack with lunch, snacks, a rain jacket, and water, then meeting up at the end of the day to retrieve your full pack.

Refusing to slack-pack had less to do with purity, and more due to the fact that I did not want to be on a schedule during my journey. I didn't want to have to be anywhere at a certain time to get my full pack. If I was having a tough day, I loved the freedom of being able to sling up my hammock for a long rest, or a nap. If I saw a wonderful campsite that looked perfect for camping, I had the freedom to stop and camp. Having a schedule, and needing to be at a certain place at the end of the day, did not fit with the freedom I sought to enjoy on my journey.

### 

The climb up "Jacob's Ladder," was steep, very steep, but not the hands-and-feet climbing some had warned about. After reaching the top I felt a little fatigued but not as much as I had the past week. So, following lunch at the Brown Fork Gap Shelter and after three somewhat slow miles to Cody Gap, I decided to stretch out my legs and test my fitness level. It was easy terrain and I covered two and a half miles in an hour. For some that's an average speed, but between my pack weight, and 50-year-old legs, it was fast for me. I passed Pebbles before slowing down and hiking with her to Yellow Creek Gap where we saw a man riding his bicycle on a dirt logging road.

As we hit the gap, he was loading his bike into his truck and introduced himself as Jimmy Dean, and said, "I've got something you probably haven't seen in a while." I hoped for some trail magic, and sure enough Jimmy Dean pulled out a nice cold can of Bud Ice beer. My joy from being handed a cold beer was surpassed only by my surprise that they still make Bud Ice! Pebbles declined a beer, admitting she was 16. I teasingly told her that on the A.T. the drinking age was actually only 16. (I felt bad later on when I learned that she actually believed me.) But she got two bananas in the deal and was happy. So was I; I got to have another beer. Jimmy was another example of the wonderful people you meet on the trail.

The next day was just over seven miles and featured another landmark, Fontana Dam. Fontana Dam is known for two things with Thru-Hikers, the "Fontana Hilton" Shelter, and the entrance to the Great Smoky Mountains. The shelter is really nice, as shelters go: flush toilets, a shower, and a solar panel charging station are as good as it gets for a shelter. But I had a resupply package at the Fontana Lodge and Hotel, and a night indoors sounded good to both me, and Pebbles.

"You mind sleeping on the floor?" I called to her. I was able to get a room, and she was welcome to stay in it. But the one remaining room at the thru-hiker rate had just one bed, and I really didn't think a 16-year-old would mind sleeping on the floor. She didn't. So, we hiked to the furthest point where we could still catch the $3 shuttle to the Lodge, the Fontana Dam Visitors Center. We lucked out and the van pulled up about 100 yards before the center, and we jumped in.

Fontana Village is a cute little tourist trap. Just a few buildings: The Lodge and restaurant, a post office, laundromat, and a general store, and a cafe that serves breakfast and lunch, and that's about the whole Village. The general store has a very large front porch, and they sell beer, which you can drink on the porch. It's hiker paradise.

The Lodge is also a paradise for car and motorcycle clubs because of its proximity to mountain roads such as the Tail of the Dragon, boasting 318 curves in just 11 miles. We arrived on a Friday, along with scores of Volkswagen Golf car enthusiasts.

We did laundry, resupplied, had lunch, hung out with other hikers, and basically had a great day. Pebbles enjoyed two salads at the Lodge, while I enjoyed a fantastic dinner of locally caught trout. Tomorrow, we would enter the Smokies.

## CHAPTER 5: ARE YOU F***ING KIDDING ME?!?

*I ain't heard that much worth listenin' to. There's a lot of guys layin'
down a lot of rules and regulations.*

Paul Newman
*Cool Hand Luke*


Rules and regulations. That's the greeting hikers receive upon entering the Smoky Mountains National Park. Unlike anywhere else on the entire A.T., the Park charges Thru-Hikers a fee to hike through the park. Twenty bucks a head for the permit that gives you the privilege of being harassed and irritated by a bevy of ridiculous rules and regulations. Within yards of entering the Park, a "Ridgerunner" was there asking if we had our permits. We did, and we were graciously allowed to continue.

In addition to the permits, hikers are required to camp only in shelter areas. In fact, we were required to first fill the shelter to capacity before anyone would be permitted to set up a tent or hammock outside. As a hammocker, I didn't carry a sleeping pad, and there was no way I was going to sleep on a hard wood shelter platform.

But what bothered me most about shelter policy is that it prevents deciding for yourself how many miles to hike each day. If shelters are spaced 7 or 8 miles apart on average, you can't do an 11, or 12, or 17-mile day; your hike has to be structured to the distance between shelters.

Despite the rules, I was enjoying hiking with Pebbles. She was vegan and carried her food in a hard-plastic bear canister, unlike most who kept their food in a lightweight bag, hanging it from a tree, or cable, or pole if provided, to protect it from critters. Hanging your food is said to keep the bears from getting it, because after all, there are dangerous ravenous bears everywhere, right? Far more food bags are raided by mice than any other wild creatures, but where's the fun in hanging a "mouse bag?"

Pebbles enjoyed not having to find a suitable place to hang her food, so she didn't complain about the extra weight of the bear canister. In fact, Pebbles didn't complain at all. She didn't complain about the cold, she didn't complain about the heat, she didn't complain when a restaurant didn't offer vegan dishes, she didn't complain that I ate meat, she didn't complain about the hills, she didn't complain about bugs, she didn't complain about other hikers. She didn't complain about anything.

But I did. I complained about the heat. We had been endlessly warned about the freezing conditions we were sure to encounter in the Smoky Mountains. Stories were being told that a week earlier, no less than four hikes had been medevac'd from the Park suffering from hypothermia. But by the time we got there on April 16, it was summer. I was carrying my winter gear in 80-degree temperatures.

The first day in the Smokies seemed all uphill. Starting at Fontana Dam we were 1,700 feet above sea level. Seven miles later, we were over 4,500 feet. As always, leaving town with full, heavy resupply, the trail was up a mountain. We'd had a later start to the day, and after heading uphill almost the whole time, we stopped at the Mollies Ridge Shelter after a 10-mile day.

It was now Day 21, and I was up at 7:00 a.m., very early by my standards, and on the trail by 8:15. The hiking was nice, not too difficult for the first six miles before stopping for lunch at the Spence Field Shelter. It was near this shelter, a month later, that a black bear "attacked" a Thru-Hiker. Nevertheless, the hiker managed to escape with only a bite on the leg.

It was really a bear bite, and not a full-blown "attack," and he was most likely a victim of his own stupidity. If a sleeping human being is attacked by a 300-plus pound black bear, his chances of survival are not great. The bear likely smelled something in the man's tent, and hoping for a snack, took a bite. At first there were rumors the hiker was wearing coconut oil sunscreen, which he claimed was untrue.

The idea that the bear just randomly appeared out of the woods and bit this poor hiker is hard to believe. If that really happened, bear bites would be quite common on the trail. They are actually very, very rare. Yet the culture of fear remains.

We hiked on to the Derrick Knob Shelter, where I enjoyed my evening coffee watching a beautiful sunset. We had a nice fire going, and there was a lot of laughter as we huddled around the flames on that chilly night. A hiker from Indiana reminded us all about why we were out here. He told us how, after hiking over three miles off Albert Mountain he began to wish he had stayed and camped at the fire tower to see the sunset and then wake to the sunrise. So, he hiked back up the hill and saw both, and it was beautiful. He said he didn't want any "I wish I would have" stories on his journey. He said he had too many of those in his life already, drawing laughter with, "I wish I would have kissed Susan Harris in the 5th grade." But he was right; this should be a journey of no regrets, no "I wish I would haves."

It was now three weeks, and 189.3 miles into the journey, and the strain on some was beginning to show. The next morning an older hiker headed out early, on the wrong trail. I brought it to his attention, and a couple of us pointed to the northbound trail. He didn't thank us, he just mumbled something under his breath, and seemed frustrated and not enjoying himself. I felt sorry for him, why take on such a wonderful journey if not enjoying it?

In the heat, poor 007 was sweating and wearing a long sleeve wool base layer after getting sunburned the previous day. I had a light-weight, long-sleeve hiking shirt in my pack that I wouldn't mind getting rid of, and he sure wanted to get that base layer off, so, he took the shirt before we headed up to Clingman's Dome. Clingman's Dome is another iconic landmark on the A.T., the highest point above sea level on the whole trail. 007 joked that from there it would be just a slight downhill pitch to Katahdin.

It's another place to enjoy the attention that comes with being a Thru-Hiker. Visitors from all over the country and the world come to the Smokies, and almost all of them visit Clingman's Dome. We posed for pictures, talked about our hike, and enjoyed the attention. At that point, we only had a little over three miles to the shelter. The trail had been hard and rocky throughout the day, and as I descended Clingman's Dome, with my feet hitting a hard surface with every step, I began to feel a slight pain in my right foot. It felt like gout.

*GOUT!! Are you fucking kidding me, Gout, on the trail?? Really...GOUT?!?*

I had lost weight and gotten into shape to avoid this bullshit. *Gout!?!* I realized I hadn't been drinking enough water, and combined with the pounding my feet were taking, I shouldn't have been surprised, but I was still pissed. *Fucking gout.* After the three plus miles to the shelter, I was sure it was gout pain, and I still had a half mile side trail to the Mt. Collins Shelter.

After setting up my hammock, I walked tenderly to the spring, where I forced down a liter of water, and filled up three additional liters for that night. I did my best to drink as much water as possible, as dehydration is a factor in gout. I sat in my hammock wondering if this would be the ailment that takes me off trail for a few days, or even a week. In addition to the water, I also threw down "Vitamin I," ibuprofen, like it was candy. I took seven or eight to start, then three or four more before bed, wondering if tomorrow would be my first unplanned zero day.

Some say you should not take ibuprofen to mask pain or injury to continue hiking. I agree with the injury part, but to not mask pain with Vitamin I? Not a chance. Those who advise against it never had gout, or persistent back pain, or the incurable condition of turning fifty.

I kept the pills in the pocket of my hammock, so when I woke up, they were within reach. In the morning, I downed a few more and laid back down, before getting up to test the foot. I sat up in the hammock, and slid my foot into my boot before slowly putting weight on it. I realized that I would be able to hike today, but not without considerable discomfort. I slowly packed up, waiting for the morning dose of pain killers to kick in before hitting the trail.

After I got going, the foot felt better. It was uncomfortable, and in some pain, but not a problem. I hiked 7.3 miles to the Icewater Spring Shelter, where again I loaded up on water, and just a little less ibuprofen. I had to decide if the foot would allow me to make a mad dash and get out of the Smokies in two days. But that would mean a 19+ mile day tomorrow, or the next day. My thought was let's see how I feel in the morning.

I was in crappy mood as I hiked the next day, because the idiotic rule of having to camp in a shelter area. I could go 7.2, 12.1, or 19.8 miles, those were my "choices." The discomfort in my foot wasn't that bad, just bad enough to add to my shitty mood. This would have been a great day to do 13 or 14 miles, and leave about 15 for tomorrow. But no, in the Smokies you had to hike *their* hike, not your hike. But as the sun was setting, my mood improved.

There is something I love about evening and night hiking. It's far quieter, not just because there are no other hikers, but a certain serenity seems to envelop the forest. The coolness of the night made the hiking enjoyable, and for the first time in two days, I was really feeling good. I was pleased that doing almost 20 miles was not killing me, and knowing I would wake up just 8 miles from the Northern boundary of the Smokies had me feeling pretty good. I was done being pissed off at the Smokies... I thought.

Other than a thru-hiking couple named Snorelox and Music Box, who also didn't mind night hiking, everyone else was asleep at the Crosby Knob

Shelter when I arrived after 10:00 p.m. Posted all around the shelter, and on many trees, were "Danger" signs, warning hikers of a "problem" bear that had been seen in the area, and reminding us that leaving any food near you would likely result in a painful and tortuous death at the hands of a black bear.

A "problem" bear isn't necessarily aggressive, or dangerous. It's just way too familiar with humans, to the point that an encounter becomes far too likely. Contrary to the belief that attacks are more likely from mother bears defending their cubs, almost all fatal bear attacks are done by solitary male bears.[ii]

As I passed by a set of bear cables, I looked up and muttered, *"what the...?"* Hanging on the cables, where I expected to see just food bags, were full backpacks hanging in the night.

Once again, I was pissed at the Smokies, and at my fellow hikers for playing into the culture of fear by hoisting their backpacks up to the cables. As I set up my hammock, I heard Snorelox and Music Box lower a cable to hang their food. The weight of the backpacks on the cable and pully made a metal-to-metal screeching sound that woke up everyone in the shelter area, if not all of East Tennessee.

I was not about to disturb everybody again by hanging my food bag up with the backpacks. And I was too tired, too lazy, and just too pissed off to make the effort to hang my food from a tree. So, risking the danger of being mauled to death by a ravenous black bear, I stuffed my food bag in the bottom of my backpack, under everything else, and placed it under my hammock for the night.

Against all odds, when the sun rose the next morning, I was alive! My backpack and I had survived the dire warnings of a "danger bear," and made it through the night. With just over ten miles to the Standing Bear Hostel, I saw no need to get on the trail early. Most hikers were long gone by the time I got up. There were three hikers left, so I walked to the shelter to have my late morning coffee. As we talked, I realized it was a good thing I arrived as late as I did the previous evening.

The hikers informed me that it was not the danger signs that had made people hang their packs from the bear cables, but an officious Ridgerunner who visited the shelter before I arrived. Ridgerunners are hired by the local trail clubs and the A.T.C., and could be considered the eyes and ears of the trail, and most are really nice, and very helpful to hikers. This Ridgerunner was not. I was told by the three hikers that she was condescending, and quite nasty, as she ordered the backpacks be hung on the bear cables.

At this point I was sure glad I wasn't there last night. After having to pay to hike the Smokies, putting up with their stupid rules, all topped off with gout pain, I don't think a rude, obnoxious Ridgerunner would have fared well with me. I had a renewed faith in my fellow hikers, as all day I heard my own thoughts repeated to me as hikers told me how happy they were to be leaving the Smokies as well. My mood improved as I descended Davenport Gap to Pigeon Forge River, and out of the Smoky Mountains National Park.

As I entered lower elevations, it became spring again. It was mid-April, and the higher elevation of the Smokies had not yet been touched by spring, but as I descended toward Pigeon River, the forest was alive. As cold fresh streams hurried past on their way to the river, it was green everywhere. I crossed paths with Cautious, a 21 year-old from Kentucky - slender, with curly black hair, and always wearing a smile. He told me that he hadn't packed enough food, since he ate the last of his food for lunch. Given that we were about an hour from resupply, I believe he packed the perfect amount of food. A few steps later, I was out of the Smokies!!!

After the rules and regulations of the Smokies, I entered what is sometimes called the "wild west of hostels," the Standing Bear Farm. If I was looking for a place without the insane rules and regulations of the Smokies, I found it. The property is adorned with cottages, treehouses, a bunkhouse, and a common area with a fire pit and self-serve kitchen. A small building serves as a self-serve pantry, with items sold on the honor system, and a tiny shack housing both mail drops, and a refrigerator, from which they sold beer.

Beer flowed (and joints were passed) as we sat around the fire pit. For $15 you could set up your tent or hammock wherever there was room. I strung my hammock up about 40 feet from the fire pit and common area, sipping a beer as Free, a hiker in his 60's, played "Hey Porter," by Johnny Cash and America's "Tin Man," on one of the guitars available in the common area. Before dark, a light rain sent the hikers under cover. Given Standing Bear's reputation, it was a pretty quiet night.

*Figure 8 - "Free" strumming a guitar at Standing Bear Farm.*

Cell phone service is spotty along the trail. And since searching for a signal seems to drain a phone's battery, I kept mine on "airplane mode" most of the time, using it only as a camera. Service was especially bad in the Smokies, so at Standing Bear I was able to have a nice call with my wife.

Most days on the trail I would find an area with cell service; usually on higher ground, or when closer to cities. So I talked with, or at least left a message for my wife almost every day. Many nights there is no cell service, because shelter and camping areas are located near water, off the tops of hills and mountains. But regardless of cell coverage, I could always text her with the emergency satellite tracker I carried. Despite the extra ounces of weight, I made the concession with her to carry the device for her piece of mind.

It rained lightly on and off throughout the night, but the real downpour waited until 11:00 a.m., when I was ready to hit the trail. For most hikers, this was just the excuse they needed to call Standing Bear home for one more night. I waited for any break in the downpour, then headed out, alone. At the trailhead, I saw a hiker with a heavy pack, and a large heavy poncho covering both her and her pack, preparing to head out in the storm. It was Viking, the mother of Pebble's friend Princess. What she lacked in hiking experience and physical ability, she made up in grit and determination.

She let her daughter hike ahead at her own pace, then would "yellow blaze" ahead to meet up. Yellow blazing is skipping part of the trail, by getting a ride forward. It is named for the yellow lines on the road.

There is something to be admired in young, fit, slender hikers that can routinely do 20-mile days, but I've always been motivated by those not born with a hiker's build, who were not slender, or young, but still managed to get themselves up every mountain. She very easily could have been dropped off ten miles north, but instead, there she was, in the storm, climbing every one of the 2,475 feet up Snowbird Mountain.

It was a short 6.9-mile day, and I hit the Groundhog Creek Shelter just before 4:00 p.m., and had my rain-fly up before the rain got heavy again. Despite the rain, Whipper-Snap, a trail volunteer and 2010 Thru-Hiker, just kept working, with an occasional jab at us soft 2016 hikers, standing under the shelter, afraid of a little rain. The rain soon stopped and the fire was stoked up again. We were joined at the fire by a father and his 5-year old son, on his first overnight backpacking trip, carrying his own gear. I talked with him briefly, and he was clearly enjoying himself, but a bit shy around our group of smelly, unshaven Thru-Hikers.

Before sunset, Viking made it to the shelter...grit and determination.

*Figure 9 – Despite the rules and regulations, the Smokies are beautiful.*

The shelters in the Smokies were plastered with signs stating the rules. The need to have a permit, no tenting or hammocking, if you collect too much wood we'll remove the fire ring. But one sign also contained one the best pieces of advice I received on my journey. It was handwritten by a hiker at the bottom of the sign, and simply said: *Don't let the hiking, get in the way of the hike.*

Don't let the desire to complete 2189.1 miles get in the way of enjoying yourself today. Don't judge the journey by the miles, but by the experience. I had a certain sympathy for the "early to bed, early to rise" hikers, who never seemed to find time to just relax, and enjoy the journey. Every day they planned their miles, and stuck to that plan. They knew just how much time they could stop for lunch and breaks throughout the day. They were at work.

Perhaps they learned that from trail legend Warren Doyle, who has thru-hiked the trail 17 or 18 times depending on who you ask. He holds a workshop for people wanting to thru-hike, and tells them, "Hiking the entire Appalachian Trail is not recreation. It's an education and a job." I have one word for that advice: Bullshit. Sure, it's tough, but to treat it as a job? You might as well stay home and go to your cubicle farm every day. I decided that if I wasn't having fun, if I had to force myself to hike, and if I felt like going home, I would just go home. But that never happened.

Not that I skipped my way to Maine, whistling a happy tune. It was hard, but not as hard as getting up to an alarm clock and dragging myself to work every day. The trail was an adventure, an escape from the Rat Race. It sure as hell wasn't a job.

Finishing the trail was important to me, very important. But it wasn't the most important goal. Making it to Katahdin wasn't as important as enjoying myself, and experiencing what this journey had to offer. Yes, there was blood, toil, tears, and sweat, or in my case sweat and toil, very little blood, and certainly no tears.

I was now 250 miles into my journey, meaning I had hiked 230 miles over 24 days since receiving trail magic. On the south end of Max Patch Bald, a couple were set up with a pickup truck serving soda, candy bars, and fresh strawberries. The strawberries were quite a treat, as was the soda, but how was I to know this would just be the appetizer round of trail magic that day. At the top of Max Patch, one of the most beautiful vistas on the entire A.T., a young couple informed me of some *real* trail magic on the other side of the bald.

As I hiked down Max Patch, I was feeling great. The beauty of the bald was breathtaking, and the major uphill of the day was behind me. As I headed down the mountain, I saw a group of tents and canopies, and hoped it was the trail magic I was told about. As I got closer, it became obvious it was, and I was about to get my first taste of *real* trail magic from a group of former Thru-Hikers. A crude sign read: "2014 Hiker Trash Hangout" I realized then they had beer, *they had beer!!!*

Frank Sinatra once said: "I feel sorry for people who don't drink. When they wake up in the morning, that's as good as they're going to feel all day." As I enjoyed my first cold one, and looked at the abundant supply, I knew the morning would not be the best I would feel tomorrow. I didn't get drunk, but enjoyed not worrying about miles, or time, or Maine. I just had a good time with other hikers. There were Thru-Hikers, section-hikers, and overnighters all having a good time around the fire and loving the outdoors. One thing, for damn sure, was that no one felt like it was a job.

I stayed about three hours; others stayed the night. I wanted to make Hot Springs, N.C. the following day, and that would be just over 13 miles if I made the Walnut Mountain Shelter, 5 miles away. It was six o'clock, and the sunset was coming later every night. The majority of the hike would be downhill, and making the shelter by 9:00 p.m. would be pretty easy. It was dark when I got to camp, and after the feast I had been treated to, I wasn't hungry, so on a cold, breezy night, I climbed into my hammock, then into my sleeping bag, warm, and happy.

I woke up feeling pretty good, knowing today I would hit Hot Springs, N.C., the first town where the Appalachian Trail actually goes right through town. The sidewalk along Bridge St. is part of the A.T., with white blazes painted on telephone poles. Imagine the joy of stopping for lunch and a beer without leaving the trail! But before I walked down my first A.T. sidewalk, I learned a lesson I would not forget.

Some say the best way to hike is put your guide away, not pay attention to where you are, and just hike. I tried it today, and it proved to be the worst advice I ever heard. I hiked for what I thought was seven or eight miles before stopping for water, at a place the guide, which I hadn't been looking at, described as a "brook with cascades." At the cascades Full Throttle said, "You're 5.2 miles in." I felt good about that, so I responded, "Cool, 5.2 miles in to Hot Springs?" "No," he said, and then informed me that I had eight miles left to Hot Springs, I had only hiked 5.2 miles for the day. Lesson learned. From then on, I checked the guide frequently and kept a pretty good idea of where I was.

The water from the brook was nice and cold, so I half-filled my bottle and started chugging, "You're not filtering that," I heard Full Throttle ask with incredulity. "That's how Brother Blood rolls!" answered M&M. I repeated M&M's refrain, with a laugh "that's how I fucking roll." No, I don't play into the culture of fear. Consequences be damned.

Full Throttle was hiking with his wife, Grasshopper, and both were really nice, cool people. They were always encouraging, and despite not possessing the tall, slender hiker's build, and probably having ridden this planet around the sun a few more times than me, their positive attitude was contagious. I was always in a better mood after seeing them. Except today.

As I drank my unfiltered water at the "brook with cascades," I was not happy that I had more miles than expected to Hot Springs, but thought to myself, "no worries, the town will still be there when I arrive."

Unless it burns down.

For a while we had heard about trail closures around Hot Springs. Fires north of town had closed about nine miles of the A.T. from Hot Springs to Hurricane Gap. We could see the smoke from the hills and stranded hikers were starting to fill the tiny town of Hot Springs to capacity.

Very much a river town, Hot Springs also has steaming hot spring baths, which gave it its name. Its population has never reached 1,000, and now stands at about 600, give or take a dozen. It has a couple bars, a couple places to stay, a resort where the hot springs are, a convenience store called "Tobacco Road," and since we're still in the South, a Dollar General, of course.

The fires in the mountains just north of town, provided quite a show after dark. The "Silver Mine Fire" created a logjam of thirsty, hungry, dirty hikers. Which led to the second big story of Hot Springs for 2016 northbound hikers, the legend of the "Dumpster Beer." It remains unclear exactly why it was tossed out, but as many as 70 cases of cold beer were found in a dumpster. The rumored causes ranged from passed expiration dates, to a lost liquor license. But nobody really cared about the reason - it was free beer.

As hikers converged on the brew bonanza, the dumpster doors were locked, and a log placed on the top door in the vain hope it would keep the hikers from getting to the discarded beer. Guess how well that worked.

The grounds of the Hot Springs Resort and Spa had become the makeshift headquarters for firefighters. The rest of the town became a makeshift camp for hikers unable to proceed north. The local outfitter ran shuttles to Allen Gap, 15 trail miles from Hot Springs. But with free beer, and a desire not to skip any portion of the trail, many hikers were content to wait it out until the trail reopened.

I stayed with my friend Robert, "The Cleaner," in nearby Greeneville, Tennessee, but after two days, I was restless, and wanting to get back on the trail, so he drove me to Hurricane Gap, where I would only skip nine miles of the trail north of Hot Springs. The outfitter's shuttle took hikers to Allen Gap, six miles further along the trail, since getting to Hurricane Gap involved a long stretch on an uphill dirt road. So, for the first time on my journey, I had a stretch of trail all to myself. The six miles between Hurricane Gap and Allen Gap are fairly easy, and this afternoon was just a 1.7-mile slightly uphill hike to the Spring Mountain Shelter, for a night of solitude. For the first, and only time of my journey I was all alone at a shelter. After setting up my hammock, I collected wood, built a nice fire, and sipped my flask while two mice ran roughshod through the shelter. It felt good to be back in the woods, to be back home.

*Figure 10 - Robert "The Cleaner," right, and Brother Blood at Hurricane Gap*

My time alone in the woods alone was short-lived, I hiked just over four miles to Allen Gap, where I met my friend Maps, who had given me the great advice before starting my journey. She had beer! She had worked with me at REI in Virginia, before transferring to the Asheville, N.C. store. As we finished the beer, another hiker, Be-Bop, needed to get to Asheville, so the three of us jumped in Maps' car and headed out.

It was a nice evening, drinking wine, and having a great dinner in town, but after spending three of the past four nights indoors, I was ready to be living in the woods again. A little hungover, but happy, with a full belly after Maps' homemade breakfast, I was back on the trail just after 10:00 a.m. It was uphill again with a full resupply, today a 2,500-foot ascent. While taking a break for lunch, I was reunited with Pebbles. I had 1.3 miles and 1,000 feet uphill to the summit, and believed the hike to the shelter after that would be fairly easy. It wasn't. The guide described a part of the next 6.5 miles as "rocky and strenuous." It was a perfect description. I made Jerry Cabin Shelter by 6:00 p.m. Between the logjam caused by the fires, and the natural bottleneck that occurs after town stops, the shelter was quite crowded, and somewhat loud, including one hiker playing a guitar he carried with him. I moved a fair distance from the shelter, and camped near Pebbles, Chedda, Thumper, Texas Hippie, Spaceman, Stonebridge, and Wok Man.

My friend Robert was named The Cleaner, after Harvey Keitel's character in *Pulp Fiction*. Not part of any trail group, The Cleaner took it upon himself to adopt the Jerry Cabin Shelter and keep it clean and well-maintained. Another of the hundreds of wonderful souls that take their time to make the Appalachian Trail what it is.

The next morning was a rare treat. After a 2 mile, 700-foot uphill to start, the trail gave us seven not-too-difficult, slightly downhill miles. It wasn't until 9 miles in that I hit the first and only real uphill of the day, 1,500-foot Lick Rock. After 500 feet down, then 500 feet back up, it was nice arriving at the Hog Back Ridge Shelter to a quieter, more subdued atmosphere than last night.

A young lady at the shelter had a unique trail name. She had been a vegetarian from the age of eight, but when hiker hunger got the best of her at a trail magic gathering, she bit into her first ever bacon cheeseburger. The taste was so overwhelmingly wonderful, she broke into tears. I had met "Bacon Tears."

The Trail was still buzzing with the tale of dumpster beer. And when Tetradactyl arrived, we all had a good laugh listening to his animated tales of what happens when hikers find a free beer treasure trove.

I had been told before my hike that if I made the first three weeks, I would make it to Katahdin. I was now on week five, and April was coming to an end.

My first decision of the day was whether to push a few extra miles to make the town of Erwin, Tennessee the next day. That decision was an easy one, considering today was Saturday. Why push extra miles to arrive in a Bible Belt Town on a Sunday?

I was again one of the last hikers to leave camp. As I headed out I crossed paths with a man heading south with a shopping bag in hand. I thought he was heading up to the shelter to do some maintenance, so I asked what he had in the bag. It wasn't maintenance supplies at all, it was... donuts! He also had some bananas hanging off his fanny pack, I took one for the road. "Yonder" was his name. He thru-hiked in 2003, and enjoyed surprising hikers with morning donuts.

He mentioned there was more trail magic 2.5 miles ahead at Sam's Gap. But as I approached the Gap, all I saw was a trash bag, and a cooler labeled "trail magic," full of nothing but trash. So much for more trail magic I thought to myself. At Sam's Gap, the trail joins a road that passes under US I-26, before heading back in the woods. As I got closer to the overpass, I could smell charcoal burning. A barbecue! Trail magic! Trail magic with barbecue! I bet they have beer! They did!

But it wasn't just beer, they had laid out a feast fit for a king, and I feasted like royalty. They had homemade pasta salad, barbequed chicken, homemade muffins, homemade cookies, homemade potato salad with bacon, coffee, soda, chips, homemade chili, and more. They were a group of geo-cachers, a hobby in which people place small "caches" in the woods, or elsewhere, and others navigate with their GPS to find them.

After three hours of stuffing my face, I headed out in hopes of making it almost 8 miles to the Bald Mountain Shelter. I didn't even make it four. Feeling like I was carrying an extra 20 pounds in my stomach, with a storm approaching, I hit Low Gap campsite after 4:00 p.m., just in time to set up before the storm hit. I quickly fell asleep. I woke up again just long enough to realize I still wasn't hungry, and fell asleep for the night by 7:30 p.m.

It's easy to let your mind play tricks on you on the trail. Hiking up Big Bald the next morning, my belly aching, the creative side of my brain kept asking, "did I drink some bad water?" "Do you think it's giardia, maybe norovirus?" The more intellectual side of my mind would causally reply, "Yeah, it's probably bad water, couldn't be the chili and Fritos, cookies, beer, soda, brownies, chips, BBQ chicken, pasta & potato salads, and then more beer. You're right, it's gotta be bad water."

Of course, it wasn't norovirus, or giardia. And after a short walk off trail with toilet paper and my lightweight hand shovel, I was feeling better. As I ascended Big Bald, a hiker that looked too familiar was heading south at a pretty good pace. I asked his name, and where he was headed.

"I'm Tater, I'm hoping to make Erwin today." I did remember him, he had passed me just yesterday. For a moment, I worried that I was headed the wrong way, but again the intellectual side of my mind was correct. He was the one going the wrong way.

"Which way are you headed?" I asked.

"Northbound."

"I don't think so," I added, before we looked at our guides, and realized he was indeed heading the wrong way.

He thanked me, and with his same positive attitude and pep in his step, his turned around to go back up and over Big Bald for the third time in two days. I heard later that despite adding 12 miles to his hike, he did make Erwin that day. Soon after, I crossed paths with Princess and Viking slack-packing southbound, who jokingly tried to convince me that I was the one heading the wrong way! Didn't work.

Big Bald Mountain was beautiful. Cloaked in a cover of fog, I hiked through a cold and windy mist, which felt wonderful going uphill, but chilled me to the bone as I hiked down the other side. I stopped for coffee and a Clif Bar at the Bald Mountain Shelter, before hiking down to Spivey Gap, and then it was an easy, slightly sloping downhill three and half miles to finish at the No Business Knob Shelter. There I would enjoy the two beers I carried out of Sam's Gap, but had been too stuffed and too tired to drink the night before.

A fire was already burning nice and warm when I got to the shelter, where I rehydrated some my wife's homemade chili and had the first beer. It was dark, and a little quiet around the fire when I cracked open the second can of beer, making everyone a bit jealous. But I had carried a pound and half of beer all day, and would be carrying out the empty cans, so I wasn't in a sharing mood. Plus, they had weed; they'd be fine.

Soon after crossing into North Carolina, the trail follows the state line separating North Carolina and Tennessee. At many crossings, roads are split; a Tennessee road to the west and a North Carolina road to the east, often paved on one side, dirt on the other. But the biggest difference is that in Tennessee, most of the shelter areas do not have privies. Instead they provide a shovel, with a sign leading to a "toilet area." With thousands of hikers passing through each year, it takes only a small percentage not digging cat-holes to turn these "toilet areas" into turd minefields.

With only seven miles to Erwin, I was in no real hurry to get going. As usual, everyone else seemed real anxious to get to town, and again, I was the last one out. It was a beautiful day, so I took my time, and along the way made a reservation at the Super 8 Motel in town. After a 1,000-foot downhill to the Nolichucky River and Erwin, I came upon Uncle Johnny's Hostel.

Uncle Johnny's is another trail landmark, another "vortex" where hikers are known to get sucked into staying for three or four days, despite every night saying that they will be leaving the next morning. I had a resupply box waiting for me at the hostel, and asked if the shuttle could take me into town to the library, where I could download videos and pictures. I had been told that Johnny would give me the hard sell to stay at his place, which he did. He tried to sell me a private cabana-like room for the same price as a room at the Super 8, I declined. There was no fee for the shuttle, or holding the mail drop, but I gave him $10 anyway, $5 for the mail drop, $5 for the shuttle. He does run a business after all. Every day Johnny loads up his passenger vans for lunch at the all-you-can-eat Pizza Plus, and today his daughter took me the extra few miles to the Post Office. I tipped her $4, making the total for the free shuttle and mail drop, $14. Worth every penny, Uncle Johnny treats hikers very, very well.

At the motel, Bacon Tears, Lewis, Texas Hippie, Thumper, and I met Jake, staying there while working on decommissioning areas of the Nuclear Fuel Services plant that supplies enriched uranium to the U.S. Navy. To no one's surprise, it had polluted the local groundwater with radioactive material. Jake asked if we needed a ride anywhere, so five hikers jammed into his small rental car and headed out for mango margaritas as an appetizer, then dinner a few doors down at Primo's Italian restaurant, a bring-your-own-beer-and-wine eatery. It was our good fortune that a store in between was a liquor store. I bought wine for dinner, and a small bottle of sipping whiskey for the trail.

The next day it seemed a lot of hikers were ready to get back on the trail, just raring to go. But when I arrived back at Uncle Johnny's, I was once again reminded how little rain it takes to keep a Thru-Hiker off the trail. It was just a drizzle, but the beer at the hostel was enough to delay most hikers. As more beer showed up, the Uncle Johnny's vortex sucked a few hikers into staying one more night.

### ###

While in Ervin, I checked Facebook and saw a message from my neighbor Carlotta that she had mentioned me and my journey to her first-grade students. She said the kids were quite interested and excited about my hike, and were following me from the satellite tracker I was carrying. She asked if I would answer some of their questions. Just over a week later, the first batch of questions showed up on Facebook:

*How are you today?*

*Do you ever take a break and rest?*

*Where do you get your food? Your water?*

*Where do you sleep?*

*Do you go anywhere to eat?*

*Where do you charge your phone?*

*What electronics did you take with you?*

*What color is your phone?*

For the next few weeks I had fun recording videos on my cell phone for Mrs. Moulder's class. I showed them the shelters, my hammock set-up, flowing springs, and how I filtered my water - when I actually filtered it. I talked about why I was hiking and about the wildlife I had seen.

The questions kept coming until the school year was about to end. And of course, the final request from the first graders was to please take a picture of a privy. I obliged with five pictures ranging from nice, new privies, to one more primitive and run down.

### 

As uphill hikes go after resupply, this one wasn't bad, a gradual 1500-foot climb out of Erwin to Indian Grave Gap. A nice 8.4-mile day. I laughed to myself thinking about when I once thought 20-mile days would be routine by now. All day I had been leap-frogging with Lewis & Clark. I had worked with Clark at REI, and he and his girlfriend, Lewis, were great people to be with on the trail. First World problems were the last thing on their minds. That night around a fire, as I shared some of the Wild Turkey American Honey I bought in Erwin, one young man made a passionate plea for his political views. That night I realized just how well a campfire and booze can work to block out background noise.

The next morning, I woke up early, but didn't get up early. Like most days I nodded back off to sleep before waking up for good, When I woke the second time my phone's clock read 9:36, which is pretty late even by my standards, thank goodness I didn't care. At that moment, I felt bad for the hikers who feel a sense of guilt if they sleep past the time they wanted to be on the trail. I always felt that the day I worried about what time I got up and started hiking, would be the beginning of the end of my journey. At that point, it would just be a job, and an education.

After leaving at around 10:30 a.m., I made it a full 200 yards or so, before I was greeted with trail magic! A gentleman, who called himself "Brother Tom," was serving hot coffee, homemade banana bread, and brownies. And it was good. As he was handing me a cup of coffee, he asked something about my religion. I recall answering in a friendly tone that also hinted it wasn't something I wanted to talk about, "can't say I'm a very religious person." At that point Brother Tom made my day, by simply respecting that and not trying to have a religious discussion.

Between a good night's sleep and Brother Tom's trail magic, I felt great on the trail that day. I felt like I was finally getting my "trail legs," and the uphills weren't as challenging. I decided to hike on into the night, and was feeling good enough to pass by several nice campsites and pressed on to the Clyde Smith Shelter. By 9:30 p.m. the temperatures were in the 30's and it was sleeting. Of course, everyone was asleep in the shelter when I arrived at almost 10:00 p.m., but my cooking woke up Loudmouth and we shared some kind words before he laid back down in his cocoon of down and fell back asleep.

Loudmouth earned his name because of his very soft voice. He was tall and slender, some might say lanky, and was hiking the trail with his friend M&M. Loudmouth possessed a genuine warmth, far too lacking in the world. I always enjoyed seeing him. I set up my hammock as I let my dinner rehydrate. Despite not stressing about miles, I was proud that I did 18 miles. Sleep came easy that night.

## CHAPTER 7: HAPPY CINCO DE MAYO

No surprise, I wasn't up early. It was a chilly morning, but unlike most days, it was not warming up as I started hiking, but getting colder. It was really cold by the time I was three miles in, but at a road crossing I came upon a couple hosting trail magic. With beer!

After a while, the man hosting the trail magic asked, "How about some real trail magic?"

I wasn't sure exactly what he meant, but he soon revealed that in addition to hot dogs, hamburgers and beer, in his pocket he had a stash of neatly rolled joints for weary hikers. Happy Cinco De Mayo! Say what you will about pot smokers, but they are a generous bunch, I was always offered a hit whenever joints were being passed.

I've never really been a pot smoker; as politicians used to say, "I experimented" with it, as if I was testing some long-held hypothesis on the science of getting high. But there is one opinion I have held for a long time, and it was validated on my journey: Legalize it. The idea of anyone having a criminal record for the recreational use of marijuana is inherently wrong, and runs counter to what we understand to be individual freedom. I never once witnessed anyone making trouble, getting loud, or causing any trouble after smoking pot. The same cannot be said about alcohol.

Legalize it, tax it, and use the money the fight the real problem with drugs and alcohol: addiction. The war on drugs has always been a war on people, minorities to be specific, and it has been one of the most colossal failures in American history, in both human rights and effectiveness.

# # #

In front of me was 2,000 feet up Roan Mountain. I could see that the summit was getting a blanket of snow, and I actually looked forward to a snowy trail. My feeling of wonder at snow and its beauty is as alive in me now as it was when I was seven years old and we moved from Memphis to Youngstown, Ohio. My brothers and I were so excited about a winter with snow. Nothing has changed for me. A snow forecast still makes me restless, drawing me to a window every 10 minutes to see if snow is falling.

I was not disappointed; the snowy forest was beautiful. It was quiet, and cold, but not windy, a true "winter wonderland." As I made the final ascent of Roan Mountain, I came upon a very slow, older hiker, of course nicknamed "Turtle." His name was Dave, and he explained how he had undergone a "heart procedure," just months earlier. He said his friends had hiked forward to the shelter. I stayed close for a while, to make sure he'd be okay, and while he was very slow, he seemed confident he would have no problem making the shelter. After a while I hiked on, but couldn't shake the nagging feeling, that someone should keep an eye on Dave.

I got to the shelter where his friends asked me if I had seen him, I let them know I had, while thinking to myself, "some friends these guys are." The High Knob Shelter on Roan Mountain sits at the highest elevation of any shelter on the entire A.T. at 6,193 feet. It is more of a two-story rustic cabin than a shelter. It is completely enclosed, and even has windows, poorly sealed, drafty windows. By now it was bitter cold, and I decided to fill up with water, and have a snack before heading down to lower ground for the night. I decided that if Dave had not made it to the shelter by the time I returned from the spring, I would go make sure he was ok. I was relieved to see Dave at the shelter when I got back. When I mentioned that I was hiking on to lower ground, Dave said once I got down to Carver Gap, I'd have about "half a mile" over a bald, then I'd be back in the woods again.

After heading out I saw two young ladies, Moonshine and Sunshine about a quarter mile down the trail, apparently searching for the shelter which is not visible from the trail, especially in the snow. The sign pointing the way to the shelter is very small, and also hard to see in the snow. After confirming they were indeed looking for the shelter, I directed them back and described the small sign that lead to the shelter.

Sunshine & Moonshine I would guess in their mid-20s, using their journey as a way to increase awareness of Suicide Prevention. That night they tented in the snow and provided an example of how stories circulate on the trail.

The A.T.'s informal communication network is legendary. Between trail angels, shelter journals, and word-of-mouth, a Thru-Hiker can normally be located in a matter of hours. And just like social media, stories certainly are, shall we say, "embellished," along the trail. The following day I started hearing horror stories about the cold and the snow at the High Knob Shelter. One story told of two young ladies whose tent had completely "collapsed" on them from the weight of the snow. I knew it must have been Moonshine & Sunshine.

Soon I was believing the ladies had barely escaped serious hypothermia, and I didn't think I'd be seeing them on the trail again. It sounded pretty bad.

### 

As I reached Carver Gap and prepared for the half mile over the bald, I didn't bother checking my guide. After all Dave had told me he knew this area quite well.

My journal entry for that evening perfectly describes my hike forward that afternoon:

*I hadn't decided how yet, but this much I knew: Turtle would have to die. I was going to kill him.*

*The day was cold, very cold. After a morning of a little trail magic, I saw snow at the top of the hills I was about to climb. I made the climb up Roan High Knob. It was beautiful. Trees outlined in snow, with the sun peeking out just enough at times to make a stunning portrait.*

*I had passed Turtle on the way up, he was slow, but in good spirits. At the shelter, his friends seemed a little worried about him, yet didn't think of actually leaving the shelter to check on him. Some friends.*

*After getting water, Turtle had indeed made the shelter, and was in pretty good spirits. I told him I was moving to lower ground where hammocking might be more comfortable than up here. He said that I had "a bald ahead, but it's only about 1/2 mile across it, then back in the woods."*

*Those were his fateful words.*

*I hit Carver's Gap and was ready to bear the wind and snow for a 1/2 mile before hitting woods again.*

*My pack cover was blowing off, so I stuffed it in my rain jacket pocket and looked ahead into the wind, snow, and fog. Just a 1/2 mile, right? It was well over a mile of crossing the bald when I decided to check the guide. Half mile my ass, the bald was over 2 1/2 miles across. I did finally hit the woods. It was still cold, really cold, but the wind was not as bad in the woods. Not long after I came to a small shelter, with just one occupant, Yosh the Oracle. He was what some might call an earthy, hippy. But his positive outlook, and desire to work together to make the shelter as comfortable as possible is just what I needed. We used my hammock rain tarp to block the snow blowing in from gaps under the roof in the back of the shelter. I set up my hammock in the shelter, he laid down, partly under my hammock.*

*I had my winter gear, so before long I was toasty in my sleeping bag and ready to ride out the snow.*

*I made it across the bald and was warm again. I guess Turtle will get to live, this time.*

Despite the freezing temperatures, Yosh made it a great night. My rain fly stopped most of the snow that had been blowing in, and what little continued to blow in from the front of shelter, wasn't enough to create problems.

The next morning, I was no hurry to get out of my toasty sleeping bag, and neither was Yosh. We had the exact same sleeping bag from REI good down to 19 degrees, so I knew he was warm as well. He strummed his ukulele, using his sleeping bag as a blanket, as the martyrs started hiking by. They were wet, and cold, telling us it wasn't too bad once your body warms up. I took their word for it, and stayed nice and warm in my sleeping bag.

*Figure 11 - Snowy trail from inside the Stan Murray Shelter on Cinco de Mayo*

The weather started to break just after noon, so I eased myself out of my bag to make coffee and get in at least a few miles that day. I packed up and was on the trail at 2:30 p.m., with the temperature back up to the low 50's. The Overmountain Shelter, converted from an old red barn was only two miles on. When I stopped for lunch a couple told me that the night before over 50 people had stayed there – and it sounded like a real mess. I was really glad I'd stayed where I had.

It was after 5:00 p.m. before I was on the trail again, prepared to go over Little Hump, and then Hump Mountain. After getting over Little Hump in no time, I swore I heard something. I listened again and sure enough, it was the sound of a ukulele. There on a rock was Yosh the Oracle, picking at his instrument, looking content. He had set up for the night in a small group of trees in a ravine. A storm was definitely moving in, but looked like it might be moving north and just miss us. I gambled and decided to climb Hump Mountain. The guide had warned of several false summits before reaching the summit, but on the A.T., it seems like every hill has false summits.

The false summits were no worse than on most mountains, and my gamble paid off as the storm moved north and I stayed dry. The weather was actually quite pleasant as I headed down Hump Mountain for two and half miles to Doll Flats, where the trail stops straddling the North Carolina border, and fully enters Tennessee. Doll Flat is a very nice campsite with one exception; like many places in Tennessee it doesn't have a privy, so there were areas that were turd minefields.

The winter storm was over. I built a nice fire and camped with Sun Dial from Albuquerque, New Mexico. He earned his trail name when one time he headed out in the New Mexico desert without a compass and tried to navigate using the sun. Care to guess how that worked out? Sundial admitted he was well off course when his experiment finished, but how can you not love a person willing to go out try something like that?

With the short winter storm behind me, I was back in short pants and short sleeves again, glad to have experienced snow, but also glad the cold didn't last. Throughout the day I crossed paths with Frisbee & Stubbs, Redneck (now calling himself Refill), and Cruiser, who I hadn't had seen since Georgia. That evening I set up my hammock and rain fly right before the rain started falling. With the brief winter storm in the rear-view mirror, I was on my way to Trail Days.

But not before crossing paths with Moonshine & Sunshine. I was surprised to see them after hearing of their harrowing experience in the snow with their tent collapsing. They chuckled as they explained the snow had merely built up on the outside of their tent, and they had to knock it off.

It was the first of May, and Trail Days was just around the corner. While hiker festivals along the Appalachian Trail are now commonplace, Trail Days in Damascus, Virginia is the granddaddy of them all. The three-day festival held in mid-May attracts 15-20,000 hikers and trail enthusiasts to this town of less than 1,000 residents.

Some hikers had taken great pains to be in Damascus for the weekend. I hiked into town on the first day of the festivities, Friday, May 13th, by sheer coincidence. I headed to the Post Office, where I ran into Old Spice, and his son Axe. They enjoyed doing big miles and were pretty fast hikers. A couple hours earlier I had seen them at the Tennessee/Virginia line where they said they wanted to make the Damascus Post Office before it closed at 4:00 p.m., I assured them they would make it. As they waited outside for the end of the postal employees' lunch hour, Old Spice described perfectly what the last week on the trail had been: "a rolling frat party."

For a good week before Trail Days, the trail south of Damascus was crowded as hikers either sped up, or slowed down to reach Damascus for the party weekend. The trail took on a party feel, with an abundance of trail magic. When I hit Dennis Cove Road on Mother's Day, Sunday May 8th, a group had laid out a spread highlighted by "fix your own" burritos and tacos.

I didn't stay too long as I wanted to climb the 1800 feet to Pond Flats and give myself a short hike into town Monday. While enjoying a burrito, I heard perhaps the funniest, and possibly most sad comment relating to Trail Days. A hiker in his early twenties was explaining his excitement about festival, and commented, "I'm looking forward to doing some good drugs, no hard drugs or anything serious, maybe just some acid."

The trail magic had no beer, but several hikers remedied that by getting a ride for a beer run, and setting up camp at the trailhead, just off the road, stocked with cases, upon cases of beer. It had much more of drunk party feel than I was in the mood for, and since I was planning to be in town the next night, I decided to hike on.

At Laurel Falls the trail becomes a ledge above the water downriver from the falls, not dangerous, but certainly beautiful. There was a one-mile side trail to Hampton, TN, but that would mean starting out the next day with the 1,800-foot hike up Pond Flat. No thank you. The hike was indeed strenuous, confirming my decision to do it now, instead of the morning was a wise one. At the summit, I camped with Loudmouth and M&M, and built a raging campfire. I sat at the fire with the flask of honey bourbon, but despite my offers, they each settled on just one sip of the whiskey, leaving almost a full flask all to myself. With just over three miles to the trailhead tomorrow, I felt no need to get to sleep early, so for the first time on the journey, I just laid in my hammock with earphones on listening to music late into the night.

In the morning, the hike downhill from Pond Flat to Rt. 321 was an easy stroll. I called the Americourt Hotel in Elizabethton, TN and booked a room, then called a cab to get me there. I did laundry, and had a good dinner with wine. The next morning, I was stuck waiting for a ride back to the trail until after noon, and then encountered trail magic right where I was dropped off, on the shore of Watuga Lake. After enjoying some red beans and rice it was 3:00 p.m. before I hit the trail. After a relaxing three-mile path around the lake and across Watuga Dam and up a small hill, I crossed Wilder Dam Rd., where steps lead up from the road to a small primitive campsite along the trail. I climbed the steps, looked to my right, and realized I was not alone. From about 25 feet away a black bear was staring right at me, not one bit scared or apprehensive about my presence. Causing me a bit of concern.

There had been signs posted about a problem bear in the area, and no doubt, she was it. I saw one cub several yards behind her, and decided backing off was probably smarter than pushing my luck. Now I know what is written about what to do when encountering a black bear, but I also know who doesn't read that: the bear. The mama bear was acting territorial pacing back and forth while keeping her eyes on me. I wasn't scared, but extremely cautious. I moved up to the steps with my video camera, when she turned towards me and angrily thrust her front paws forward as if to make a charge. I backed off pretty damn fast. Now, I was a little scared. It's called a bluff charge, and it was enough for me. If she wanted to stay there all day, I would let her.

I only caught a half second or so of the bluff charge on video, before rushing back to the road. Soon, another hiker arrived, and once the bear was out of sight, we headed up the trail. I'm sure that the next half mile, was the fastest uphill hiking I did on the whole journey.

The Vandeventer Shelter area provided awesome views of Watuga Lake and the surrounding hills, and luckily, I was again set up and dry when the rain came. I woke at dawn to a beautiful red sky, but remembered the saying, "red sky in morning, sailors take warning." Almost before I finished that thought...the winds came. And they came strong, blowing up the ridge and up under my rain fly. I held out one hand to hold the tarp in hopes of preventing the stakes from being blown out of the ground. After a few minutes, my hands were cold enough that I decided to trust that the stakes would hold and let go of the rain fly. The stakes held.

Like most cold, wet mornings, I watched and listened as those with their self-imposed schedule packed up in the rain and head out for the day. As the rain lightened, I finally emerged from under my rain fly, and prepared to hit the trail. All day the skies were threatening, but somehow the rain held off.

Throughout the day I'd been hearing about the famed "Riff-Raff" trail magic party just past TN Route 91. And as I crested a hill just past the highway, I walked into a pasture with tents and hikers everywhere. Someone announced my arrival with the shout of "hiker!" and the crowd let out a cheer. Something told me they had beer.

They had beer and when the supply got low, they quickly dispatched a crew to the local package store for resupply. I donated $20 to the cause, although they did not ask for contributions. I figured they would return with five or six cases of cheap beer, but I was wrong. It was cheap beer alright, but at least 20 cases were being hauled up from the road. I enjoyed a few by the bonfire that was being faithfully maintained by a Riff-Raff member. I called it night around midnight. The party continued until around 2:00 a.m. when a downpour sent the revelers to their tents for the night.

### 

Riff-Raff is a trail group started by former Thru-Hikers and their stated mission is to "throw the biggest parties and deal out the most fun on the Appalachian Trail." It's fair to say they've succeeded. The party starts almost a week before trail days, with many hikers simply staying at the makeshift trail city for days. They pack up the day before Trail Days starts and take their part of the rolling frat party to Damascus, where the party continues.

The morning sun hit my rain fly as if it was a solar panel. It was the hottest morning yet. A little hungover, I took my time knowing that

I had less than 20 miles to hike over the next 2 days. The Riff-Raff folks had their caravan just about ready to go as I headed out just before 10:00 a.m., hiking through a herd of cattle to start the day. The trail was still buzzing with the excitement of the upcoming Trail Days weekend. I was actually looking forward to getting past all the partying.

That evening the skies were again threatening when I made Abington Gap Shelter. The shelter area was packed with section hikers, including a dozen or so college students. They were all very nice, but I wasn't in the mood to camp with a group, so I loaded up with water, and hoped to find a campsite before the approaching storm hit.

I wanted to hike until 7:00 p.m. and then claim the first decent spot to camp. At 6:30, I found a nice little opening, and was deciding whether to stop when the sound of rolling thunder made it an easy decision. After getting my rain fly up, I collected some wood and stored it underneath and keep it dry, to start a fire after the rain stopped. The rain did come, and soon Spaceman and Firefly came hiking into camp, barefoot. They asked if I would mind them setting up camp; I asked if they wanted a sip of hot coffee. They had decided earlier in the day to do some barefoot hiking, to see if their feet would get used to it over time. I never found out if it worked.

They were both really nice, and easy to spend time with. The thru-hiker rumor mill had them becoming a trail couple, but I really didn't care. I wasn't into trail rumors or drama. The rain did stop, and Spaceman and I got started building a nice warm fire. One of the nicest things about a thru-hike are the times you get to really relax and talk with people you've met on the trail in passing. Tonight was one of those nights.

I had knocked out over 13 of the 20 miles remaining to Damascus, so it was just 7 fairly easy miles into Damascus and Trail Days, passing the Tennessee/Virginia line along the way. I rolled into Damascus just before 2:00 p.m., when I ran into Old Spice and Axe waiting outside the Post Office. Rather than waiting for it to reopen after lunch, I walked across the street to the Old Mill Restaurant, for a bottle of wine and lunch. It was there I met the bartender Pauly, preparing for their busiest weekend of the year. The Old Mill was a not party place, so it became my go to place over the weekend.

The Post Office reopened and I picked up both my resupply, and my "bounce box." My bounce box contained my laptop, beard trimmer, and miscellaneous items, that I would mail from point to point, on the trail. I used the laptop to download videos I had taken. Damascus was the last place I received my bounce box, since it was just one more thing to worry about.

Doing a bounce box is a hassle, so I decided going forward to just keep my videos saved on thumb drives and SD cards.

Trail Days is really two huge celebrations. First there are the activities in town, such as auctions, raffles, free concerts, along with food vendors, gear repair stations, and authors of trail books. It's family oriented, with no alcohol served outside. Vendors from the largest gear companies down to the mom and pop purveyors of hand cut walking sticks are there peddling their wares.

But on the outskirts of town, just about a mile down South Shady Avenue, three days a year "tent city" springs up. Tent city consists of a couple municipal baseball fields, and the woods behind them. It's the biggest hiker party of the year. Five dollars grants you the opportunity to camp wherever you can find a spot, from Thursday to Sunday. As I entered, I was given one simple piece of advice: if partying late into the night go to the right; if not, go to the left. I went to the left.

I set up in tent city and decided to keep some of my more expensive gear in my backpack and with me. Then, being the fool I often am, I drank wine and beer throughout the day and night, without complimenting it with a fair amount of water, resulting a hangover the next morning. But today was a zero day, so I laid in my hammock, drank what little water I had, and slept it off, until after noon. Although touted as a three-day festival, Saturday is when almost everything happens: the hiker parade, auctions, raffles, and the "hiker prom," where many of the male hikers get dolled up in dresses to dance and party the night away.

I took it easy, visited some of the vendor tents, ate some crappy carnival food, hung out at the Old Mill, and made sure to drink plenty of water. I ended the night at the Old Mill, which was far more crowded than the previous night, and found myself stuck next to a former Thru-Hiker extolling the virtues of slack-packing.

I felt better Sunday morning, and as I prepared to head back to the woods, there was Pebbles. She was arriving and hoping to enjoy the final day of the festival, but most people, and vendors were packing up to leave. As I headed out, it would be last time I saw Pebbles.

She had found a nice group of hikers to head north with and I knew she'd be okay. She was starting to do big miles and soon left me in the dust in Virginia.

I stopped at the Old Mill for coffee, a burger, a hard cider, and a chance to thank Pauly for how wonderful she had been over the weekend. As I headed past the vendors packing up, one asked if me if I wanted to try out his lightweight hammock. "Why not?" His gear was made in Tennessee, which qualifies as "made in the USA," despite Gen. Longstreet's efforts in the 1860's. I gave it a try, and it was comfortable, and not as wide as the double wide hammock I was currently using. He said he'd give it to me for $50, including the suspension straps to hang it. I told him I was happy with my straps, so he offered $30 for just the hammock. I left Trail Days with one new piece of equipment, by Yukon Outfitters. At an outfitter in town, I mailed my heavier hammock home, and began my hike through Virginia.

I had completed four miles, or 7/10th of 1% of the A.T. that runs through the Commonwealth of Virginia. Just 546 miles to West Virginia. A friend had warned me weeks ago: "It will be so crowded after Trail Days, there will a line at the springs to get water." It was one of many warnings I received about the mess that would be the Appalachian Trail north out of Damascus following Trail Days. As I prepared to rejoin the trail, I was not looking forward to the rolling frat party continuing.

I was anxious to be heading north again, but leaving town I noticed an ice cream shop and stopped for a treat. Finally leaving town I came to the intersection of the Appalachian Trail and the Virginia Creeper Trail, created where a railroad once ran. The A.T. turns left, up a mountain, while the Creeper Trail takes a smoother, flatter path and re-connects with the A.T. about 12 miles north. Ahead of me was a group of hikers I call "creepers," Thru-Hikers who, instead of making the turn back into the woods and over mountains, decided to stay on the easier Creeper Trail.

As a purist, that's just not my style. I know each person can hike their own hike, but I just couldn't see getting to Katahdin and raising my arms in triumph if I had skipped even inch of the trail, so up the hill I climbed. I passed signs about a detour of the trail, due to a footbridge being washed away. The purist in me wanted to see just how bad the water crossing was, before taking the detour. When I got to where the bridge was supposed to be, I was surprised that anyone would think a bridge was needed to cross. The water was moving, but wasn't even close to knee high. I put on my flip-flops, and waded through. Always the purist!

When I got to VA Rt. 58 I was happy to have not detoured around any white blazes. On both sides of the road I saw a large Ziploc bags with several sheets of paper inside. I was not surprised when the contents warned the world is going to hell and rapture will soon come. The author also mentioned her ability to faith heal. I was happy to add two large Ziploc bags and some fire-starting paper to my gear. As far as faith-healers, I know the only thing they can rid you of is the money in your wallet.

As I started out the next morning, my feet were chafed and irritated. The night before I had picked at some hardened skin on my heel, hoping it would feel better. Sigh. Fifty years old and still thinking that picking at something will make it feel better! But I soon stopped thinking about my feet, and enjoyed a nice day of hiking.

The fears of a crowded trail melted away as I realized that Damascus and Trail Days served as the jumping off point for many hikers. Many had planned to hike to the festival and head home, while others had spent far more money in the first 500 miles than they expected, so they headed home after the weekend of partying. I was ready to hike through Virginia, where I was promised the trail flattens out. "Flat" Virginia started out with an 1,100-foot ascent, then a 2,400-foot climb to Buzzard Rock. Along the way, I saw several "creepers," as they rejoined the A.T. "It's their hike," I told myself. At least for them the first part of Virginia was pretty flat.

After the crowds at Trail Days, I was hoping for a night of solitude; and just after 7:00 p.m., the trail provided it. Near the summit of Buzzard Rock, I found a nice little area, with a small fire ring on uneven ground. Uneven ground means no tents. I would likely be alone. Not long after, I had a fire going when a couple hiked by and I told them that they were welcome to set up here, if they could find a flat spot. They hiked on, and I had my night of solitude, with abundant firewood. I was happy.

It was now Day 51 of my journey, and I reached another iconic A.T. landmark, Grayson Highlands State Park. The Grayson Highlands are known for herds of wild ponies that roam the park, but the term "wild" is used pretty loosely. While it is true they are not penned in nor owned by a farmer, they are far from "wild." Not only are they not skittish around people, they are downright friendly. In addition to the ponies, I noticed something else about the park. It's beautiful. Of course, natural scenery has a hard time competing with the novelty of friendly ponies, but I was pleasantly surprised by the beauty of the highlands, which no one seems to talk about.

The landscape has a western prairie feel to it, something I imagine is similar to the hills of Montana. That evening I arrived at the Wise Shelter just outside the park's boundary, where the biggest challenge was finding a place to camp free of pony turds. Hardly the worst problem to have in the world.

*Figure 12 - Ponies at Grayson Highlands*

But the next morning, I realized I had an issue that I hoped would not come for at least another few hundred miles. My boots were failing. I hoped to complete the journey using two pairs of boots, but after the 500-mile mark, the first pair was already shot. And again, the skies looked ready about to open up at any time. Seven miles in, I stopped briefly at the Old Orchard Shelter as rain started to fall, ever so lightly. That was reason enough for several hikers to put off getting back on the trail. Those that did hike on came to a sign at Rt. 603 from a local church that read, "Hiker Picnic 6:00 p.m., Wednesday 5/20/2015." Today's date was Wednesday 5/18/2016, but word on the trail was that the church simply used last year's sign, and the picnic was indeed today.

All of the hikers that didn't stop at the shelter, stopped there. I pushed on, alone.

This time the rain did come, and it came hard. But it wasn't cold, and it wasn't windy, just a steady hard rain. After leaving the hikers waiting for the Hiker Picnic behind, I didn't see another person for four and a half hours. It was just me, the trail, and the rain.

I was enjoying the hike; my feet were not. With my boots falling apart, mud and water seeped in where the sole was separating from the rest of the boot. The mud turned my socks into a fine grit sandpaper which rubbed against the tops of my toes with every step. But there was nothing I could do, changing socks would only have been effective for mere minutes, so I just hiked on, into the night.

It was well past dark when I arrived at the Trimpi Shelter, just north of Troutdale, VA. I cranked up my stove to prepare a well-earned cup of coffee, and slowly removed my boots and socks. My feet looked horrible. The one hiker I had seen earlier on the trail, Turkey Bait, was there, so I shined my headlamp on to my chewed-up toes for some confirmation of how bad they looked. I wonder if any doctor has ever figured out why we feel so much better when someone agrees how bad something looks. I was worried that maybe I pushed too hard, and my feet might need a day or two off.

With my coffee ready, I was in my flip-flops and ready to head down a small, but muddy and slippery slope to the spring to fill up with water. So, with a water bottle in one hand, hot coffee in the other, I tried to ease myself down the slope in flop-flops. I made it about halfway, when to no one's surprise, I slipped and fell, but managed to spill only about half the coffee.

I'll call that a win.

The water flowed from a piped spring, so I moved my foot under the water waiting for the sting that comes with cold water hitting raw, worn skin. But it didn't sting. The water actually felt good on my feet, I thought, "I'll be okay."

With a light rain falling, I laid in my hammock the next morning, realized my feet were dry, and felt pretty good. My goal was to make Adkins, VA the next day, so I really didn't have to push miles today. I taped over where my toes had been rubbed raw, and hit the trail.

I know why people like to say the trail "flattens" out in Virginia. It is because of days like this. The first 10 miles were pretty easy compared to what I had become accustomed to, and my mind got to thinking that I could make Adkins that night. I had already made reservations at the Relax Inn for the following night, so if I could make it tonight, I would earn myself a zero-day tomorrow. I was thinking, "why hike until 7-8:00 tonight, just to set up camp, and break it all down in the morning to do just four or five miles to town." The idea of making it to Adkins was growing on me.

When I arrived at the Partnership Shelter at 3:30 p.m., I was 12.5 miles from Adkins. The group there was still in party mode from Trail Days, and I wasn't in the mood for a loud shelter. The Partnership Shelter is in close proximity to a road, so it's one of the few shelters where a hiker can get pizza delivery. Like all shelters close to a road, there is also a prominent, "No Alcohol" sign, which is proof that there will be a lot of alcohol brought in. After a quick snack I was back on the trail.

It was getting close to 4:00 p.m., and in my mind, I was calculating when I might be able to make it to Adkins. I first thought maybe 10:00 p.m., but as the miles clicked off, I starting thinking about maybe 9:00 p.m. Then my thoughts turned to the two things that made me determined to get to Adkins by 9:00, beer and pizza. If a small town like Adkins had pizza delivery, I really didn't think it would be available late on a Thursday night. Then a troubling, very troubling, thought entered my head: "What if Adkins is a dry town?" I was almost paralyzed with fear. As I tried to expel the demon of a dry southern town from my mind, my legs raced forward. I called the Relax Inn and booked a room for that night as well.

The AT Guide lists every feature of the trail on an elevation profile, and as evening set in on rural Virginia, I hiked past them all as I headed for Adkins. *Spring, stream, Chatfield Shelter, USFS 644 (dirt), footbridge, stream, two powerlines, VA 615 Lindamood School.* Now it was just 2.8 miles to go, and still not dark. I went through the fence stile, over the railroad tracks and just before 9:00 p.m. I hit VA 683, and the Relax Inn was right there! Next door was a Sunoco station with Hunt Brothers Pizza... paydirt! Lewis & Clark were there and handed me a Pabst Blue Ribbon as I headed to the office to check-in.

I got to the gas station just after 9:00 p.m. They had beer! I asked about a pizza, but a woman informed me the oven had been turned off. I didn't care, I wouldn't go hungry. But in the next breath she said, "I just turned it off. It's probably still hot, I can make you a pizza." She turned the oven back on and asked what toppings I wanted.

Her name was Theresa, and it was people like her up and down the trail that really make the journey what it is. When people ask me about special places on the trail, I know they want to hear about hiking up a mountain and looking out at the horizon, and having some philosophical, life-changing moment. But the life-changing moments I experienced on the trail were at places like that Sunoco station, where with one small act of kindness, Theresa helped restore my faith in humanity. As small as that act was, I thought about it many times on the trail, and thinking about Theresa making that pizza helped me get over few mountains on my journey.

The next day a few of us piled into the motel owner's car for a cramped ride into Marion, where I hoped to buy a good pair of new boots. I had arranged the shuttle, and acted like a jerk when hikers started piling into the car. The town's outfitter didn't have boots, so I settled for a cheap pair of running shoes from the Shoe Show discount store. After a bite to eat, and buying some resupply, we piled back in the car to head back to the motel. I apologized to my fellow passengers, admitting that I had been a jerk, and they all accepted the apology, without malice.

By now rain was an everyday occurrence, which I hoped would help with the fires in North Carolina and Shenandoah. Storms were forecast again for Saturday, when I would be leaving Adkins. While enjoying my zero day, I met a trail volunteer, and as we chatted I could tell he was no fan of the Appalachian Trail Conservancy. "They're all about money," he told me. He said while he and others are out working on the trail, for free, all they're doing is talking about money and increasing revenues. And he's right.

It really doesn't matter what kind of group you're talking about, once they hit a multi-million-dollar budget, it becomes more about money than anything else. Salaries and fundraising become the focus, rather than the original, stated mission. Whether it's the NRA, a teachers' union, or the ATC, money tends to control the group's focus. While it describes itself as a "volunteer-based" group, their Chairman was compensated over $200,000 in 2015, and seems to me to do little more than take credit for the volunteer work of local trail clubs...and raise money.

Some accountants are the modern-day equivalent of snake oil salesmen, the used-car dealers of yesteryear. Their job is not to simply count and record where money is raised and spent. A second-year accounting student could do that with a simple spreadsheet. No, some accountants are hired today for their creativity, to make the numbers look good, in a public relations sense. And to show the public how an organization is spending every dime they take in for their stated purpose.

At the end of 2015, the ATC was sitting on over $8.4 million in stocks and bonds, $7.5 million of that in their "endowment" fund, a sum that has skyrocketed from just $3 million in 2008. They do a great job protecting and growing their assets. Despite this cash hoarding, their accountants make it look like the group is putting everything it raises back into the A.T.

Despite the warning that a hard rain was gonna fall, I decided to head out on Saturday anyway. For once, I left before check-out time. I made it to the Barn Restaurant five minutes before the 11:00 a.m. cut-off time for breakfast. I had the "hikers special" with coffee, and then more coffee. Not long after hitting the trail, I ran into some volunteers at the site of the former Davis Path Shelter. I asked one if he was Jim, the man I had met yesterday. He wasn't. I said that Jim thinks the ATC is just about money, to which the volunteer quickly responded, "We all think that."

With the promised storm approaching, I set up my rain-fly and hammock, and enjoyed lunch protected from the heaviest rain of the storm. After the rain slowed, I hiked a few more miles, before making camp just past Rt. 42, and was set up just before the storm again unleashed a deluge. I changed into dry camp clothes and enjoyed dinner in my hammock, nice and dry.

### 

The rock just missed my flip-flop clad foot. Had it landed just a few inches to the right, my hike might have ended, or at least been delayed right there. I was setting up a fire ring, and carrying a large rock over some rocks scattered with leaves, when my foot hit a soft spot and I lost balance, dropping the rock just inches from my exposed foot. I felt lucky, and stupid. I would have had no one to blame but myself. On a trek of 2,189.1 miles, over some difficult terrain, it stayed in my mind that one misstep, one mistake could send me back home. This time I dodged that bullet.

The day had started with a steep 625-foot climb, up Lynn Camp Mountain. It was a 2,000-foot hike up to the Chestnut Knob Shelter. In "flat" Virginia. Chestnut Knob is a bald, with a fully enclosed shelter at the summit. The shelter was filling up as I ate dinner, and with a chilly wind cutting across the bald, I decided to hike on to find a better campsite. In two and half miles I found a great site near a rock outcropping on Garden Mountain, and after my close encounter dropping the rock, I waited out the rain and got a fire going. I sipped on Junior Johnson's Apple Pie "legal" Moonshine and enjoyed a chilly Virginia night.

My wife had planned to join me on Memorial Day weekend when I would take a few days off the trail. We were to meet on Thursday, May 26th, with the only question being where. The easiest place to meet would be Pearisburg, VA, but that was 64 miles ahead. I decided I would try to make Pearisburg, but that would depend on the next two days, so I decided I would hike into the night to make miles. I wanted to have my dinner before dark, so when I got to camp it would be just coffee, and bed. I wasn't in the mood to be cooking and cleaning after 10:00 p.m.

Of course, the rain came just when I thought it would be a good time for dinner. So I just kept hiking. The weather broke just before 8:00 p.m., and I had a dinner of homemade dehydrated chili mac, and then hiked on in the dark. After almost 22 miles, I got to camp after

10:00 p.m., had a snack of peanut butter on a mini-bagel, then slept wonderfully.

The next morning began with almost a mile walked before being back on the A.T. They're called "sideways miles," and they suck. These are the miles going in or out of a shelter area, a side trail to get water, or anytime you are walking, but not making any progress toward the 2,189.1 miles to Katahdin. This morning I walked 0.3 miles to the spring, 0.3 back, then the 0.3 side trail back to the A.T. The shelter had been home to about a dozen hikers last night, a far cry from the 50-60 at the shelters in Georgia. And again, I was the last one to leave.

### 

Cankerworms are small caterpillars that drop from trees and dangle on a silk string before falling to the ground. Today was the first hot summer day of May and they were everywhere. Sometimes just hanging there, sometimes dropping right in front of you, and sometimes right onto your head.

Again, the hiking was moving along at a good pace, and I hoped to be relaxing in my hammock well before dark. I came to what was supposed to be a campsite along Dismal Creek, but only found a tiny area, unsuitable to hang a hammock. But then a man named "Dusty" came over, offering mini-chocolate bars, and told me of a place just up the trail perfect for hammocking. He was so friendly it reminded me why I love the trail community. I filled up my water bottles with untreated water from Dismal Creek, and headed up trail. Sure enough, there was a really nice area to set up, Dusty was there in his tent, and welcomed me. I was relaxing, in my hammock, with coffee by 7:30 p.m. A day that started with emergence of dangling caterpillars all along the trail ended with me wishing, for the first time, that I had my bug net as I sat in my hammock, swatting bugs, and drinking unfiltered creek water.

After hiking almost 40 miles in two days, I now had no need to push miles to make Pearisburg on Thursday. That was good since I woke up Wednesday morning with a pressing need to dig a cat-hole. I had some pep in my step as I headed into the woods with an aching stomach. Even after finishing my business, my stomach was still churning, so I rested in the hammock before setting out for the day. Was the creek water a big mistake? I was on the trail by 9:30 a.m., with my stomach feeling a little better.

I misread some landmarks and thought I was hiking pretty slow, before hitting the Wapiti Shelter and realizing I was actually making pretty good time. I had a long lunch before heading up a 1,300-foot hill in "flat" Virginia.

By 3:30 p.m. my stomach was hurting again, nothing horrible, but I started looking for a place to string up my hammock and rest a few minutes. It wasn't until 4:30 that I found a place to set-up and relax. I was very close to the Woods Hole Hostel, another iconic stop on the trail. I had already decided I would be moving on. I'm not a big fan of staying in hostels, plus I was about to be indoors for three straight nights.

As I relaxed to let my stomach settle, a hiker who was staying at Woods Hole, came hiking past, slack-packing with a daypack provided by the hostel. The pack featured child star Hannah Montana, the character played by Miley Cyrus. I remembered thinking what a sweet, innocent young girl she was when she played Hannah Montana. For a moment, I was sad, to think what has happened to that little girl, the daughter of Billy Ray Cyrus. And it just broke my heart, My Achy-Breaky Heart.

I arrived at Docs Knob Shelter by 7:00 p.m., and was feeling pretty good. Tomorrow would be day 60 on the trail, and I would spend a weekend with my wife, seeing her for the first time since I started. I was already 40 pounds lighter.

Something happened that night I won't ever forget. It was well past dark, and was lying in my hammock with my pack underneath, when I reached over to get something out of the pack. It was sitting among some ferns and weeds as I dug in and found what I needed. It was then I realized that being in the middle of the woods, sleeping over ferns, felt as natural as if I just reached for something on a nightstand. I was totally at home living in the woods!

That night, I thought to myself, "I'm tough, this stomach bug was nothing." The next morning, I felt the same, believing the worst of the stomach bug was behind me. I was wrong. I was looking forward to seeing my wife, and enjoying a couple of zero days. But first, there were miles to be made up in Hot Springs. I didn't want to summit Katahdin, and then figure out when to get back to Hot Springs to make up the nine miles missed earlier due to the fire. And while it's true that missing miles due to trail closures does not negate it being a true thru-hike, I wanted to do every inch. Always the purist.

I can't say my wife was thrilled at the prospect of driving another three and a half hours to Hot Springs, after driving four to Pearisburg, but I reminded her that I did not forfeit my driver's license by hiking the A.T. She was glad I'd be doing the driving to Hot Springs. I had also agreed to take Loudmouth and M&M with us, so they could make up the 15 miles they missed. The hike to Pearisburg was under 10 miles, followed by a strenuous uphill road walk to town. Even the pick-up trucks were laboring as they ascended North Main St. and headed to town. Perhaps not wanting to break their momentum heading up the hill was the reason no one offered a ride to this smelly hiker.

The climb was worth it, at the top I hit the outskirts of town and an all-you-can-eat Chinese buffet. I felt pretty good as I ate plate after plate, before my wife arrived at the restaurant. We headed out to pick up Loudmouth and M&M who had chosen the most out of the way trail crossing possible at Lickskillet Hollow. But soon, a car of three smelly hikers, and my wife, was heading back to North Carolina. We arrived in Hot Springs and settled into the Alpine Court hotel, whose owner was not thrilled to be talking about the "dumpster beer" episode of a month ago. It's pretty clear that more than a few residents of Hot Springs were not happy about unlimited free beer for hikers. I don't blame them. I was feeling pretty good as I sipped wine with my wife for the first time in two months.

My stomach was a mess again the next morning, but it wasn't going to keep me from hiking. Loudmouth and M&M decided they would slack-pack their 15 miles, while I, of course, insisted on carrying my full pack. The heat was bearing down on me as I left town and headed up the first steep climb of the day. I was chugging Gatorade in the hope it would have me feeling better as the day progressed. It didn't. The first hill was followed by another 1,300-foot hill, and I was feeling as bad as I've felt on the journey. Then, as I trudged up the hill, the skies opened up and a downpour cooled everything down. I still didn't feel great, but felt better without the sun beating down on me.

It was slow hiking, but I made it to Hurricane Gap just before my wife arrived after bravely driving up the long gravel road that the shuttle drivers wouldn't. I had a couple of beers with some hikers, before heading to Allen Gap to pick-up Loudmouth and M&M. We headed back to Virginia, stopping along the way for fast food, a real treat for Thru-Hikers. I felt hungry, but my appetite was subdued as my stomach was still aching. This might be a long night.

We struggled a bit to find the trailhead at Lickskillet Hollow, but eventually Loudmouth and M&M were back in the woods, and my wife and I decided to stop at the first decent motel we could find. It was late, and after laying down, I knew something was wrong. My stomach was tightening up and causing real pain. I went and sat on the toilet, and started to think I might be getting really sick. It soon became evident that I should get up and kneel in front of the toilet, but I was hurting and didn't want to move. So, I reached out with my right foot and slid the cloth bath mat under me, and let the purge begin.

After emptying my stomach, I started feeling a little better, still tender, but better. A few minutes later I laid back down, starting to feel even better. Slowly my stomach began to settle, and I knew I'd be able to sleep. Was the worst behind me now? By the next afternoon, I was sitting on the banks of the New River in West Virginia, sipping raspberry mimosas with my wife. The stomach bug was gone. I do remember at one point during previous night my wife asking me, "Do you think you'll be more careful about treating water now?" My answer: "Of course not." The next day we visited a winery, and enjoyed a lazy night, I did not miss a day on the trail due to the stomach bug.

I did clean the bath mat in the motel's laundry room the next day. It just wouldn't be fair to leave it for the housekeeping staff.

It was now day 64, and after lunch with my wife at the Dairy Queen, it was back to living in the woods. As always, leaving town with a full resupply means uphill hiking. Today the first six miles took me up 1,600-feet before starting to level off. It became a somewhat relaxing evening hike. Whatever was blossoming on that ridge north of Pearisburg must be very tasty to black bears. In less than a two-hour span, just after 6:00 p.m., I saw six bears. All very wild, and very afraid of me. In that short time, my bear sightings for the journey jumped from two to eight.

I caught up with Loudmouth and M&M where they had set up camp just past the intersection of the Groundhog Trail. As I cleaned up after dinner, I noticed a pair of eyes just a few yards from camp. They seemed somewhat low to the ground, but not a racoon or squirrel. As whatever it was walked off, I told my two camping partners, and Loudmouth grabbed his headlamp and joined me in pursuit of the animal. I thought maybe a bobcat, or fox, or something exciting. But we were soon disappointed when we discovered it was just a deer. It must have been conducting reconnaissance, because throughout the night we were visited by a group of four or five deer roaming through our camp.

### ###

Some hikers swear by trekking poles, adjustable ski poles that allow a hiker to use their arms, taking pressure off the legs, much like using a handrail going up, or down stairs. I've even read where trekking poles can reduce the pressure on your knees by up to 20%. The author then calculated that it means tons of weight taken off your knees in the course of a hike. I say Bullshit! That's the same logic drunks use when joking about doing "12-ounce" curls. If that were true, drinking a six-pack is the equivalent of doing a 29 ¼ pound curl. I did the math. I agree trekking poles might make the hiking easier, but I like having a free hand while I hike, and for me, a stick does just fine. A lot cheaper too.

But the night before I broke my hiking stick by hitting a tree, to alert a bear of my presence. And today I was becoming obsessed with finding a new one. My eyes kept darting from one side of the trail to the next looking for that perfect fallen branch. It cost me a fair amount of time, and I only found a branch that would work temporarily. It was hot, and I was frustrated for allowing myself to waste so much time looking for a walking stick. One will present itself soon enough. Then around 6:30 p.m. I came across a couple setting up camp, planning trail magic the next day. I was invited to stay, but wanted to get a few more miles in before calling it a day. They did give me a Granny Smith apple and an Orange Crush. It's amazing how something as small as an orange soda lifts your spirits. It wasn't beer, but it was good enough. Plus, if they had beer, I would have spent the night. Instead I hiked on and set up at a primitive camp after another couple miles.

It was now June, and as I hiked on, I thought what a cruel joke it is tell people that Virginia is flat. I was lucky that I knew from past hikes not to believe the "Virginia is flat," fairy tale. Early in the day I had a 1,700-foot climb that wasn't bad, but after heading right back down the other side, I then encountered a smaller, maybe 900-foot, ascent. It kicked my ass. As I finished the second hill and the terrain flattened out, I checked the guide to see how far it was to my goal of the Sarver Hallow Shelter, when I realized that I hadn't looked at the sideways miles to the shelter, it was 0.4 miles off trail, and I was sure it would be all downhill. No one minds a downhill hike into a shelter area; the part that sucks is walking back up the next morning almost a half mile just to get back to the A.T. But I had no water, so I was stuck making the trek down to Sarver Hollow. I was thinking on the way down just how far, and how much uphill I would be walking in the morning, just to get back to the white blazes. But as it turns out, it was worth it!

## CHAPTER 10: NO RAIN, NO PAIN, NO MAINE...NO THANKS

Sarver Hallow Shelter was a nice new structure, serving as that night's habitat to just one other hiker, Beef Jerky. I had casually crossed paths with him over the past few weeks, and this became another example how nice it is to actually get to know someone on the trail. In his late sixties, he hiked circles around many younger hikers, including me. He made me feel better when he talked about how the second smaller, but steep hill that day made him feel like he was going to throw up. After dinner, I popped some popcorn for us to share, every hiker loved when I made popcorn. He explained to me that his brother-in-law, a dear friend, had recently passed away and that he was going to be leaving the trail briefly to attend the memorial. That night I let him use my phone to text his wife since he had zero coverage. As I laid down in my hammock that night, his wife texted and asked me to relay the message that he was asked to deliver the eulogy at the service. I was glad that I was there to relay that message, and it meant a lot to Beef Jerky to be asked to do that for his friend.

It's times like that that really drove home the reason I was on the trail and savoring life in a way that reminds you what's important. At times like this, it's hard to even comprehend complaining about things as trivial as a crowded car ride, or hills, or cold, or rain... or taxes.

But he wasn't the only reason I was so glad I made the walk down to Sarver Hollow. The shelter area sits on the homestead of the Sarver family. The water source is a walk-in spring that is as old as homestead itself, dating to before the Civil War. The spring sits at the bottom of a large stone box, about five feet deep, with the stones beautifully showing their age. There are steps down to the spring, where the water is just as fresh, cold, and delicious as it was 170 years ago. It was some of the coldest spring water I had on the entire trail. Just past the spring sat the ruins of a small cabin, somehow still standing, and beyond that only the chimneys still standing from the Sarver cabin.

Records about the Sarver family say at least two family members served in the Civil War. One who helped build the homestead, John Elmore, died in Pickett's Charge.

Beef Jerky was well on his way by the time I had my morning coffee. I spent some time just checking out the ruins in daylight; it was definitely worth the almost half mile trek back up to the trail. Again, Virginia teased me with fairly flat and some downhill terrain, before heading up Brush Mountain. The first part of the climb was hot, and slow. But a summer storm was moving in to bring relief.

It had been a pretty wet May, and with June came summer heat. And with summer heat comes thunderstorms, heavy thunderstorms. It was June 2nd and today I faced another 1,000-foot plus climb in *flat* Virginia. Hiking 1,500 feet in summer heat is not easy; it's not just the elevation, but the summer sun is against you as well. In the heat, all you think about are the climb and the distance to the top. The heat conspires against you along with the elevation.

But as they say, "*No Rain, No Pain, No Maine.*" To make the promised land of Maine, you must endure pain and wetness and suffer endlessly for that wonderful moment when you summit Katahdin. It's an oft repeated phrase on the trail.

And it's Bullshit.

Putting on a rain jacket can be a fool's errand. Some buy in to the "breathable" material marketing hype, but there is no such thing as "breathable' waterproof material. Every hiker has a temperature at which a rain jacket is useless. A temperature where after a few hundred yards in a rain jacket, you are drenched with sweat. For the first time on my journey, the temperature hit that threshold. It was well over 80 degrees, and I was about to go up 1,400 feet. I saw the storm coming in, and said to myself, "if you're going to bring it, bring it strong." Mother Nature complied.

Accepting my challenge, the storm unleashed its wrath on this solo hiker. And it was awesome.

As the storm unleashed its fury, I was liberated. I climbed the hill not thinking of the heat, or the elevation. I was scanning ahead with trepidation of a blown-down tree ending my hike. I was thinking about the storm as I paced up the hill with a spring in my step that only a storm like this could produce.

I was alive!

The rain paused before I reached the summit, but soon a second surge came and got me up the rest of the mountain. It was only when I reached level ground, and the rain had stopped, that I felt the decline in temperature the storm had brought. It was only then, for warmth, I put on my rain jacket.

I hiked along level terrain on Brush Mountain until I reached a short side trail near the summit. It led to a monument near a spot where a small plane piloted by Herman Butler crashed, killing six people. On that spot, May 28, 1971, Medal of Honor winner, and the most decorated solider of World War II, died. Audie Murphy was only 45 years old. Visitors had left dog tags, service medals, and even a beer can with the label, "Freedom Isn't Free."

The rainstorm had passed and I had five miles to my home for the night, the Pickle Branch Shelter. Despite the storm, it was still going to be a warm night. It was the first night I slept without my under-quilt around my hammock. Summer was here. The water source for the shelter was a stream at the bottom of a steep 0.2-mile path. The rain had turned the stream into a muddy brown raging river. So for the fourth time on my journey, I filtered my water.

There is something about wet, stormy days. They don't confirm the idea of "No Rain, No Pain, No Maine," they completely destroy it. If my evening cup of coffee in my hammock was great after a dry day, imagine how wonderful it was being dry and warm, taking that first sip of hot coffee after a day of being soaked to the bone. It was a time to savor the coffee and feel an immense joy over the simple pleasure of being warm and dry.

The next morning, as I sipped my coffee, a man was pacing from campsite to campsite, asking each person if they knew the weather report. It was pathetic. After all, if he made it through the storm yesterday, he should be just fine today. His girlfriend didn't seem to care at all about the weather, as he implored her to ask people nearby if they had the forecast. As he approached me and inquired if I might be the chosen one with cell service and a forecast, I simply replied, "100% chance of weather." He was not amused.

###

"You're almost there," are perhaps the worst words to hear from a hiker heading in the opposite direction. Same goes for: "It's just around the corner," or "It's not far," and "half-mile, maybe." Today it was Dragon's Tooth, south of Catawba, VA. She probably thought it was encouraging to tell me I was "almost there." But it wasn't, the ridgeline that looked so flat in the guide, was really a series of small steep ups and downs, and her words had me believing that Dragon's Tooth was just beyond the next small hill. Then the next hill, then the next hill, then the next. It's demoralizing to think you are getting close to the next landmark, just to realize the person was being nice in not telling you how far it really was.

But today, I was meeting my wife, and hoped once past Dragon's Tooth, I might have a smooth downhill to our meeting point at VA Route 311. I shouldn't have gotten my hopes up. The descent down Dragon's Tooth is a very popular day hiking trail, because of its challenging rock scrambles and excellent views. Perfect for young hikers with small day packs, not so much for a 50-year old carrying over 35 pounds. As with every rock climb, the downhill sucks more than uphill, and I just kept thinking, "one mistake here can end my journey," or worse.

My attitude was not that great as I inched my way down the rocks until I remembered my own thoughts about what's really worth complaining about in life, and it helped, just a little. But as with every obstacle, I got through it, hit smooth trail and picked up my pace. My attitude picked up along with my speed. I crossed paths with a high school cross-country runner, who said how much respect he had for what I was doing. I told him the respect was mutual as he dashed off up the trail.

My wife arrived, with beer, soon after I made it to the trailhead. I always asked her to bring extra beer in case there were other thirsty hikers, but between my being slow and one of the last to leave every morning, most hikers were well ahead of me when the beer showed up. Their loss. Just one hiker, Scarab, was dropped off at the trailhead by a shuttle, and enjoyed a beer with us before my wife and I headed off to a quiet cabin for two nights.

### 

It's the most photographed site on the entire Appalachian Trail. McAfee Knob is a rock ledge that jets out over the Virginia landscape, where every hiker gets their picture taken near, or right on the edge of the protruding boulder. I sat on the edge with my feet dangling over what looks like a drop of thousands of feet into oblivion. My wife was not too happy seeing the picture, but at the risk of upsetting those who want their friends to believe they risked death, I will tell you that the tree tops are only a few dozen feet from the ledge. Trust me, if I can sit on a ledge without soiling my pants, it can't be that scary.

*Figure 13 - Sitting on the edge of McAfee Knob.*

The day at McAfee Knob was one of the greatest of my journey, and not just because I hit the iconic landmark. I had hoped to do over 11 miles to Lamberts Meadow Shelter, but signs were posted that the shelter was closed due to "Problem Bear Activity." Hikers were being diverted to a temporary campsite at Hay Rock, over 5 miles past the shelter. The signs also stated the campsite did not have a water source, and that Lamberts Meadow was the only reliable water source before Hay Rock. I guess they didn't mind if you were mauled by a bear when filling up water, just not while you were sleeping.

I decided I would camp less than a mile north of McAfee Knob at the Campbell Shelter. I would not be doing the miles I had wanted, but glad not to be pushing it. Just after starting the day, I missed where the A.T. veers off from the easier, fire road trail to the Knob, and being the purist, backtracked to where the trail split from the fire road trail, not to miss any white blazes. Near the Catawba Mountain Shelter, I was sitting on a rock next to the trail snacking on some peanut butter, when a young female hiker came down the trail. We chatted for a second before I stood up and noticed a black bear sitting like a dog in front of a tree, watching us from about 50-60 feet away. It slowly got up and nonchalantly walked off, completely unafraid. This was the problem bear. Bear count now at nine.

Not long after, I was standing on the iconic ledge of McAfee Knob. I took pictures for some couples on day hikes, and of course had my picture taken standing on the ledge. I made a cup of coffee and relaxed before heading downhill to camp at Campbell Shelter. I got a fire going and said hi to the hikers in the shelter, when El Duce asked if I wanted to head back up to the Knob for sunset. I hedged, but as I sat by my fire, I couldn't think of any reason not to. El Duce and his dog headed up first, I followed about 20 minutes later. At the Knob, I took pictures and video of him and his dog, and then handed him my camera. It was then that he took the picture that freaked out my wife. I was unsure about dangling my feet off the ledge, but El Duce convinced me that as I Thru-Hiker, *I had to*, so I did.

Before the sunset, we could see rain and storms heading our way. It was quite beautiful to see the weather systems making their way across the landscape. But since they were heading our way, we headed back down to camp.

The rain was brief, and had passed through before sunset. I could see that a stunning skyscape was just beginning. I went down to the shelter to see if El Duce wanted to make one more trip to the Knob, but he declined. I had another scare as I slipped on the wooden steps leaving the shelter and fell pretty hard. El Duce jumped up to see if I was okay. I was, just frustrated. I headed back up to the Knob, and the sunset was breathtaking. I was all alone, and felt like a little kid on a great adventure. I would set my phone's camera to a 10-second delay, then try run across the rocks to the ledge for a picture at sunset. It was fun feeling like a kid again!

I got some good pictures and video, and some not so good. But it was fun. I headed back to camp reminded that the journey is not about the miles, or suffering through rain and pain, just to make Maine. It's about feeling free, and like Thoreau at *Walden*, "to live deep and suck out all the marrow of life."

### 

It was June 6th, day 72 of my journey, and the first time in my life, I littered on the Appalachian Trail. I did it to send a message. Not a message of civil disobedience, or to bring attention to social injustice. No, the message I sent by leaving a piece of paper on the trail was much simpler:

Rattlesnake under rock with white blaze. 6/6 11:15 am.

I had seen my first rattlesnake on the Appalachian Trail! In my three previous years of backpacking, I had seen many black snakes and garter snakes, but never a venomous snake. But there at Tinker Cliffs, sunning itself on the rocks was a fat, lazy rattlesnake. It didn't care too much about my presence, so I took out a selfie stick to attach my video camera. A section hiker next to me feared that I was going to use the stick to pick up the snake. I don't think so. As I started filming, the rattler decided it would be more comfortable under the rock, so it turned toward us and slithered under the rock. I decided to leave the note in case the snake was spooked and ready to defend itself.

### 

It's at this point some hikers start suffering from what is known as the Virginia Blues. The trail magic parties are gone, we've hiked about 250 miles into Virginia, and aren't even halfway through the state. It was raining just about every day, and we hadn't completed one third of the entire A.T. And, Virginia is NOT flat like we were told. The journey can start to feel like a grind. Because of the rain, people were in their tent, the shelter, or under their hammock rain tarp in camp, so there was less socializing. People were also trying to do more miles, realizing they weren't even close to where they thought they be by now. And, to repeat, Virginia is not flat.

I found a lot of reasons in Virginia to keep from getting "the Blues." Being close to the one third mark means you're still on the trail, after many hikers have headed home. Plus, you're also about 150 miles from one of the least difficult, and for me, one of the more relaxing sections of the trail, Shenandoah National Park.

Instead of getting the Blues, I was figuring out what I could do to make the journey more enjoyable. I focused less on the number of miles I was hiking. I had given up on the crazy idea that by now I would easily be able to do 20-mile days, and realized how much I enjoyed relaxing in camp and watching a fire, "caveman TV." A fire also tends to bring people together, and creates a more social atmosphere. When alone it served as a great companion. I started making an effort to get to camp with enough daylight to eat dinner and collect firewood before dark.

### 

No one is going to mistake the wine sold in small cardboard cartons as much more than cheap fermented grape juice. But as I sat by a fire at Blackhorse Gap just off the Blue Ridge Parkway, I realized how everything is better on the trail. Even cheap box wine tastes like a fine vintage.

It was day 74, and I was starting to get up earlier. Today I was actually on the trail before 9:00 a.m. And today Virginia actually was pretty flat. I put in almost 15 miles by 4:30 p.m., when I came across some trail magic at Cross Jennings Creek. I had decided I would stay at the Middle Creek Campground that night, where I had a resupply box waiting. I called for their shuttle, and before I could finish one PBR, the shuttle was there. As we pulled away I asked if she gave rides to buy beer, and she did, but for a fee. No problem, I mean how much could the shuttle be? Seven, maybe ten dollars. We we're almost to the store when I asked. "Twenty dollars" was the answer, I was about to buy the most expensive 12-pack of my life. It was still worth it!

I didn't head back to the trail until after noon the next day.

### 

"She offered me a Snickers, then a banana, when I said 'no,' she said, 'how about some meth?'"

We should have changed his trail name to "Snickers and Meth" immediately. Of all the stories I heard on the journey, that one takes the cake. But he stuck to his story and swore it was true. He swore that upon entering a fairly run-down hostel, the middle-aged host offered him meth that he claimed was being cooked in small outhouse-like building in the backyard!

It was a short day since again a shelter area ahead was closed due to bear activity. It was almost all uphill again in flat Virginia, so I stopped at the Cornelius Creek Shelter after just nine miles. As I got a fire going the conversation turned to politics. One retired military guy was explaining, in detail, exactly why Hillary should be in jail. I just tended the fire and grinned, thinking to myself that all those Congressmen and all those lawyers going after Hillary just had to ask this guy hiking the A.T. to crack the case... then they could "lock her up." It was nice letting go and not engaging in the discussion, after all I had a half-liter carton Chardonnay chilling in the creek. Just as I poured the first glass of wine, Snickers and Meth started talking about his fear of the government turning on the people. Unlike most times I had wine, I felt no guilt that night about not sharing.

Though I was no longer obsessed with miles, doing nine or ten miles a day would not get me to Maine before Baxter State Park closes on October 15th, so the next day I hiked until dark, doing almost 18 miles. At lunch I ate my first, and last, portion of Spam for the journey. Is it possible that stuff has gotten worse over the years? It was close to dark when I arrived at Matt's Creek Shelter and ate my dinner while bugs had their dinner with my legs.

The conversation was better tonight, as Moss Man was wearing a hat reading, "The Heart is A Lonely Hunter." Discussing classic American literature sure beats politics and talk of a government takeover, though not quite as interesting as a hostel peddling Snickers and meth.

For the first time of the journey I was on the trail by 7:30 a.m., 7:18 to be exact. The day started with a relaxing flat hike along the James River, before crossing the longest foot traffic only bridge on the A.T., the James River Foot Bridge. The bridge is a footbridge, but called the Foot Bridge because it is named after Bill Foot, a trail volunteer whose efforts helped lead to its completion. So, I walked over the Foot footbridge. Soon it was back uphill, 2,300 feet, followed by another 800-foot to the summit of Bluff Mountain. It is on this mountain where in November of 1890, little Ottie Cline Powell strayed from his classmates while collecting firewood, and somehow made it to the top. He was within a week of turning five years old, when he died at the summit. Right next to the trail is a memorial, exactly where his body was found the following spring.

After making it down the other side of Bluff Mountain, I was ready to camp wherever the opportunity presented itself. Frustrated at the inability to locate a campsite the guide had listed 0.2 miles off the trail, I continued on to the 800-mile mark where I found a nice little camp spot, and built a fire ring. But again, the bugs were having a field day. Redwing and Cheeks, another rumored trail couple, joined me, and I tossed and turned all night unable to sleep in the hot weather.

Even though I was still tired from not sleeping well, I was again on the trail before 8:00 a.m. That morning I crossed into familiar territory; a section that I had hiked three years earlier. I enjoyed passing through the Brown Mountain Creek area, home to a community of freed slaves in the late nineteenth century. I stopped to chat with four ladies section hiking, and shocked them by drinking untreated water right out of Brown Mountain Creek, I guess I'll never learn. Then it was back uphill, 2,700 feet up Bald Knob, which is not a bald. But my climb was interrupted - by two former Thru-Hikers who had driven from Indiana to do trail magic. At Route 60, 700 feet into the climb, I was treated to Mountain Dew, pudding, chips, Fritos, bread sticks with cheese, cookies, and two Pop-Tarts. My belly was full as I leapfrogged with Elf and Tsehay up the mountain before calling it a day at Hog Camp Gap after 12.5 miles.

I really enjoyed getting to know Elf and Tsehay by the fire. Elf was Canadian and learned about the A.T. on a motorcycle tour of the states, so he decided to return and hike it. Tsehay was Eritrean, and her trail name means sunshine in that language. She was in her mid to late twenties and one of the most intelligent people I met on my journey.

As the sun began to set on our camp, things couldn't have gotten better, until they did. A man suddenly appeared at the campsite bearing gifts of beer. He had thru-hiked the trail 30 years previously, with the trail name "Odie," as in Odie-Doe, Over the Hills We Go. Over a couple of beers, we talked about how different hiking was back then. He said access to money is a big difference. On his hike he carried a one-page tri-fold brochure that listed every ATM machine in the country that was in his network. Western Union was the preferred method of receiving funds for hikers. I liked Odie because he didn't lecture us on how much harder it was back when he thru-hiked. It's not uncommon for thru-hikers of years past to talk about how ultra-light gear, smartphones, and access to cash make the trail too easy.

The night before, I couldn't sleep because of the heat at 1,000 feet; tonight it was too cold to sleep at 3,500 feet. It was not the lowest temperature I would experience on the journey, but it was one the coldest nights as I tried to stay warm in my summer gear. Odie just grabbed a sleeping bag from his truck, and stretched out right on the trail. The next morning, he told us how he laid awake looking at the Milky Way. He had brought some homemade pound cake, and was making fresh coffee by pouring water he boiled on a camp stove into an automatic drip coffee maker. Fresh brewed coffee, and homemade pound cake as the sun crept over the mountains to warm us up. Wonderful!

Earlier that morning, as I rose and put my pants on, I realized I had a decent size bug bite on my ass. I didn't think much of it but to laugh. Tsehay also found it funny as I told her and Odie. At which point Odie told me that if it turned black in a week, and abscessed an inch, it was a brown recluse spider bite. My heart sank as the words came out of his mouth. And not because I feared it was a venomous spider bite.

All I could think was, "*Et tu Odie?*" The culture of fear even affects a Thru-Hiker of decades past? Heart-breaking.

It was Monday, and I was deciding whether to push it and make Waynesboro by Wednesday, or take it easy and arrive Thursday. It didn't take long to decide on Thursday. The decision to take it easy gave me the time to take a side trail and climb Spy Rock to take in some beautiful views of the Virginia landscape.

I'd spend the night on top of a mountain simply called The Priest. There it was evident just how many hikers had gotten off the trail. The Priest

Shelter structure was empty, and only five Thru-Hikers were camped on the grounds. While I was there I was reminded how wonderful the trail is when I met a mother hiking with her college-age daughter who were on a 30-day section hike. The trail was their way of maintaining closeness and a bond as the daughter grows up.

I wasn't looking forward to the descent of Priest Mountain because I remembered from three years ago how the hike down had sucked. But as I continued down the mountain, I realized the only thing that sucked was my memory. It was nice smooth trail all the way down the Priest, which was nice, because on the other side was the 3,000-foot climb up Three Ridges Mountain.

### 

He called himself "White Walker," my guess was due to his white hair. His wife's trail name was Archer, for reasons still a mystery. We were at the Maupin Field Shelter area. As they looked for a place to set up their tent, I suggested a flat area not far from my hammock. They settled on a place that was a few yards further away, yet still close enough to talk. He was retired U.S. Army, over 30 years; I had put in three years of active duty. We soon realized that we had both served at Fort Ord, on California's Monterey Peninsula. As we talked I realized he must have had a high rank when his service was complete. For Army officers, there are very clear and distinct lines drawn in rank. Achieving the rank of Lieutenant Colonel, the fifth in line, is almost mandatory. But getting over the hump, to that level of O-6, "Full-Bird" Colonel, is a monumental step. So, it was with some trepidation when I asked his rank at retirement, "You must have been a Full-Bird?"

I couldn't have been more wrong. He replied, "No. I was a Major-General." Now it had been almost thirty years since I left the Army, so I asked "how many stars is that?" Two Stars. I was sitting in camp with a two-star General, yet at this point in life, and at this point on the trail, we were just two guys hiking. The trail can be the great equalizer. The next morning as we would part ways, I reached out my hand and offered a firm handshake worthy of a professional solider. He earned it. I wasn't about to offer an A.T. fist-bump; he deserved better.

On my section hike three years ago, I remember setting up camp on a ridge overlooking Waynesboro. It was great looking out to the city lights. That was the first time I had "stealth" camped, that is not sleeping near a shelter or camp area. I wanted to visit that spot again and have a cup of coffee or maybe even lunch.

But it was not to be. The trail had been re-routed, and the part of the A.T. where I set up my tent overlooking Waynesboro, was now a side trail designed for day-hikers. I wasn't in the mood to do extra miles just for the sake of nostalgia, so I continued following white blazes for a few miles to the Paul Wolfe Shelter, a great place to spend an evening. It has a nice front deck overlooking Mill Creek, 50 yards to the front. There are ample camping areas, and close to the creek is a granite bench dedicated to Virginia hiker John Donovan who died after straying off the Pacific Crest Trail in the San Jacinto Mountains.

I was looking forward to getting to Waynesboro, so when I woke up at dawn, instead of putting my head back down like I did most mornings, I was out of my hammock. It would be a pretty easy five miles to Rockfish Gap, and then a short ride into Waynesboro. Along the way I ran into the couple who had given me the apple and Orange Crush a couple weeks ago, now on a hike of their own.

Rockfish Gap lies at the southern end of the Shenandoah National Park, where the Blue Ridge Parkway meets Skyline Drive. At the Gap, hikers are welcomed by a food trailer selling gourmet popcorn and hot dogs, against a backdrop of completely run-down buildings that are falling apart. At one time, it was a typical 1960s travel stop: a Howard Johnsons, a motor court consisting of small cottages, and a motel at the summit of the hill. But now it's just a dilapidated eyesore. Some residents are trying everything they can to revitalize it, from asking the government to take over the property by way of eminent domain, to begging and pleading with the owner, Phil Dulaney, to sell the property. But Dulaney, who let the property fall into ruin was reported to have told one person he wouldn't sell the property because he said, "it's like one of my children." The person responded by saying, "If it was one of your children, the state would have taken them a long time ago."[iii] After a soda and a snack, I walked across Route 250, and for the first time during my journey, stuck out my thumb to oncoming traffic.

In most trail towns, hitching a ride is pretty easy, and today was no exception. In less than ten minutes I was in a car and dropped off not just in town, but at the front door of the Quality Inn where I was staying. Because of my early arrival, a room was not ready, so I headed out to find a restaurant with a patio, so my hiker stink would not pollute the inside of the establishment. Soon I was sipping a hard cider at the Tailgate Grill, outside, when I was surprised see a text from my hiker friend, Navigator.

A graduate student studying physical therapy, I met her the past summer on my section hike with the Lawyers, when she was on her first section hike, alone, with less than ideal equipment, but loving it. Now she was interning in Waynesboro and asked if I wanted to have dinner together? Navigator is another example of how quickly friendships develop on the trail: we had only crossed paths one night as we headed north, and she headed south.

I let her know I'd be at the motel's pool. She arrived, and immediately said, "You're too skinny to be Brother Blood!" We had a nice Italian dinner, she drove me the Kroger for resupply, then after I dropped the food off at my motel, she dropped me off a sports bar in town. Since it was her first week at the internship, she declined a late-night drink.

## CHAPTER 11: SHENANDOAH IS NOT THE SMOKIES

I turned a corner on the trail, and on a branch, maybe 15-20 feet away, stood a brown owl. As it turned to look at me, I noticed its massive talons gripping the branch. I took a backward step. I've never heard of an owl attacking a hiker, but seeing those talons, I did not want to be the first. Logically I knew if I startled it, the owl would just fly off, so I stood there for a moment, until the bird focused on its prey and ever so quietly swooped down to capture its snack.

I was in Shenandoah National Park.

Many of the hikers that were as disgusted as I was about the rules and regulations of the Smokies were worried about entering another National Park. Were we entering another land of rude Ridgerunners and a genuine unfriendliness toward Thru-Hikers? I had assured them Shenandoah is different, for starters the "Backcountry Permit" they require is free, and available at a kiosk right on the trail at the entrance of the park. No need to find a computer to print it out, no credit card needed, and no squad of Appalachian Trail Conservancy employees hounding you about the permits. No, this is not the Smokies.

The terrain is much easier as well. I had little difficulty doing 20 miles a day through the park. After a late start, I planned to make it to the Blackrock Hut. (They call shelters "huts" in Shenandoah). I'd be hiking after sunset, but days were longer this time of year. I was just 0.7 miles from the hut, when the trail crossed Skyline Drive, and I stopped to retrieve my headlamp. As I removed my pack, a car slowed and a young lady asked if I was okay, and if I needed anything. As I told her I was just putting on my headlamp and heading less than a mile to the hut, I realized she was a Park Ranger. We chatted briefly, and soon I was on my way to camp. Yes, Shenandoah is different than the Smokies.

I enjoyed dinner and wine in my hammock knowing that tomorrow would be just 6 miles to where I would meet my wife at the Loft Mountain Campground, for another night indoors... and more wine. I got to the campground early, and there, just showing up for work, was the young lady who had asked me if I needed anything the night before. I thanked her, then had a conversation with another Ranger who had thru-hiked in 1974. His only peeve with today's Thru-Hikers was all the electronics we carry, especially smartphones. I never really paid any attention to former hikers that complained about our smartphones, had the iPhone been around back then, I am sure they would have carried them.

But then he gave me a small box of Whitman Sampler chocolates. Chocolates in exchange for having to listen to him complain about smartphones for 30 seconds was a fair trade-off. Soon my wife was there, and we were off the Comfort Inn in Waynesboro, AARP rate, of course. Being 50 has at least one benefit.

For the second time in three days, I was in a pool in Waynesboro, VA. This time it felt like a pool party with several couples hanging around and drinking beer. That night it was margaritas and a Mexican dinner, before I called it an early night.

My body wasn't used to sleeping in a bed, and I woke up with a stiff back and looked forward to sleeping again in my hammock. I was planning a short day, so I was in no hurry to get back on the trail. We headed into Shenandoah and enjoyed a little wine, mine with Taco Bell, before my wife dropped me off at the trail around 2:30 p.m. The combination of bean burritos, tacos, and chardonnay made for some uncomfortable hiking for me that afternoon, and probably much worse for anyone behind me. But it was just seven miles today and I was in camp by 6:30 p.m. - just after seeing bears number 10 and 11 of my journey.

I was hoping my back just needed a night in my hammock, and I was right. I woke up feeling good and was on the trail by 8:30 a.m. for a 20.6-mile day to Bearfence Hut. One nice thing about Shenandoah is the camp stores and waysides on, or near, the trail. The waysides are gift stores/snack bars, where I had seen many Thru-Hikers on my previous section hikes in the park. And today, as a Thru-Hiker, I would be hitting the camp store at the Lewis Mountain Campground. The big question was whether or not I could make it by the 6:00 p.m closing time. Initially I didn't think so, but Shenandoah is not the toughest terrain on the A.T. By 12:30 I thought it was a possibility, and by 2:00 p.m. I made up my mind I would make it. After all, they sold beer.

Before long I was well ahead of schedule to make the camp store by closing time. Along the way I spotted two bear cubs in a tree with mama on the ground keeping an eye on things. New bear count: 14. A few hundred yards ahead was Pocosin Cabin, and a trail magic dinner.

I skipped the dinner, but did take the young daughter of the trail angel and a fellow hiker back to see the bears. There's just something really cool about showing a young person a live bear in the wild.

I made the camp store with time to spare, and bought a six-pack and some snacks for later. The Bearfence Hut is a very easy 0.7 miles from the camp store, so after dinner, I carried out four of the six beers (or as hikers say, "I hiked out four beers") and a bag of chips for later. Along the trail to the hut my bear count increased by 1 to 15.

### 

Bearfence Hut is the shelter where I met the Lawyers two years previously, on a hike at the end of July. I was lucky my wife had convinced me to take my forty-degree sleeping bag instead of my idea of just a lightweight Army poncho liner. The Lawyers' wives did not do the same for them. I was building a fire, since the forecast was for temperatures in the low forties. I looked up and saw a hiker coming down the side trail to the shelter wearing a Shenandoah National Park sweatshirt, holding a Shenandoah National Park blanket, and other gear just bought at the camp store. It was Silver Fox, who soon explained how he had only brought a thin sleeping bag liner for warmth. After all, it was the end of July. About 10 minutes later, Maverick headed down the same trail, and like his friend, his arms were full of warm gear from the camp store.

We hit it off as we chatted around the fire, and I said that I would give them a ride to Dulles Airport when their hike was over in four days. I can't imagine any other way in the world I would have met, and befriended, two very successful attorneys from Florida and Georgia, except on the Appalachian Trail.

The day after meeting Silver Fox and Maverick, I did my first 20-mile day on the A.T., 22.4 to be exact, to Byrd's Nest Hut #3. That night the hut was filled with young hikers I assumed were Boy Scouts. But learned the next morning that they were actually a group that had broken away from the Boy Scouts, in protest of the Scouts allowing gay members. The group is called Trail Life.

I was saddened to think that adults would use the outdoors to preach hate towards LGBTQ individuals. And I was downright angry when, a year later, Backpacker Magazine did a feature article glorifying the hate group. I immediately cancelled my subscription. What they did is no different than doing a story about a Ku Klux Klan all-white hiking group. Backpacker magazine even called the homophobic, anti-LGBTQ hate-group's effort, "a worthwhile endeavor." Sad.

I would do the same 22.4 miles today as I did two years ago, only this would be the day I would have one of the Park's famous blackberry milkshakes. For years, I had heard how wonderful the shakes were, but decided I would not enjoy one until on my thru-hike. So after seven miles, I took a 0.4 mile detour to the Big Meadows Wayside. Lunch was a black bean burger with a blackberry milkshake. The shake was worth the two-year wait.

Later, as I passed Rock Spring Hut, I passed some soaking wet southbound hikers, who were surprised that I had not been rained on. I thought perhaps the storm somehow passed me by. But, as I reached the summit of Hawksbill Mountain, Mother Nature unleashed her fury with vengeance. In addition to what had to be 40-50 MPH winds, I was being pelted with hail. The poncho I had traded my rain jacket for didn't stand a chance; it was worthless.

My only real concern in a storm like that is a tree blowing down. So while trying to shield my face from the hail, my eyes darted back and forth for any sign of the ground losing its hold on a tree's roots.

But the storm was brief and three miles later, I made it to the Skyland Restaurant, still soaking wet. I changed into dry clothes and went to the bar and joined Frisbee and Stubbs, the same couple I met on day one at Springer Mountain. They offered me a spot in the cabin they had rented, but I was hellbent on making it to the Byrd's Nest Hut. After three beers, I had a fried chicken dinner with a bottle of wine. I only drank a half a glass of wine from the bottle, the rest was going with me, along with a roast beef sandwich from the restaurant's deli. It was close to sunset when I changed back into my wet hiking clothes and hit the trail for some buzzed night hiking. I had six and half miles to Byrd's Nest.

I stopped twice along the way to enjoy chardonnay in my 2.4 oz. plastic wine glass, extra weight most hikers wouldn't carry, especially the ultra-lighters. I didn't make camp until 12:30 a.m., with half the wine and the full sandwich. At 1:00 a.m. I was drinking wine and eating a sandwich on my Appalachian Trail thru-hike. It was 2:33 a.m. by the time I laid down to sleep after a great day of the journey.

### 

"My Dad's a 'City Slicker,'" my 9-year old hiking companion would tell people who thought we were a father/son duo. His dad was a neighbor and friend. A single father of two, he was indeed a "city slicker." His son had watched videos I had taken while section hiking, and wanted to experience the A.T. for himself. When he was eight, we went on day-hike on a local trail which he carried a small pack. After finishing the six-mile hike, he exclaimed, "this trail's nothing, I want to do my first overnight on the Appalachian Trail before I'm ten." I started planning to make that happen.

The following July, 2014, we headed out to the Shenandoah National Park to hike from Elkwallow Wayside to Gravel Springs Hut for the night. During the drive, I mentioned something about the fact I was getting old, which caused my 9-year-old buddy to have an almost visceral reaction. "you're not old, you go hiking up and down mountains, and sleep in the woods, most people can't do those things. You're not old." I really couldn't disagree with what he had said.

I told him bring a can of food for lunch, expecting Spaghetti-O's or Beefaroni, but when I asked what he brought, he surprised me saying, "mixed vegetables." We stopped for lunch a few miles in at a large rock he thought would be a good place to eat. We started up my PocketRocket stove and he went to work cooking up Ramen noodles, with mixed vegetables. We then looked up and realized a storm was coming.

We made a small shelter using our ponchos, and sat eating lunch, nice and dry as the thunderstorm hit. With rain coming down in buckets, we saw a young couple running down the trail. As they approached, my young friend jumped out from under the poncho and yelled, "get in, get in!" The couple was soaked, but we all rode out the rest of the storm in our crowded little poncho shelter. Before long the sun returned, the couple moved on, and we headed north. A little while later, my friend mentioned the couple again and said, "the girl was kinda hot, huh?" For the second time that day I couldn't argue with something he had said.

The shelter area was empty when we arrived. He quickly started exploring the area, when I heard the privy door open, he yelled out, "Oh man, that stinks!" It was less than 15 minutes later he told me, "I have to take a dump." He pleaded to just dig a hole, and not use the privy, but I told him in the shelter area, he had to use the privy.

Since we were the only ones there, I told him I'd prop the door open with a rock so he would have some fresh air while doing his business. He was worried someone might show up. I told him if anyone did I would tell them he was in the privy and they would leave him alone. He looked back at me, and with all the wisdom of a 9-year old exclaimed, "What if it's a pervert!"

The next day we saw a young bear and enjoyed hot dogs and ice cream at the wayside before getting in car to head home; he slept the entire ride.

## CHAPTER 12: ANYTHING WORTH DOING...
## IS WORTH DOING HORRIBLY
### REMEBERANCE OF HIKES PAST

*It's destroying the next generation of musicians! Musicians should go to a yard sale and buy an old fucking drum set and get in their garage and just suck. And get their friends to come in and they'll suck, too. And then they'll fucking start playing and they'll have the best time they've ever had in their lives and then all of a sudden they'll become Nirvana. Because that's exactly what happened with Nirvana. Just a bunch of guys that had some shit old instruments and they got together and started playing some noisy-ass shit, and they became the biggest band in the world. That can happen again! You don't need a fucking computer or the Internet or The Voice or American Idol*

Dave Grohl

I sucked at backpacking.

In 2013, after my first two overnight hikes since leaving the Army twenty six years ago in 1987, I was ready for my first section hike on the Appalachian Trail. A friend picked me up at the IHOP in Centerville, VA, and gave me a lift to the trailhead at Route 211, east of Luray in Shenandoah National Park. The plan was simple enough, 13 miles on day one to Gravel Springs Hut, 19 miles on day two to the Jim & Molly Denton Shelter, 18+ miles to the Rod Hollow Shelter on day three, and then finish with *just* ten miles to Bears Den Hostel where my car was waiting. Simple enough.

In the Army, at Fort Ord, California, we did those kinds of miles in 2 ½ days, max. And I was carrying the 13.75 lb., Vietnam-era PRC-77 (prick 77) radio, and the 4.9 lb. Vinson voice encrypter, in addition to my regular military pack. My total pack weight had to be over 60 pounds, probably closer to 70. But I was also 19 years old. Now I was 47, and carrying at least 60 additional pounds of body weight as well.

With a pack weight of 38 pounds, I headed north from Route 211. It was a steady uphill, and soon the bargain pack that had I bought online was digging into my shoulders, and my muscles were starting to burn. I told myself they would loosen up. They didn't. I was hurting when I got to the Elkwallow Wayside, and still had six miles to go. I met some Thru-Hikers and agreed to buy two, half-liter cartons of wine, one red, one white, if they would carry them to shelter.

It was near dark when I got to the Hut, and the white wine was gone. We opened the red, and I enjoyed a cup as they shared the rest. I was sure I would feel better tomorrow. I didn't. The next day was a grind. I loved being in the woods, but my body was killing me by the time I made the Denton Shelter. I had a great time at the shelter, and loved talking to the Thru-Hikers. I cooked my dinner on a fire made by "Grandpa," who prided himself on making a fire every night, regardless on the conditions. He was very skeptical about whether I could actually do the nearly 19 miles the next day. *I will show him,* I thought to myself.

I did those miles that next day, but it was brutal. I was hurting right from the start, and by the time I took my first break at the Manassas Gap shelter, I must have looked pretty bad. Javaman, a Thru-Hiker, gave me some powdered Gatorade to help me get up the next mountain. Grandpa showed up and was convinced I would only make 10 miles. More motivation for me. I crossed paths with Grandpa again at Dick's Dome shelter, as I headed out for the final 8.4 mile stretch to Rod Hollow Shelter. I was actually feeling better when I hit Sky Meadows State Park where a bench at the side of the trail provided a nice break.

Soon I was striding down nearly three miles of slightly downhill trail to Ashby Gap at Route 50 on a path cut through what looked like a pasture. I did it in one hour and was feeling good and thinking to myself, *I got this!* But upon crossing Rt. 50, everything changed. The clear blue skies quickly gave way to dark ominous clouds. Within half a mile, a steady rain was falling, and it was getting darker by the second. The intensity of the storm steadily increased until I was hiking by headlamp in tornado warning conditions. I came to a sign that marked the side trail to the Potomac Appalachian Trail Club (PATC) Myron Glaser Cabin, which according to my map, left about 1.5 miles to the shelter. I continued on, desperately hoping my headlamp would not succumb to the elements. After what I thought was at least a mile, I saw a wooden sign on a tree, *I made it! I was at the shelter!* But, I got closer to the sign in the driving rain, I saw an arrow with the words, "Myron Glaser Cabin." The cabin had two side trail entrances, about a mile apart. I still had over a mile to go.

My headlamp was 45 lumens of brightness, not even close to the 150-plus lumens most hikers carry. So I inched along, in the storm, straining to see the white blazes that were obscured by the driving rain. The thunder and lightning were right on top of me, but I had no choice but to hike on. The storm was still raging when I finally saw the shelter's entrance sign. After crossing a stream that was normally a trickle, but now well over my ankles, I saw some tents but couldn't find the shelter. About 200 feet ahead up a slight hill, I saw the lights of a vehicle, maybe a pick-up truck. No way could there be a pick-up truck out here. There wasn't. Some of the hikers in the shelter saw my headlamp, and me wondering around, and turned on their headlamps to guide me in. One white, one red, like the front and rear lights of a pick-up.

The Thru-Hikers were a bit surprised at my determination to hike through the storm. They moved around to make just enough room for one more hiker to sleep in the shelter. Like many first-time hikers, I believed my pack was waterproof enough not to require a rain cover. Of course I was wrong. Luckily, my sleeping bag remained dry in its stuff sack, but most everything else ranged from soaked, to at least damp. I stripped down and jumped into my sleeping bag, laying my head on a mostly wet pillow. As I was zipping up my sleeping bag, my headlamp died.

The next morning was damp and chilly, as I ate my freeze-dried dinner meant for the night before, I was in no hurry to get going. I chatted with an Army veteran named Rodney who had fallen asleep, just off the trail the previous evening, without setting up his tent, and was woken up by the rain. I also talked to 'Grrrrr,' who I had seen the previous two days. He was at least 20 years my senior, and used a hearing aide, which he said was the result of Howitzers in Vietnam. He had a rough exterior, and my first impression was that of a somewhat grumpy, unsocial man. But first impressions can be very wrong. Grrrr remains one of the kindest souls I have ever met on the Appalachian Trail, or anywhere for that matter.

I mentioned how it rubbed me the wrong how Grandpa kept insisting that I couldn't do the miles I planned. But Grrrr said I should be thanking him instead for the motivation he provided. And then Grrrr told us the story of the Deaf Frog.

*One day a group of happy-go-lucky frogs were mindlessly hopping along when they fell into old abandoned well. Soon the other animals in the forest gathered around and watched as the frogs hopelessly tried to jump out of the well. Knowing they had no chance of escaping the well, the other animals waved their arms and shouted to the frogs to give up and not pain themselves trying to escape. And soon the frogs began to die off, one by one, except for one. That frog continued to jump and struggle until somehow caught a hold of a crack in the well's wall and climbed out.*

*The animals were astonished and asked the frog why it kept trying to get out when they were yelling to it to stop because it was impossible. It was then that they discovered the frog was deaf. One of the animals knew sign language and asked the frog why. The deaf frog responded that it kept jumping and trying because of the motivation and encouragement everyone was giving him.*

Grrrr explained how it's not what people say, but how we choose to interpret it, that really matters. I realized that Grandpa did indeed motivate me to push myself, regardless of what his intentions might have been. I also realized that Grandpa had no ill-will towards me, and in his own way was trying to get me to ease up on the miles and enjoy the hike more. Either way, it was good lesson.

That day would be just 10 miles to Bears Den Hostel, and the completion of my section hike. But the Rod Hollow Shelter is the starting point of the famed Virginia "Roller Coaster," 14 miles of constant ups and downs. The climbs are only 400-500 feet each, but come in rapid succession. After three tough days, the Roller Coaster got the best of me, and after seven miles, I was beat, and a storm was coming in. I stopped at the Sam Moore Shelter, and decided that it would be home for the evening. I had agreed to give Grrrr a ride to Harpers' Ferry that evening, but there was no way I was making it to Bears' Den Hostel. I couldn't remember being this exhausted in my entire life. I quickly fell asleep for a short nap. I ate dinner and did some reading, but my body needed rest, and soon I was out for the night.

I'm not sure if I ever had a tougher three miles as I did the following day, but by noon, I arrived at the Bears' Den Hostel. Grrrr had left a note on my car that he found a shuttle to Harpers' Ferry, and hoped I was doing well. As I started the drive home, I felt great! By the time I got home, I was thinking about my next hike, and more importantly what to do different to enjoy it more.

I learned more about backpacking on that first section hike, than I've learned since. Because anything worth doing is worth sucking at until you get better.

### ###

The present. June 22, 2016. Day 87 of the journey.

This would not be an early morning. The shelter area was cleared out by the time I rolled out of my hammock, but I was excited. This would be the start of retracing the steps of that first, ill-planned section hike. I had three miles to Rt. 211 where I started that hike, so I would actually be doing more miles than I did three years ago. As I headed down Mary's Rock, I passed a large group of students on a field trip hiking up. Some were really enjoying it, others not so much. "How much longer do we have to go?" I was asked by many on their way up. To which I would jokingly respond, "Oh, Georgia is just a little over 1,000 miles." They would ask in a surprised voice if I really hiked all the way from Georgia. I can be such an attention seeker! I tried to encourage them by telling them that view was worth it, but also was honest in the fact that most of them still had a way to go.

It was 4:00 p.m. by the time I made it to Elkwallow Wayside, and all of the other hikers had already moved on. I enjoyed a couple of beers and a bacon cheeseburger with guacamole. I did a minor resupply and was thrilled that they stocked Original Flavor Corn Nuts. Most hikers have one or two go-to snacks that for some reason they don't get sick of. I was tired of beef jerky, I was tired of dehydrated bananas, but I never got tired of Corn Nuts and hard Sourdough Pretzels. Perhaps the most annoying thing about America today is the replacement of original flavors with bullshit flavors, I mean, who the hell eats Chile Picante, or Ranch Flavored Corn Nuts? Life on the trail can be so hard.

Shortly after leaving the wayside I stopped and watched a bear snacking in a small field. Later, on my way to the Gravel Springs Hut, I saw a mama bear and one cub, completely unfazed by my presence. My bear count had jumped to 18. I gave myself some credit for what I had accomplished in that first section hike; even 1,000 miles into my thru-hike, it was not easy. "Feeling pretty damn tired," was the final sentence of my journal entry for that day. With rain on the way, I enjoyed some wine I had carried for three days and a sandwich from the wayside, and quickly fell asleep.

The rain did come, along with thunder and lightning, and the skies were still threatening in the morning. I thought the dark clouds would keep several hikers in the shelter, but I was wrong. Again, I was the last person to leave. Perhaps those who didn't like hiking in rain had been weeded out in South and Central Virginia where it seemed to rain every day. Or hikers were just getting used to hiking in the rain, or even enjoying a break from the summer heat. Either way, I relaxed and decided not to focus too much on recreating my first section hike, and just enjoy the day. Before leaving Shenandoah National Park, one more bear sighting took my count to 19.

It turned out to be a great day. The terrain was not tough, and the miles clicked off pretty fast. Near Rt. 522, where the trail borders the backyards of a neighborhood near Front Royal, VA, were some chairs and a cooler of beer. I sat alone and enjoyed a beer, then took one for the road. After crossing Rt. 522 the trail was scattered with freshly downed trees, as if a tornado had cut a path across the trail. I would weave through the wreckage of two or three trees, the trail would be clear for a hundred yards or so, and then a few more trees would be down. This continued all the way up the hill.

Near the top of the mountain, I turned a corner and saw two bear cubs scurrying up a tree. My initial reaction was wanting to hold them and pet them, they were so cute. But I knew they didn't decide to climb that tree themselves, mama made them do it. My desire to get a picture was heavily outweighed by my desire not to piss off the mama, so with some pep in my step, I moved along. Bear count now at 21.

I hit the Jim & Molly Denton Shelter at dusk, to be greeted by Old Spice. He had been derailed by shin splints after pushing big miles early in his hike, but looked good and was back to doing pretty serious miles. I had become really fond of him and his son, who was now switching between calling himself "Axe," and "Just Joe." I also saw Duchess, with whom I'd been leapfrogging since Central Virginia. In addition to the Thru-Hikers was a group of high school boys celebrating their last day of school.

The kids were joking and laughing well into the night but were far from unruly. I slept wonderfully and woke up well-rested before 6:00 a.m. By now I had become proficient in leaning over and making coffee without leaving my hammock. Does that mean I wasn't hanging my food bag every night? Yes. Old Spice was already heading out. I was on the trail at 7:03 a.m., one of the rare times I was one of the first to leave.

After crossing Rt. 55, I came across a couple saying goodbye to each other. They were section hiking, but after one day and night, he was done, and she was pushing on. As unprepared as I was on my first section hike, she was worse. Even after giving her machete to her boyfriend to take home, she had to be carrying at least 60 pounds, and wearing jeans, a cotton t-shirt, and beat up old sneakers.

At the Manassas Gap Shelter I chatted with "Crusty Hiker," and his 11-year old grandson Zack, on his first A.T. hike. I was eating when the woman hiker I had seen saying goodbye to her boyfriend arrived, looking as bad as I did three years earlier. Her name was Amanda, and she told me her gear actually had belonged to her father. When she pulled out an ancient Coleman stove and began working the fuel pump, I realized her father most likely got the gear from *his* father. Her goal was to make it to Harpers' Ferry by 11:00 a.m. on Sunday. We were over 40 miles away, and it was Friday. I remembered how I felt on my hike, and how wonderful Javaman's Gatorade was. So, I offered her some Gatorade, which she quickly finished off, and asked for more. Three years ago, it took me two more days to get to Bears Den Hostel, almost 20 miles closer than Harpers' Ferry, and I didn't make it by 11:00 a.m. I told her that getting a shuttle from Bears Den to Harpers' Ferry wouldn't be too hard, and that was a far more reasonable goal. We crossed paths again about two hours later, and she said that sounded like a better idea.

I hope that the determination she showed on that first section hike will lead to the same joy I have experienced in this wonderful passion. I hope she will think of me the way I think of Grrrr, Javaman, and the crew of Thru-Hikers that were so supportive during my tumultuous first section hike. Even Grandpa. I hope someday to cross paths again with her on the trail, with better hiking clothes, and better, lighter gear, and see her helping and providing support to a new hiker. The Appalachian Trail is not always about the hills we climb, or the miles we accomplish, but how we, as a community of hikers, can truly change our lives and the lives of others with such small acts of kindness.

With less difficult terrain, I was actually enjoying the fact that I was retracing that first section hike. The 3.5 miles between the Manassas Gap and Dick's Dome Shelters were a breeze. For nostalgia's sake, I wanted to take the side trail to Dick's Dome, but sideways miles were not very appealing to me, especially just for nostalgia. I now looked forward to the bench I remembered at Sky Meadows State Park. A couple hours later, I took a seat on that bench and looked forward to the easy downhill hike through a pasture to Rt. 50 and Ashby Gap.

The bench was exactly how I remembered it, but the hike to Route 50, not so much. It wasn't a difficult hike, but it wasn't the easy slide through a field I remembered. Either my memory sucked, or they had re-routed the trail west, through the woods, but soon I was crossing Route 50, and heading uphill again, remembering the storm three years ago. As I headed uphill from Route 50, I again gave myself some credit for what I had done on that first hike. I smiled as I passed the entrance sign for the second side trail to the Myron Glaser Cabin. I made Rod Hollow Shelter by 5:00 p.m., and realized how different things are on a fair day, versus a tornado warning storm.

There were still hours of daylight, and I looked forward to laying in my hammock and reading. I slid the power button of my Kindle, and...nothing, it was dead. I had dinner, chatted with some hikers, and went to bed just after 8:00 p.m. At this point of the journey, it was the earliest I had been up, and the earliest I had gone to sleep. Tomorrow was the Roller Coaster.

I don't like going downhill. It's a misconception that going down is easier than going up, it all depends on the slope. A slight uphill is far less difficult than a steep downhill, especially with 50-year old knees. Every step requires slowing your momentum as to not allow your body to build inertia and have your legs helplessly trying to keep up with your careening body. I was even slower than most thanks to the aforementioned aging knee joints. Section hikers often passed me down the first few hills of the Roller Coaster, but uphill, they didn't stand a chance. With pride, I blew through the first 10 miles of the Roller Coaster and was hitting Bears Den Hostel around 2:00 p.m.

Bears Den was built as a "faux Medieval castle," according to bearsdencenter.org, "by Dr. Huron Lawson, a professor emeritus in obstetrics and gynecology at The George Washington University, and his wife, Francesca Kaspari, a soprano singer, as their summer home." It more resembles a large stone summer cottage, which it really was. It is built on a small slope, so it has a one-story front, but the back reveals a lower, second story. The lower story today serves as a hostel of simple bunk beds. But the main floor is beautiful. Stone walls and hardwood floors with the charm to be expected in the summer home of a well-healed couple.

When they died, a development company bought the cottage and land in hopes of building a "country club-like community." But failure to secure proper permits killed the project, and for years the company tried to sell it for $1 million. In 1984 the Potomac Appalachian Trail Club bought the property, and less than three months later, sold it to the Appalachian Trail Conservancy "at cost."

Today, Bears Den is known by hikers for their $30 Hiker Special: hostel stay, a Tombstone Pizza, laundry, and a pint of Ben & Jerry's Ice Cream. I wasn't planning on staying, but I thought a pizza, and resupply of snacks would be just the thing to get me up the next mountain. But, I was SOL (shit-outta-luck.)

I didn't check its hours of operation in the guide; after all, if every run down, two-bit hostel from Georgia to Maine is open all day during the thru-hiking season, why wouldn't the hostel owned by the A.T.C., be open as well. But like I said, I was SOL. You see, I was just a hiker wanting a little resupply, maybe a pizza. And for that I was greeted with a sign at the door, "Private Party, Do Not Disturb." A small wedding party was taking pictures in the front lawn, and I was not welcome.

The Bears Den Hostel store is only open from 5:00 – 9:00 p.m. to hikers, so we do not interfere with the fundraising activities conducted there. Most Thru-Hikers don't have much money, unlike the families of the bride and groom that are so much more important to the A.T.C. We're just hikers, why should we expect anything from Appalachian Trail Conservancy? As I headed back to the trail, I remembered the trail volunteers in Adkins, VA, who told me, "all the A.T.C. cares about is money."

It was the only time during my journey that I was really mad. I actually felt rage. The A.T.C. was far more concerned with using Bears Den as a fundraising instrument than doing anything for hikers. I read in Kyle Rohrig's book "Lost on the Appalachian Trail," how he pushed himself to make Bears Den by 9:00 p.m. to enjoy a pizza, only to arrive at 9:07 and be told the kitchen was closed. Rohrig described the 20-something kid working at the hostel as "rude and cocky." I'll bet the young caretakers treat the well-healed guests of "private events" much better than they treat hikers. I then remembered showing up just after 9:00 p.m. in Adkins, to have Theresa restart the pizza oven just for me.

On the bright side, there is something to said about hiking when angry. Whatever chemicals the body produced at that time created an energy that propelled me over the final four miles of the Roller Coaster in no time at all. I had seen a sign just past Bears Den, at the Rt. 7 trailhead, about a "Thanksgiving in Summer" dinner being offered that night at the Blackburn Trail Center. It would be hard, but after a few angry miles, I believed I just might get there it in time for a turkey dinner.

The hike to Blackburn Trail Center is along a ridge, with a long, fairly steep drop to the right, or east. The trail center itself sits about 300 feet down a series of small stone steps, so it's not always a popular stopping point for Thru-Hikers, given that the next shelter is only three miles ahead, and does not have a 300-foot decent from the trail. The center consists of a large house, with a wraparound screened-in porch, and a smaller, less charming house where the caretaker resides. The camping area is much larger than most and could easily accommodate dozens of tents. There is also a small bunkhouse, which has a wood-burning stove for the winter.

The Blackburn Trail Center was empty when I camped there for my very first overnight hike on the A.T. in 2013. But tonight, the porch was populated by a combination of both thru and section hikers, along with several volunteers. I was just in time to get a plate of turkey, stuffing, and vegetables. The mashed potatoes were gone. Shortly after dinner ice cream was announced, causing a rapid, but orderly, dash to the kitchen. I sat on the porch chatting with Crusty Hiker and his grandson Zach, who I'd met days earlier. Unlike Bears Den, we were treated wonderfully at the Blackburn Trail Center.

Now is a good time to draw the distinction between the local trail clubs, and the A.T.C. All the trail really needs are the men and women that roll up their sleeves and do the work. From clearing fallen trees, to building and repairing shelters, to building steps on steep embankments, and more. These are the people that keep the trail going. Over the course of my journey I met people of all ages donating their time and money to maintain the trail. These are not the people who sit on endowments of millions of dollars and claim to be preserving the trail. These are the true stewards of the trail. These are the people that make up the local trail clubs. Just like the men I met in Atkins, Virginia, who were out working on the trail while the A.T.C. was thinking up better ways to raise money.

These are the people that helped restore my faith in humanity.

The camping area at Blackburn was well populated, including a group of Boy Scouts. I was glad their leaders did not allow them to partake in the turkey dinner. The next morning, I met a section hiker who would soon be heading back to school for his PhD in physics. Finally, I thought to myself, someone who will get my joke, and proceeded to tell him that I had been seeing in trail journals, the name "Heisenberg," and based on his progress I knew how fast he was going, but never knew where he was. Some of you will get it.

Today I would hit Harper's Ferry, the ceremonial halfway point to Katahdin. The actual halfway point lies 80 miles North, but this is where Thru-Hikers stop at the A.T.C. headquarters to have their picture taken and marked with what number Thru-Hiker they were to have reported in for the season. The hike was fairly easy, and soon I knew I was approaching Harper's Ferry because of the increasing number of day-hikers on the trail. Day-hikers always lifted my spirits. They loved to ask about my journey and share their own trail stories. Some hikers refer it to it as thru-hiker "celebrity." It's also not unusual for day hikers to offer a snack or something to drink. In Central Virginia one family gave me a full bottle of Powerade.

It was Sunday, June 26th, day 92 of my journey, and Harper's Ferry was packed. I had just enough time to get ice cream cone before my wife arrived. I would be spending my first night at home in three months. People ask what I missed the most while on the trail, which is a difficult question for two reasons. One, you really don't miss anything that much; and two, you miss different things at different times. One of the small pleasures I missed at times was enjoying wine with my wife on our deck on summer evenings. My wife felt the same, so I agreed to take off and spend two nights at home.

Despite my apprehensions about the A.T.C., I did stop at their headquarters to register. The volunteer working the counter said that there was no official register and offered to take my picture. I declined. I was ready to get home and enjoy a night on the deck.

## CHAPTER 13: HALFWAY

After a zero day at home, I was in no hurry to rush back to the trail, so it was 3:00 p.m. before we left for Harper's Ferry. The skies had been threatening, but once I was back on the trail, just after 4:30 p.m., they were clearing up. Today would be a short hike, a little over six miles to the Ed Garvey Shelter, and along the way, I'd pass one of my favorite places on the A.T., as well as one of my least favorite. After crossing the Potomac River into Maryland, the trail is part of the C & O Canal towpath for three miles. It's flat, and boring. The C & O Canal towpath is a wonderful bicycling trail, running 180 miles from Washington D.C. to Cumberland, MD. But I like hiking in the woods, not on a 20-foot-wide dirt towpath built for mules.

After three miles on the towpath the trail heads back into the woods, and of course, uphill. The uphill leaving Harper's Ferry is not bad (about 1,000 feet in a little over a mile), and just over halfway up there is a short side trail to Weaverton Cliffs, a wonderful rock outcropping looking down at the Potomac River. I hiked in a beer to enjoy on the Cliffs, and just lounged around, taking in the view. I told a few Thru-Hikers that it was well worth the short detour to the Cliff, they agreed. We chatted with some section hikers and prepared to get back on the trail. It was then a hiker went by moving furiously up the hill huffing, puffing, and sweating. I tried to tell him the view at the Cliff was awesome, but he barely acknowledged me as he plowed forward, in a hurry, making miles.

As he continued up the hill, I said to the others, "if I ever get like that, I'll just quit hiking." Everyone agreed. Maybe I'm not being fair; everyone has to "hike their own hike." But when I see people using the Appalachian Trail as a proving ground, doing faster and more miles as if it was a race, I feel sorry for them. I feel sorry they are not getting to know the wonderful people on the trail, like Boomer, who I talked to that day. I think we had crossed paths earlier, but today was the first day we actually talked. He was an unassuming, funny, awesome young man. He seemed to like hiking with other people as much as he liked hiking alone. I got the sense he had been considering whether to continue his journey and seemed to have decided to go on. And he did.

Reaching the Ed Garvey Shelter was special, since it's where I had spent my second overnight hike on the A.T. It's one of the newer shelters built by the PATC, and it looks more like a log home than a traditional shelter. It only has the three walls, but is two stories, with a plexiglass wind break at the front of second floor.

The shelter area was somewhat crowded that night, between Thru-Hikers, section hikers, and a group of young people on a club outing. I'm always cautious about youth groups on the trail since coming across the Trail Life group. But these young people were different. As I ate my dinner I talked to a young lady who couldn't have been more than 14 or 15 years old. But she spoke with a wisdom beyond her years which lifted my spirits. She talked of her goal in life of pursuing social justice. She truly understood, at such a young age, that the pursuit of happiness, and equal rights for all is what this country is, or at least should be about. She helped restore my faith in humanity.

It's very possible that her group, like Trail Life, was Christian based. Which offers a valuable lesson I heard eloquently given by the Dali Lama when I was in college. He spoke of education as merely a tool, that can be used for good or bad. Just like religion. Some people, like those in Trail Life, use religion to train young men to, "have the skills – the manly skills – that are necessary to go and take back our culture."[iv] While others can use that same religion to teach kindness and caring to create a better world based on equality and justice. No religion instills hate in people, yet people use religion to instill hate. Some also use it to do wonderful things; it's just a tool.

### 

The Maryland section of the A.T. is not strenuous, and I was enjoying the miles after a good night's sleep at the Garvey Shelter. Five miles on, I hiked through Gathland State Park, the first of Maryland's historic sites on the trail. Gathland was built by a retired war correspondent to honor his profession. It's a combination of monuments, ruins, and historic markers and plaques. For hikers, the best attraction is the restroom with running water and a spigot to refill water. From there it was a relaxing day of hiking, with a stop for lunch at the Rocky Run Shelter. After lunch, I would hit the next two historic sites. First, over South Mountain, where Robert E. Lee's Army of Northern Virginia first clashed with Union forces outside of the Confederacy, days before the Battle of Antietam. Alongside the trail, where it crosses Reno Monument Rd, stands a large memorial to Union General Jesse Reno, as well as a smaller monument, resembling a gravestone, for Confederate General Samuel Garland.

Next was the Washington Monument near Boonsboro, MD. A 40-foot circular tower, it is the first monument completed to honor our first President. A spiral staircase leading to the top provides a stunning view of the countryside. As I sat in a pavilion near the monument enjoying a snack, a hiker's phone alarm sounded. It was 4:20 p.m. The hiker began to retrieve his stash of weed, and commented it was 4:20, and people all over the country were lighting up. I didn't think this was the right time to discuss the concept of time zones. No one likes a buzzkill.

I was in camp well before dark at the Pine Knob shelter, with a sore foot. After a few Advil relieved the pain, I knew it was nothing to worry about.

Packing up the next morning, a bird took almost perfect aim as I rolled up my hammock and crapped right on my head. Luckily most of the load missed. And while I'm not a hunter, if a shotgun had been available at that moment I would've blown that turd-dropper out of the sky. It was a beautiful morning, and my foot wasn't hurting as I headed out for 13 not-too-difficult miles.

Along the way I met Jane, who had traveled from England on an extended vacation to hike from Harpers Ferry to Katahdin. She dropped herself right into a bubble of Thru-Hikers who had over 1,000 miles under our belts, so there was no way she could keep up. But she had a great attitude and I liked her immediately.

I was relaxing in my hammock while taking a break at the Ensign Cowell Shelter, when someone mentioned trail magic at the Rt. 77 crossing. For a moment, I thought the trail angel might be Sheryl. But I quickly dismissed that thought; after all, we hadn't talked since Georgia. But when I hit the road, there she was. She fulfilled her promise to do trail magic, so I joined Frisbee, Stubbs, and Jane for snacks and soda.

Sheryl drove me to a Subway for a sandwich and a liquor store where I bought myself a bottle of wine, and some small bottles of Fireball for the crew. Upon arriving at the shelter, I found Jane nursing a sore knee from a fall she had taken during the day. She recreated the experience at the shelter when she tripped on a root. By then I had a nice fire going and a bottle of wine. The day started with a bird shitting on my head and ended with Pinot Noir by a fire.

The next morning was coffee, a Clif Bar, and Pinot Noir for breakfast. It seemed like a waste not to finish the glass of leftover wine.

I took my time and didn't get on the trail until almost 9:30 a.m., and not long after ran into Jane again. Her knee and ankle were holding up well, and I decided to slow down and hike with her to the Mason-Dixon Line. I normally don't like hiking with other people, but Jane was fun, witty, and cussed like a sailor. It didn't hurt that we shared similar political views as well. We came to Pen-Mar Park at the Pennsylvania border, where we relaxed in the park pavilion. Soon a man with the trail name Pappy came striding into the pavilion with three pizza boxes. I figured it was leftovers from a family picnic, but I was wrong. It was three fresh, hot pizzas, soon accompanied by a cooler of sodas and Gatorade. We devoured pizza as Jane drank her first ever Mountain Dew.

Back on the trail we stopped for pictures at the Mason-Dixon Line marker, then on to Rt. 16, where she would hitchhike into Waynesboro, PA. She had obviously never hitchhiked in the States, so I stood with her with my thumb out as well, figuring anyone with bad intentions was less likely to pick up a woman with a man. Soon a pickup stopped and Jane was off to enjoy her first shower since stepping foot on the A.T.

*Figure 14 - The Mason/Dixon Line*

Five miles further, I came upon a stretch of three shelters in just 3.6 miles. They are nice shelters and have a feature unique to that stretch of Southern Pennsylvania. Some of the shelters are actually two small shelter buildings, with one marked "snoring," the other, "non-snoring." The first was the Deer Lick Shelter, followed by the Antietam Shelter, very close to a road. It was now Friday, July 1st, and folks enjoying the long weekend were already out. There were three young people at this shelter, with car camping gear and a cooler full of Rolling Rock beer. Between the bugs and the party atmosphere, I knew I wouldn't be staying here, but I hung around a minute in hopes of being offered beer, a practice known as "yogi-ing" after Yogi the Bear. But they were having none of it. I think they just saw it as a cool place to camp and had no idea what the Appalachian Trail or a Thru-Hiker were. I failed to yogi a beer... a tragedy.

I arrived at the third shelter by 5:30 and decided to continue on and traverse the 1,000-foot hill ahead. I rested my feet and had a snack before heading on. I was relaxed, and would rather get up the hill tonight, than first thing in the morning. Plus, at the higher elevation, it would be cooler with less bugs. Once up the hill, I hiked until I found flat ground that would be suitable for hanging my hammock. Nothing was cleared; it was truly a primitive site.

I was all alone, sitting in my hammock that night, with my cup of coffee, when I decided to send my friend Ceci, with whom I had worked at REI, a text to say thank you. I know Pennsylvania has a fair number of rattlesnakes, and this was a perfect time to thank Ceci for explaining to me that she didn't hammock because she feared a snake would crawl into it. Thanks Ceci, for providing such a comforting thought for the night.

Tomorrow I would spend my first full day in Pennsylvania.

Anyone who reads books about the Appalachian Trail knows one thing. Upon entering the Commonwealth of Pennsylvania, the trail becomes a painful trek over jagged rocks, and nothing but rocks. Bill Bryson said it was "where boots go to die," and since then, the legend has grown. It was just last summer that I hiked the southern 64 miles of Pennsylvania with the Lawyers and Sheryl and didn't find it all that tough. Which had me believing that just north of that point is where Pennsylvania becomes the horrific "Rocksylvania."

I woke to a cool mountain morning, and it took a few miles warm up. But soon I had descended to lower ground, and it was hot. I was hiking into Caledonia State Park, where I knew there would be burgers and ice cream. The park was packed for the holidays, and I received my fair share of curious glances as I headed to the snack bar. I found one of the only open picnic tables to enjoy my hiker's gourmet meal of a cheeseburger and fries under the gaze of friendly, but curious glances. Back to the snack bar for an ice cream cone, then head north again. It was up about 550 feet to one of my favorite shelters on the entire A.T.

After the climb out of Caledonia State Park, the trail flattens out for almost a mile and a half, until you walk through a small white picket fence gate and enter the Quarry Gap Shelter. It has dual "snoring" and "non-snoring" shelters, with a covered picnic table in between. To the left was a new bench swing, and to the right is a small covered picnic pavilion. The privy stands up a hill about 100 feet, and is often not just stocked with toilet paper, but 2-ply toilet paper! Decadent. There's even a trash can, but its use is discouraged as it's marked "for slobs only," those who won't pack out their trash.

The shelter is kept in immaculate shape through the efforts of one man, whose name appears on a wooden sign reading "Jim Stauch: 'Innkeeper.'" It is rumored that after Mr. Stauch's wife passed away he began spending more and more time keeping up the shelter. He then designed and led the building of a new shelter in 1996. Whatever the true story is, his dedication to the shelter has touched the heart of many a hiker, this one included.

I had stayed at the shelter with the Lawyers the previous year. It's where I met Navigator on her first section hike. I relaxed in the newly built bench swing and enjoyed a snack. It was nice reminiscing about last year's hike, but it was time to move on. I filled up with fresh spring water and headed out. After five and a half miles, I was just a mile from the Birch Run Shelter; that night in my journal, I described the last mile as a "pine needle cushioned pleasure walk."

I soon had a nice warm fire going, and hikers started gathering around. It was July 3$^{rd}$, so the shelter housed a mix of overnighters and section hikers, as well as Thru-Hikers. One couple was on their very first overnight backpacking trip, another man on a weekend hike, and one young "LASHer" (Long-Ass Section Hiker). Thank goodness for Cruise, the LASHer, since before long the conversation somehow turned to mental illness and suicide. Certainly important topics, but around a campfire? Like me, Cruise had an irreverent sense of humor and soon the conversation lightened up. The treat of the evening came when an overnighter brought over a large Ziploc bag filled with crushed bananas soaking in banana liqueur. Kat was our hero!

My thoughts while hiking the next morning were focused on whether or not to take the "half-gallon challenge." I had ten miles to the Pine Grove Furnace State Park, and the General Store that is home to the challenge, where hikers try to eat a half-gallon of ice cream in one sitting. Almost all succeed. When I arrived, Crusher and Cruise were both working on their carton of ice cream, so I decided to take the challenge, choosing Neapolitan flavor. Upon paying six bucks for the carton, I learned it was a pint less that a full half-gallon, so the General Store would hit us up for a four-dollar pint as well. The challenge is very well known among hikers, and also very anti-climactic. Upon finishing, you simply sign the notebook, and get cheap little wooden ice cream spoon that reads: "member of half gal. club." That's it. My wife was already at the store as I arrived, and once I was bloated with ice cream, we were off to the Quality Inn in Carlisle, where I would enjoy my ninth zero day of the journey.

Two days later, well rested, I arrived back at the General Store to find Jane sitting and enjoying a snack. She remarked about how cute the driver was who picked her up hitching, and I could tell she was really starting to enjoy the hike. She was unsure of her ultimate plans but had given up on the idea of keeping up with Thru-Hikers. Smart move. I did almost 11 miles before setting up a primitive camp, having dinner and then popcorn. Fifty-five miles into Pennsylvania, where are the rocks?

My memories of the difficultly of the trail I had before my thru-hike had been consistently wrong. Some sections I remembered as very hard were not difficult at all; others I remembered as easy, were ass-kickers. I started out from my primitive camp, hoping that my memory was again wrong. I was about to enter a section I hiked with the Lawyers just last summer and hated a large part of it. For what seemed like miles, the trail skirted cornfields with the summer sun beating down on us mercilessly. I hoped I was mistaken as to how bad it really sucked. I wasn't. Maverick had really loved passing through the Pennsylvania farmland, but I couldn't wait to get back into the green tunnel.

Unfortunately, my memory was spot on for once. Hiking around the cornfields in over ninety-degree heat, and not a cloud in the sky sucked. On a positive note, it's very flat ground, so the miles ticked off pretty fast, and in between hiking past cornfields lies the village of Boiling Springs.

Depending on who you talk to, Boiling Springs is either one of the friendliest trail towns, or decidedly cool toward us unshaven, smelly intruders. I've experienced the small town of 3,225 people twice as a backpacker. Once with the Lawyers and Sheryl, and a year later on my thru-hike. Both times I experienced a less than warm reception, even from the folks at the A.T.C. Regional Office. I can't paint the whole town with that broad brush however. The Lawyers and I were treated very well by our server and busser at the Boiling Springs Tavern, a somewhat upscale restaurant with very good food.

In most towns people are quick to offer a smile and say hello, that has not been my experience in Boiling Springs. I didn't feel unwelcome, but felt as if our presence was merely tolerated. When I asked about water at the A.T.C. Regional Office, I received a fairly curt reply that there was a spigot outside the building. But I did have a good lunch and felt good as I headed north towards Carlisle.

But soon the sun and the heat were again beating me like I was a rented mule. Despite the flat terrain, I was not making great time in the summer heat. After checking the guide, I realized that I would be filling up with water a mile before the shelter, then it was all uphill. But something happened as I hiked that uphill mile; I was loving it! It's like my body was far more comfortable in the woods, going uphill, despite carrying seven pounds of water. I was in a good mood as I hit the Darlington Shelter. As I relaxed in my hammock, one of the many hikers named "Turtle" walked past. After he mentioned he had spent the night at the backpacker's campsite south of Boiling Springs, I commented, "oh that little crappy one?"

He must have had quite an affinity for that little campsite, because soon he was voicing his displeasure at my description, stating how nice he thought the site was, port-a-potty and all. He also didn't like how people complained about everything. I found it quite chivalrous of good ol' Turtle to stand up for the honor of that crappy little campsite. And trust me, it is a crappy site.

Darlington Shelter is known for their privy, which is dubbed the "Taj-Mahal." It's actually nothing special, just much larger than other privies. "The empty warehouse" would be a more accurate name, but who cares, nothing to complain about. Like Turtle says, people complain way too much. The next morning, after coffee and a Clif bar, I sat down to sign the shelter register and see who had been by the past couple days. The most recent post was at least a half-page angry diatribe complaining about calling the privy the Taj-Mahal, when it was just a large privy, and nothing special. Signed, of course, "Turtle."

I was 67 miles into Pennsylvania and had yet to encounter the infamous rocks. But according to one hiker, this was the day. I was told that the "shit hits the fan," just south of Duncannon. The downhill hike into the town was supposed to be a baptism of fire into "Rocksylvania." It wasn't. There were a lot of rocks, but with what had to be thousands of hours of labor, the rocks were arranged to form stone steps down to the town of Duncannon. From the lookout at Hawk Rock until the trail joined Inn Rd. it was just a large stone staircase.

Duncannon is another town where the white blazes of the A.T. switch from being on trees to telephone poles. The sidewalks along Rt. 274, then Market St., then High St., are part of the Appalachian Trail. It always surprised me that many people in these towns did not realize that they were hiking the Appalachian Trail on a daily basis. One such young lady was walking on the other side of the street as I entered Duncannon. I waved and said hello, she asked if I was hiking, and then wondered if I had come from Hawk Rock. I told her I did go by Hawk Rock, but started a little south of there. When she asked where, I smiled, and said, "Georgia." She seemed surprised as I explained the painted white strips on the telephone poles mark the A.T., and it goes all the way to Georgia one way, Maine the other. Right after that, I met Ed.

It was another 90-plus degree day, and here was an older man, hiking with long pants and a long-sleeve wool base layer. I asked how he could possibly hike wearing so much on a day this hot. But I already knew, it was the culture of fear. He was protecting himself from ticks, of course. He explained that he was taking no chances, and asked me if I ever had Rocky Mountain Spotted Fever. I had not. Prompting his response, "then you don't know what you're talking about." I didn't feel like explaining the concept of lighter, cooler clothing, that comes in long sleeves... or bug repellent.

But soon we were past any acrimony and enjoying a beer together at the Doyle Hotel. The Doyle that is an A.T. landmark. The Doyle that costs just $25 a room for a night. And the Doyle that is completely falling apart.

After showering in the fourth-floor communal bathroom, I headed back down to the bar, where Ed greeted me with his plan of me buying the drinks, and him buying the food at the Doyle. I wasn't hungry, but did buy a couple beers, and enjoyed our conversation. He was certainly a caring man, and without going into too much detail, he let me know he had been quite successful, at least financially. Knowing that I was 50, without any job or idea of what I was going to do after my journey, Ed started thinking of ways I too, could be successful. He told me he had made a killing in bank stocks, but acknowledged at my age, I didn't have enough time for that. Like almost all Thru-Hikers, I had little interest in thinking about my future, let alone discussing and planning it. Soon Ed figured that out, and we moved on to other topics.

Ed was a very nice guy, and despite his desire to discuss my future, I enjoyed sitting with him at the bar. I then noticed a bumper sticker behind the bar saying something about being a proud "Perry County Scumbag." The bartender, probably forty-something, was wearing a shirt that also referenced "Perry County Scumbags." I made the mistake of taking the bait and asking. The story was nothing exceptional, the former mayor of Harrisburg, once made a comment about illegal trash dumping from a "Perry County scumbag." Yes, local politics is wonderful.

But then his telling of the story took a disturbing turn. Of that former mayor he said, "She's a *negro*." I said nothing, but my face had that, "*did you really just fucking say that*" look. He knew that look, and for good measure, to leave no doubt, he repeated again, "she's a *negro*." He stood there with his racist smirk, as if waiting for me to suggest an alternative to his racist language. I wasn't about to engage him in his race-baiting game. I finished my beer and vowed the Doyle would never see another penny from me.

As I walked the main drag, I realized why this small town, that could be so charming, sitting right on the Susquehanna River, is, like the Doyle, falling apart. The population is 98% white, and as I sat for dinner at one of town's taverns it was clear to me that many want it to stay that way.

The next morning, I was at a breakfast counter, seeing news that five police officers were shot and killed at a Black Lives Matter protest in Dallas. A local resident at the counter remarked that it was this type of event that President Obama will use to suspend the election and start a path toward declaring himself "President for Life." Without any prodding, he went on to explain that Obama had learned that from "his friend," Muammar Gaddafi. That's the kind of conversations they have in Duncannon.

As I was heading out, Red Dragon was arriving at the Doyle. Red Dragon was an easy going, friendly hiker. Another that seemed comfortable hiking with a group, or going solo. I shared the story of the bartender, and his use of the term "negro." Within minutes of telling the story, the bartender appeared, ready to start his day shift at the bar. I advised Red Dragon, an African-American, that he was the person I was referring to, and then headed north on High Street, and out of Duncannon.

It was a weird feeling leaving Duncannon. I know there are good people there. I know they all don't share the racist and conspiracy theory beliefs I heard. But it's sad that there are still places in America where that kind of ignorance and stupidity is tolerated. Yet I also realize that one need not travel to Duncannon to experience such views. While Duncannon may hold a greater concentration of such people, the same kind live in my neighborhood, bowl in my leagues, and attend our local churches and bars. We all know them. We know them when they start a thought with, "I don't have a racist bone in my body ...but."

### 

I was still waiting for the dreaded rocks of Pennsylvania. I was expecting miles and miles of jagged, hard to navigate rock fields, but to this point, nothing. I would spend just one night in the woods, at Peters Mountain Shelter, before meeting my wife again for a night in town. I met her at the trail crossing at Rt. 325, where a group called Billville, led by Trail Angel Mary, was serving up trail magic. When I was dropped off the next day to continue, a different group was at the same trail head doing its own trail magic. I was surprised to learn that there lies a slight current of rancor amongst different trail angels. First world problems.

Before returning to the trail, "King of the Freaks" had filled out a postcard, with a rambling, illegible message, I think refencing online gaming characters. He then sent the card to a random address in New England, North Dakota. Yes, sometimes a trail name fits a person perfectly.

I was feeling good when I arrived at the Rausch Gap Shelter, and hoped for a good night's sleep. I soon realized that might be tough. A raccoon, far too comfortable around humans, began stalking the camping area as darkness fell. After advising others that I knew we weren't likely to encounter bears here, and it wouldn't be a big deal if we didn't hang our food bags. Soon I was hanging my entire backpack from the intruder. Raccoons can be far more persistent than bears. My repeated attempts at hurling rocks at it were fruitless; between my horrible aim and the animal smelling food, it prowled the site all night.

The next morning, I looked down to a couple tents about 30 feet down a hill, just in time to see something walk near their campsite, a black bear, number 22 of the journey.

It was a fairly smooth trail that day, not the kind filled with rocks and roots that force you to pay attention to every step. Maybe that's why I didn't see it until it was directly under my foot. That's when I learned the immerse thrusting power of my right leg, as I propelled myself at least seven or eight feet forward. Then I looked back at the rattlesnake.

Maybe a foot or so of it was protruding on to the trail. And while I was waiting for my heart to slow and breath to return, the snake either didn't know, or didn't care that I had almost stepped on it. It was focused on something on the other side of the trail, and never acknowledged my presence. It was nice enough to remain there long enough for me to take a few pictures and some video, then moved across the trail to claim its lunch, sounding a small rattle as it crossed.

*Figure 15 - Rattlesnake I just missed stepping on*

Early evening I arrived at the 501 Shelter, so named due to its close proximity to PA Rt. 501. And like all shelters located so close to a road, it had prominent sign prohibiting alcohol. Next to the fire pit sat Cautious, who asked me if I wanted a beer. I did. Soon we had a fire going, and were joined by Frisbee (now alone), Refill, and C-Sharp. Cautious talked about how quickly he was able to catch a hitch out of town, despite being smelly and carrying a 12-pack of beer. We all chuckled a bit wondering who was going to tell Cautious he had actually brought a case. With some relief, he said it did seem a lot to pay for a 12-pack. As I settled in for the night, I looked at the guide to see what was in store tomorrow, when I realized we were now less than 1,000 miles from Katahdin. I had hiked 1,193.1 miles in 106 days.

The 501 is one of the few shelters with an actual caretaker, who lives in a house on the property. He arrived after I was already in my hammock, and asked those around the fire, "who brought the beer?" They had arrived long after the rest of us, and truly didn't know. The next morning the caretaker asked me the same question, to which I replied that I did know, but was certainly not telling. He said he respected the honesty, but wondered if it was a hiker, and not locals that brought the beer. I assured him it was only hikers. All hikers agree that shelters should not become a party place for locals.

Frisbee, Refill and Cautious had planned to cover the 24-plus miles to Port Clinton, PA that day. Cautious felt his best chance to do that would be by not letting Frisbee and Refill get too far in front of him, but they did. I met many wonderful young people on my journey, and Cautious was certainly one of them. He hiked in a pair of surfer shorts, and had the attitude to match; nothing got him down. He was warm, caring, and wouldn't hesitate to help a fellow hiker. So, it was quite disconcerting to see him laid out on the trail that day. My immediate fear was that he had been bitten by a rattlesnake. But as I approached, he looked up with his signature smile, and I knew he was okay. He had taken a wrong turn that sent him over a boulder field, that he had to cross back over again to get back to the trail. After that, he simply laid down against his pack, right on the trail for a nap. That was Cautious.

*Figure 16 – Brother Blood with Cautious*

Port Clinton, Pennsylvania is a very small borough of about 325 people, and like Duncannon, is almost 100% white. In her book "Becoming Odyessa," Jennifer Pharr Davis directed some of her harshest criticism at this little hamlet. She described a run-down town with a bar at the local fire department, where its patrons were "inebriated" by 3:00 p.m. She compared the men to Southern "rednecks," wondering if such a term could be used for Mid-Atlantic dwellers. She made clear her disdain of those gathered at the Fire Company Social Quarters. She then recalled the locals harassing her and a fellow hiker at the town's pavilion, which serves as shelter in town where hikers can sleep.

So, I expected to hike downhill into an unwelcoming, unfriendly, and possibly dangerous redneck town.

My first stop would be the Post Office, where hopefully I would survive picking up my resupply box. I was a bit worried; after all, I don't carry a gun when I hike. The Post Office was closed for lunch, so I headed across the street to the barber shop, which the guide listed as "hiker friendly," offering coffee and cookies. I was hesitant, maybe it was a trap. At this point, I was just hoping to get out of this town before any inebriated rednecks got me.

But as you've probably guessed, Davis was just showing her prejudice and ignorance when it came to people she believed to be different and beneath her. Port Clinton welcomed us with open arms. First it was the barber shop, where an older man was sitting in front welcoming us to coffee and cookies inside and offering a ride for resupply if needed. Inside were two barber chairs, wooden bench seating along the opposite wall, and a few rocking chairs. Behind the rocking chairs sat a couple of guitars, and an antique dresser in the corner.

A sign on the mirror at the barber chairs read: "Haircut $8, Flat-Top $12." I thought the sign was a throwback to the shop's earlier days, when a man could get a haircut for just $8, but I was wrong, a haircut was just $8. I really hadn't planned on getting my hair cut, but given the summer heat, I hoped it would make things a little cooler while hiking. I told the barber I would like a cut, and he put me third in line behind two local men. I asked where I might spend the night. He recommended the Port Clinton Hotel, just two blocks away.

He talked about the Yuengling Brewery, and said their porter was the only beer he drank, and about the Cabela's Sporting Goods store in Hamburg just down the road, the largest Cabela's store in the world. He told us it was the second most visited location on the East Coast, behind only Disney World. After another local customer came in, he asked if wouldn't mind letting him in line before me, I didn't mind. I told him I would go and get a room at the hotel, then return clean and showered. He liked that idea.

The Port Clinton Hotel resembles the Doyle, except that it is not falling apart. It also has communal bathrooms, and a bar on the first floor, with a restaurant in the adjacent room. It's more expensive than the Doyle, but worth it. I sat at the bar, ordered a beer and inquired about a room. Soon I was registered with key in hand. I saw Frisbee and Refill at the bar. Frisbee at the bar informed me that after 1217.2 miles, his hike was over.

It had been just days since a stress fracture forced his wife Stubbs off the trail, and Frisbee said it just didn't feel right to be pushing on alone. "We can't have a picture of us at Springer, then us at Harper's Ferry, then a picture of just me at Katahdin." He was right, and he and Stubbs had already set their sights on a 2017 thru-hike, starting again from Springer. I was going to miss leapfrogging him and Stubbs. It was always great to see them, but I was happy that he had a partner with whom he wanted to share the entire journey. I knew they'd be all right.

After cleaning up, I bought a Yuengling Porter to go, then headed to the barber shop. The door was locked, so as I had been instructed, I tapped on the window. He didn't recognize me all cleaned up, but once I told him who I was, he let me in. When it was my turn for a haircut, I reached in the bag and pulled out the bottle of beer. He said I couldn't drink it there. I informed him that I had bought it for him, and handed it over. He got a big smile on his face, and then Frank cut my hair.

Frank Russo always wanted to be a barber, like his father. He calls his barber shop a "poor man's country club." All are welcome at his shop, as Frank has said, "They're all equal when they walk in my door, doctors, lawyers, Indian chiefs, I see them all. They come from far away for not just a haircut, but an experience."[v] And the Port Clinton Barber Shop is an experience. And Frank is quite a man.

If Duncannon had shaken my faith in humanity, Frank restored it.

I went back to the Port Clinton Fire Company Social Quarters after dinner, where I had drinks with "The Dude." Now there have been more than a few hikers who have self-applied that name, which is absolutely ridiculous. After all, "The Dude was a lazy man, maybe the laziest in Los Angeles County, which would put him in the running for laziest worldwide."[vi] So, there's no way The Dude would ever strap on a backpack and hike one mile, let alone 2189.1. But The Dude looked exactly like the Big Lebowski character, and the name had not been self-applied. I left the Fire Company fairly late, and got back to the Port Clinton Hotel, just to remember that check-out time was 9:00 a.m.

Nine a.m.... really? 9:00 am? If every Motel 6, Super 8, Microtel, and Quality Inn, from Georgia to Maine can have a check out time at 11:00 a.m., is the need to have me gone by 9:00 a.m. that important at the Port Clinton Hotel? But overall, I liked the Hotel, and unlike the Doyle, no racist bartenders.

At this point I was 153 miles into Pennsylvania and had yet to encounter the dreaded rocks. One thing had changed however, the water sources. It was the middle of a hot July, and water was becoming scarce. It was now common to hike a half mile or more off trail to a water source. They were also less frequent.

Much of the day was hiking on flat, old jeep roads. And as evening approached I was within two miles of the next shelter. But then I spotted a nice camp site down a hill next to Panther Creek, so well before sunset, I settled into camp. Despite the hot temps, the creek was nice and cold, meaning the source of the creek was likely spring water, no need to filter.

"Stonewall" joined me close to sunset. He got that name when someone remarked he looked like Stonewall Jackson. To my relief, he wasn't a neo-Confederate, but the complete opposite. Stonewall was on a personal journey, carrying with him ashes of both a good friend and his dog. As we sat by the fire he told me how his dog had been killed by a neighbor, just for sport. The person had been convicted, and the sentencing was scheduled for the next day. Stonewall's journey was different than mine, as he worked to make sense of the tragedies. My heart ached as he also talked about his close friend, who he had enjoyed hiking with, that had recently passed. I would have loved to spend more nights camped with him, but unfortunately, he had started his journey at Harper's Ferry, and was not yet doing the kind of miles I was, so it was the last time I saw Stonewall.

The water situation continued to test our resolve. At the Allentown Hiking Club Shelter, I walked over a half mile off trail for water, happy to find the spring was running, as many others were now dry in the hot July weather. I knew I still had a lot of hiking ahead of me that day, but, as they say, I didn't know the half of it.

A professional player once described the game of poker as "hours of boredom, punctuated by moments of sheer terror." (A rumor says the phrase originally described war.) Hiking through the last third of Pennsylvania can be similarly summed up as miles and miles of relatively flat easy hiking, punctuated by rock and boulder fields that rise straight from the bowels of hell. Today I hit Rocksylvania.

Following a not-too-difficult 15-mile stretch, I hit Knife Edge: a long ridgeline of jagged, pointy boulders decorated with an occasional white blaze. Knife Edge became Bear Rocks after a half mile, and more boulders. The trail again flattened out, and as sun was setting I hoped for an easy mile to the Bake Oven Knob Shelter. The trail had other plans, and soon I was traversing Bake Oven Knob, a boulder field fun for day hikers, but not my cup of tea after 18 miles carrying a full pack. After passing over the boulder field by headlamp, I was dead tired when I arrived at the shelter. The shelter was a complete dump. I set up quickly and was soon asleep, hoping for a fairly long day tomorrow.

My plan originally had been to take a few days off when I hit Harper's Ferry, but my wife and I decided it would be better for me to take the longer break at the last point where it was feasible for her to drive and visit me. After that, I wouldn't see her until coming down Katahdin, which was still over 900 miles away. We decided on Wind Gap, PA as that last meeting point, 28 miles from Bake Oven Knob

Shelter. I wanted a short hiking day to Wind Gap, so my goal was to do at least 18 miles to get within ten miles. The plan seemed reasonable enough, until I crossed the Lehigh River.

The guide warned of rocky, steep trail, but you never really know what that means until you're there. But the few simple words in the guidebook could not prepare me for the climb out of Lehigh Gap. As I approached the summit, it was no longer a trail, but rock climbing over steep, sheer rock and boulder faces. By far, the toughest rock climbing thus far. As I was preparing to negotiate another boulder climb, I came across a couple on a day hike headed down the mountain. They had brought their dog, who was standing at the edge of the boulder, looking down, not trusting the female, who was repeating, "c'mon, you can do it." The dog knew better. It would have been so much fun if the dog could speak. Despite all the reassurances of its two-legged masters, the dog was having none of it. As I continued upward, the couple was preparing to carry the dog down the boulder.

*Taconite, coke and limestone, fed my children, made my pay.*
*Them Smokestacks reaching like the arms of God into a beautiful sky of soot and clay.*
Bruce Springsteen
*Youngstown*

Zinc began filling the air around Palmerton in 1898, and for the next 80 years, 3,575 tons of zinc annually blanketed Blue Mountain and the surrounding area. When the zinc smelting stopped in 1980, "much of the surrounding area had been transformed into a barren wasteland."[vii] Soil with zinc levels greater than 500 parts per million are considered unsafe for gardens and contact with children. On Blue Mountain, zinc in soil reached levels of over 32,000 ppm. It was so bad, it was declared an EPA "Superfund" site. But don't try to tell the people of Palmerton the dangers of heavy metals in their water, soil or children. To this day, many still consider the EPA the real enemy, blaming them for the smelter shutting down. One resident commenting, "I'd rather have smelly air than families on welfare."

After the rock climbing at Lehigh Gap, the trail takes a detour over a very mundane four-mile stretch across Blue Mountain. With no trees because of the zinc, the sun was relentless. The one redeeming quality of the detour trail was the abundance of raspberries and blackberries. Berries tend to thrive in acidic soil, so the berry bushes had the mountain to themselves. It did cross my mind, more than once, that maybe eating something growing on a Superfund site wasn't the smartest thing, but I doubt that nibbling on a couple berries over a two-hour period would cause any problems. I won't give in to the culture of fear.

I realized that to make it within ten miles of Wind Gap, I would be hiking well into the night, which didn't bother me. I actually enjoy night hiking; it's cooler, and there's something exciting about looking off trail with your headlamp on and seeing a pair of glowing eyes. So, I hiked on. My plan to hike well into the night came to abrupt halt at

8:30 p.m., when I "hit the wall" physically. I could have gone on, but I realized that I had reached the point of drastically diminishing returns. To hike on would have been a supreme waste of effort.

Luckily, there was a nice primitive campsite just a few yards ahead. It had a nice fire ring, with lots of good wood in the area. I set up camp, got a nice fire going, then realized I was too tired to even enjoy that. I laid down and only remember waking up to see the fire dying down into a bed of coals. It was one of the hardest days of my journey, and I was still 14 miles from Wind Gap.

As usual, my intention of being up and on the trail early took a back seat to a relaxing morning of coffee and lollygagging. But I made it on the trail by 9:00 a.m., early enough for me. If yesterday had been one of the hardest days of journey, this was feeling like one of the easiest. Flat terrain all the way to Wind Gap, doing a relaxing two miles an hour had put me in a good mood. The plan was to meet my wife at 4:00 p.m., but traffic leaving DC slowed her down, so there was no hurry to get to the trailhead.

Section hiker Johnny B was at the trailhead when I arrived and I told him cold beer was on the way. Fifteen minutes later, my wife arrived. I was off for three full zero days, and Johnny B got his cold beer.

My zero days were July 18-20, in the Poconos. We rented a house, relaxed, drank wine, and I ate whatever I wanted. I had lost 45 pounds since I started. We made a trip to Easton, to see fellow hiker Cambria, who was recovering from a stress fracture in her foot but still planning to complete her thru-hike.

I realized that I had still had a long way to go, 911.6 miles to be exact. When I returned to the trail, the heat wave was still making water scarce on the trail. But I was motivated, because while I was off trail the Republican National Convention was held, and Melania Trump inspired me with her speech saying that "The only thing we have to fear, is fear itself."

After sleeping on a not so wonderful mattress for four nights, with food and wine readily available, my body needed to recover from the time off. My back needed some good nights of sleeping in my hammock, and I had to readjust to again rationing food until the next resupply.

I was back on the trail in the afternoon and did just 8½ miles to a beautiful campsite on a ridge overlooking the Pennsylvania countryside. I laid in my hammock and watched a blood red moon rise over the horizon. Getting a good night's sleep was just what my back and body needed, I woke the next morning at 5:30 a.m. to a beautiful sunrise. It was my last day in

Pennsylvania, and I was anxious to cross another state line. I was on the trail before 6:30. By 9:00 I was heading downhill to the town Delaware Water Gap and then into New Jersey.

Shortly before Delaware Water Gap I met a day hiker named Paul who was training to climb Mt. Rainer. He convinced me that a local breakfast joint was well worth the walk, then made me an offer I couldn't refuse; he would drive. He was the Dean of a branch of a community college, and we hit it off immediately. He was planning to retire in 2018, and then embark on his own thru-hike.

Like Duncannon, Delaware Water Gap is a small borough, located on a river, but that's where the similarities end. Delaware Water Gap is a vibrant, pleasant, and diverse town. There were outfitters providing rafting and kayaking trips, bed and breakfasts, and great little cafes and restaurants. It was the kind of place where city folk come to unwind. It was an example of what Duncannon could, but will likely never, be.

We had a great breakfast, and he drove me back to the trail, to the exact spot where I got in his car earlier. Always the purist. Another brief but rewarding chance meeting on the journey.

With a full belly, and not much later than I normally start on the trail, I was hiking across the Delaware River and into the state of New Jersey. Once again, my main nemesis of the day would be the heat. Just over the bridge in to New Jersey I loaded up with Gatorade at the Kittatinny Visitors Center. The guide listed many more water sources in section ahead than behind, but the heat and lack of rain made that a cruel joke. It was just as dry as Pennsylvania. After a stop at the Mohican Outdoor Center, and 20 miles for the day, I camped just past the Rattlesnake Spring, which luckily was running. I got a fire going and settled in for the night; a very hot, restless night.

At dusk, they started coming into my camp, and as if sending word back to the others, they just kept coming, and they stayed all night. Buzzing around my hammock bug net, the mosquitoes were my constant companions. Despite enjoying some Jim Beam Apple Bourbon with Sprite after dinner, it was the worst night's sleep of the journey. Whenever any part of my body leaned against the net, the mosquitoes could slide their proboscises through the mesh of the net and feast on my blood. My knees and arms were covered with mosquito bites by the next morning. Still groggy from a lack of sleep, I didn't hit the trail until after 10:00 a.m. A coffee stop helped, and despite the restless night and heat, I hit my stride fairly early.

As I hiked along the Millbrook-Blairstown Road a bicyclist was stopped at the side of the road pointing out a very large, coiled rattlesnake about ten feet off the road. By the sound of it, the snake was enjoying the heat about as much as I was. I had seen two rattlesnakes over 1307 miles, but today I would learn why this section has a swamp, spring, and mountain, each bearing the name "Rattlesnake."

Along the way I met a woman section hiking, with the goal of possibly thru-hiking next summer. She hiked at a pretty fast pace, and despite the heat, was wearing long pants, and long sleeves. To guard against ticks, of course. As I stopped to chat with a group of day hikers, Laura, just continued on, leaving me in the dust. I was feeling good despite the lack of sleep. The trail was smooth and fairly flat, but there is always a practical joker to keep you on your toes. This one was about eight feet off the trail, and as I walked without a care, it waited until I was as close as possible, then let out a rattle that sent my heart rate through the roof. I looked over to see the second large rattlesnake of the day coiling up off the trail. Even now, I know that snake is still telling his friends how he said to himself, "wait for it...wait for it, NOW" before letting loose that rattle and scaring the shit out of Brother Blood.

The day was filled with anticipation of burgers and beers, since Branchville, NJ was 15 miles into the day's hike. The guide listed both a steakhouse and tavern just off the trail on US Route 206. It was just after five when I passed by Brink Shelter and had just over three and half miles to a cold beer! It was still hot as hell, and after another mile, I saw someone sitting on some large rocks, with her feet kicked out leaning back, it was Laura. She looked tired and beat. I asked if she was okay, and she hesitated before replying, "I'm not sure." Which always means, "No, I'm not alright."

She wasn't sure where she was. Not due to any type of heat stroke, or dementia, but because she had somehow lost the pages of the guide she had brought. She guessed she may have used them to start a fire the previous night. As I talked to her, I realized that she was attempting something like 26 miles that day. In other words, more miles than I had done in any one day yet. I let her know we were about two and half miles from Rt. 206, and she should drink all the water and Gatorade she had, and then gave her some of mine. She started feeling better, but it was still hot, and dehydration is no joke. So, I helped her up, she seemed okay, then I grabbed her pack. She thought I was going to help her put the pack on her, but instead I slung it up on top of my pack and moved on before she could argue. Brother Blood, Hero.

It wasn't long before a friend she had called met us on the trail as we were heading down toward the road. He took her pack and promised to buy me a beer and burger for my efforts. A hero's reward!

As we headed down, I was once again stopped in my tracks, by rattlesnake number three of the day. We were soon headed to Gyp's Tavern, located on the Kittatinny Lake. The lake itself is private, so I can only hope that a bar that attracts bikers and hikers is a thorn in the side of the well-heeled Jerseyites who own second homes on its private shores.

Taverns adjacent to the trail are a double-edged sword. Of course, it's wonderful to stop and have a beer and a meal after a few days of eating peanut butter and dehydrated meals, but it's easy for them to become a vortex that is hard to escape. Sitting in a climate-controlled bar, when an attractive bartender asks if you'd like another beer, it's hard to say no, and head back to the woods. I did my best not to get stuck in these vortexes, but it was hard. So if I hadn't planned on staying in a town, or had any real reason to, I hiked out that night. And Gyp's Tavern was one of those places that would be very easy to stay till closing time. When I arrived, there were a fair number of bikers, but as night fell, they were replaced by a younger crowd, several of whom just got off work at other restaurants.

The jukebox played the cover of "Sound of Silence," by Disturbed. A hard-edged, haunting version of the Simon & Garfunkel classic. The Disturbed version is a masterpiece. A hand-written sign at the bar asked patrons to be generous, because some of the employees were saving to hike the A.T. next year. Maybe it was the truth, maybe a ploy to get bigger tips from hikers. Either way, it worked.

I was close to the point of no return. I believed just one more beer, and I'd end up closing down the bar... and opening it again tomorrow. I paid my check at 10:00 p.m. and headed down Rt. 206 and turned back on to the trail at 10:30. A local at the bar had mentioned the Culver Fire Tower was just up the trail, and that sounded like a good destination for the night. It was a mile and a half, with an elevation gain of just over 500 feet. For almost an hour, I walked fairly buzzed, by headlamp, looking for any sign of another rattlesnake. When I arrived at the fire tower, I was happy. Unlike the uncomfortable heat of the previous night, it was nice and cool. Great sleeping weather.

The female day hiker waved and smiled, completely unfazed at the sight of me in my underwear, watering a tree. I said hello and climbed back in my hammock. It was 7:30 a.m., and I laid in my hammock until a pick-up truck pulled up to the radio tower. Unlike most states, New Jersey's fire towers are still in use to detect fires and guide crews. After a nice conversation with the tower watchman, I sat at a picnic table, drinking coffee, and writing in my journal. I had a short conversation with the hiker who passed by earlier, as she was headed back. I didn't start heading north again until 11:00 a.m.

By now I was in the habit of carrying extra water, which usually guarantees that water will not be scarce. It worked again. After carrying an extra two liters of water (over four pounds), I arrived at the Mashipacong Shelter, to find a cache of about 50 gallons of fresh water in the bear box. I headed out with 2½ liters, and seven miles to the High Point Shelter for the night. I had been leapfrogging with Turtle most of the day and saw him again at the High Point State Park, where he was trying to decide whether to move on or stay at a hostel. I mentioned that seven miles past the High Point Shelter was Unionville, NY, where hikers could camp for free at the village green, across from a pizza parlor. The idea of pizza and free camping appealed to him, and we both stocked up with water and moved north.

I woke up with a pretty easy seven miles to NJ Route 284. The 0.7 hike up the road to Unionville, was the toughest stretch of the day. After a quick stop at the State Line Deli, I road walked under threatening skies to the Wit's End Tavern at the edge of the small village of Unionville. I saw Turtle's pack out front, so I set mine next to his and went in for a hard cider. I never was a hard cider drinker until my thru-hike, but it was so refreshing, and went down so smooth on hot days. Turtle was sitting at the bar, but didn't stay long. The women working the bar told me he had been somewhat rude when asked not to bring his pack into the bar.

I don't remember a single restaurant or bar from Georgia to Maine that wanted packs inside. One reason is they stink, really bad. And as soon as packs are in a bar, hikers will start drying their gear, or cleaning out their food bag, or spread out all their shit looking for something. And pretty soon, the locals, the people that support the business all year, simply find somewhere else to eat, drink, and spend money. After a couple of drinks, I headed to the Post Office for resupply, and packed my food bag at the village gazebo, where I ran into three hikers currently in the death grip of the bar/pizza/free camping vortex. Turtle was there as well, still complaining about having to leave his pack outside of the bar.

I actually had a fondness for Turtle. He wasn't at all mean-spirited, but it seemed the miles were starting to get to him. He had told me that he loved camping and living outdoors, but hiking wasn't his thing. He wanted to make it to Katahdin, but just didn't think he was doing the miles necessary. He started weeks before me and was not happy with his progress.

By then I had calculated how many miles a day I had to average to finish by the end of September, and it was something like thirteen and a half. I suggested he do a couple of 14-mile days and see if he started feeling better about it. He admitted that it was a petty thing to be upset about not being able to bring his pack in the bar, but insisted on repeating why he should have been allowed to bring it in.

After loading my food, I had a piece of pizza, bought a little more food resupply at the general store, then was ready to head back to the white blazes. But not before stopping for one more drink, of course. The rain had held off, but the skies were getting really dark, so I decided to have one more. Soon, the locals were starting to show up for their after-work ritual. I was on a stool near the corner of the bar, with a man sitting around the corner, maybe five feet away. I offered to move if my trail stink was too much. He said he couldn't smell it, but said that I was first hiker to have ever offered. That surprised me.

Outside the skies opened up and a summer nor'easter came charging through. I decided on one more drink. At this point I was joined by the three hikers caught in the vortex. They were planning to get back on the trail... tomorrow. I ordered another drink, and now the owner was there, telling jokes from his mental rolodex that must have contained thousands. Dave was a retired professor from SUNY (State University of New York), who loved the hikers that wondered in. It was easy to see why the locals loved this place. Dave was a warm, fun host. As he started every joke, the young lady in vortex group would ask if this was another joke. Dave would say "oh no, this really happened." She fell for it at least five times.

*Figure 17 - Dave and me at the Wit's End Tavern*

It was getting dark, so I had another drink, and soon I was playing pool, and feeding dollars into the jukebox. I joined Dave at the bar, for some more jokes, actually telling him one he hadn't heard, when he asked if I would do a shot with him. I did, of course. With the Rumple Minze down the hatch, I started to think about getting back to the trail, then ordered another beer.

It was well past dark when I actually exited the Wit's End Tavern. The storm had passed and it had cooled down enough to be very comfortable hiking weather. With a pretty good buzz on, I hiked nearly a mile back to the trailhead. The trail became road walking, and after almost a mile on Carnegie and State Line Roads, I started walking the perimeter of the Wallkill Reserve. It was a crystal clear, moonless night, as I moved at a snail's pace, stopping every few minutes to look up in wonder at the blanket of stars above. It was after midnight when I arrived at the Pochuck Mountain Shelter.

I woke up in New Jersey for the final time of my journey. Tonight, I would be sleeping in New York. The last hurdle in the Garden State was the "stairway to heaven," a fairly steep 900-foot climb up Wawayanda Mountain, very popular with day-hikers. I was relieved to find the spring halfway up was still running. Little more than a trickle, but running. As I found the point where the water was coming from the ground, I began using my cup to fill my water bottles. A group of high schoolers asked what I used to purify the water. I told them I drink spring water without filtering; they were a bit surprised, one even commenting that it's probably filled with "chloroform bacteria." He seemed very impressed with his knowledge, as I sat enjoying unfiltered, crystal clear, cold, fresh spring water.

Before heading up the Stairway to Heaven I met a day-hiker who called herself Babsy. She was in her twenties, and without a pack, she hiked well ahead of me. We met again at the top, and while most day hikers were turning to head back down, she was moving on to a swimming hole she had hiked to in years past. We talked and hiked until we came to the swimming hole, which the hot, dry summer had reduced to a shallow babbling brook.

We kicked off our shoes and dangled out feet in the water as we continued to chat. She was leaving soon for a teaching gig in South Korea. She was a kind, bright, and caring person. I wish that I could have spent more time with her, but it was time to for me to continue north. She was another of the wonderful young people I met on my journey. My generation has it all wrong the way we disparage her generation.

By now the trail was pretty lonely at times, which was fine with me. No longer did hikers have to get to shelters early to secure a spot inside. But the heat remained a constant companion, 90 degrees every day, keeping many water sources dry. But as in every state through which I hiked, New Jersey and New York also played a role in restoring my faith in humanity. With water becoming harder and harder to find along the trail, volunteers found time to place fresh water at many road crossings. At one, I counted over 30 plastic gallon jugs of water.

Crossing into New York felt like a huge milestone. To the backdrop of a beautiful sunset, I stood with one foot in New Jersey, and one in New York. I was happy. I stealth camped over a small hill just off the trail, and despite being swarmed again with bugs, I was feeling good.

*Figure 18 - One foot in New Jersey, one in New York*

I never liked sleeping under the bug net. It prevents good air flow, making it hotter, and I feel somewhat constrained inside. After a restless night, I packed up without having coffee in the middle of all the swarming bugs. I was feeling sluggish, and the temperature was again in the nineties. And as if to rub salt in wound of the weary hiker, New Yorkers found it cute to run the trail up and over boulders, just for the hell of it. I never complained about humping over mountains and boulders, because how else can you get to the other side? But not here. Here the trail was routed over boulders just as an obstacle. At times, there would be a smooth blue-blazed side trail that paralleled the boulder, and then rejoined the white blazes just past the rock formation.

Southern New York was reminding me of a mud run, where people pay $50 to do a 5K run, littered with artificial obstacles, to get a "free" t-shirt to wear to the gym. Everything before this point seemed a simple point A to point B, knowing that A to B was up and over every mountain from Georgia to Maine. That's what I signed up for, but this was going up and over boulders, just to be clever.

Many times over the course of 2189.1 miles, I looked to my right, and then left, wondering if the trail had been directed over difficult terrain, just to make it harder. And almost every time, I realized that there wasn't any way to make it much easier. The Appalachian Trail is challenging enough, I wasn't thrilled to be made to climb up a rock and back down for no reason. And what's even more ridiculous is that it's already a hard section.

Turning a page in the guide is another small affirmation of progress. It represents another 30-45-mile section conquered, and on to the next. But as I turned the page into Southern New York, I missed the highlighted sentence at the bottom of the page that read: *"Despite the unimposing profile, rocks, abrupt ups & downs make this challenging."* I didn't read it until after traveling the first 20 miles in New York, and to quote the Urban Dictionary, "you ain't never lied." The first part of New York is indeed a series of abrupt up and downs.

My spirits lifted at NY Rt. 174A because I knew there was ice cream. On a thru-hike both your adult and childhood cravings become acute. You crave ice cream with same intensity you crave beer, and Bellvale Farm was not far from the road crossing. It's one of those places that locals will tell you serves the best ice cream in the country, and today, they were right. Between the heat, and unforeseen difficulty of Southern New York, Bellvale was a true oasis. On the walk back to the trail, I stopped at Hot Dogs Plus, a food trailer, where two hot dogs, chips, and a drink, was just $5.50. It is another popular joint with the locals.

At 6:00 p.m., I stopped for the night. I was exhausted, but a relaxing night lifted my spirits. By the next morning, my outlook had turned very positive, I felt enormous gratitude for the people who had left water near the road crossings. I started thinking about my long day into Adkins, VA, when I hiked over 20 miles to get to town, to earn a zero day. I thought maybe, just maybe I could push it and make to Fort Montgomery that night. It turns out that was a pipe dream.

The miles were slow, very slow. The trail was interrupted with rock scrambles and boulder climbs, including the "lemon squeezer," a tight, narrow passage, leading to a steep 8-10 foot sheer rock face climb. After six and a half hours, I had gone only 8.5 miles. I stopped just after the Fingerboard Shelter for lunch in my hammock, and a dessert of fresh popped popcorn. The trail would decide my pace today, not me.

My imagination started playing tricks on me. Was the trail not so difficult, and it was actually Lyme Disease causing my fatigue? After preaching against the culture of fear, was I going to endlessly hear, "I told you so," while being pumped full of antibiotics? Was I destined to become the poster child for every helicopter parent to point at, to keep their kids from playing in the woods? Or was I just losing my mind? At that point, I couldn't decide which was more likely...or which was worse.

But as in the path of life, a friend came to my rescue. One I hadn't seen in a while, The Appalachian Trail. My friend had come back to me. I was no longer on the Appalachian Rock Scramble, or the Appalachian Boulder Climb, or the Appalachian Obstacle Course, I was back on the Appalachian *Trail*. Back to speeding along at two miles an hour!

During a short break at the William Brien Shelter, I chatted with Sphagnum PI, a young, strong hiker who, armed with a degree in biology, loved investigating the diverse moss and plant life along the trail, which explains her trail name. She was beat, and quite disappointed and upset that she had done "only 13 miles" today. If misery loves company, we were the perfect pair. It was a relief that I didn't have Lyme Disease, nor was losing my mind.

And finally, it started to rain. As I hiked alone, I heard something just off trail, and saw a black bear scampering back into the woods. It was number 23, and the last bear I saw on the journey. It cooled down as I walked into the night, even hiking along the four-lane Palisades Parkway almost half a mile for water from a spigot at a visitors' center. The guide listed vending machines as well, but I had been informed the center closes at night, and there would be no soda for me. I proceeded to the top of West Mountain, where I camped just past the West Mountain Shelter. I was just seven miles from the Bear Mountain Bridge and Fort Montgomery.

My phone read 7:12 a.m. when I woke, with a light rain hitting my rain fly, I laid my head back down for a minute or two, then looked at my phone again... 9:46 a.m.

The hike to the Bear Mountain Bridge was as leisurely a hike as any on the entire trail. The A.T. merges with a popular day-hiking trail that was surfaced similar to a cinder running track. The ups and downs were gradual, and soon I was at the Perkins Memorial Tower, which I climbed, hoping, with no luck, to see the New York City skyline using the mounted silver binoculars at the top. As I prepared to leave the tower grounds, I chatted with a woman who was shocked that I had hiked all the way from Georgia, and had actually seen bears in the woods.

From the tower I thought it would be a gradual downhill hike on a manicured trail to the bridge. For once, I was right.

Following the hike down, the A.T. actually passes through a zoo in the Bear Mountain Recreational Area. Some of us were saddened seeing bears in a caged area, but the zoo says they were captured as "problem bears" who would have otherwise been euthanized. The zoo/park also displays a statue of Walt Whitman, and the bear cage is the lowest point of elevation on the entire A.T. I crossed paths with Hansel, who agreed about the difficulty of South New York, saying it was harder than the Virginia Roller Coaster. He was right.

I got a ride to the Bear Mountain Bridge Motel, from the owner. There I decided to shed everything I could to shave pack weight. That night, beer, wine, and barbeque had me feeling pretty good. I had crossed the 1,400-mile mark, and was feeling in somewhat rarefied air. No longer were the towns populated with smelly, hiker trash. Now it was not unusual to be the only hiker the place, as I was tonight.

Back at the motel, I marveled at the magic of air conditioning. With a remote control at my bedside, I had the immense power to choose the exact temperature for my sleeping pleasure. And at a whim, at any time, I could alter the interior climate. After exerting my newfound power, I enjoyed a deep sleep at exactly 68 degrees Fahrenheit. I packed up the next morning well-rested. I took one last look at the instrument of my power, and headed out again, into the uncontrolled climate of the woods.

I don't think I shed more than a pound during my purge of unneeded items, but my pack *felt* lighter to me. I knew it was self-delusion, and psychological, but that was good enough for me. I walked back to the trail stopping for pizza along the way and was heartened by the kindness that the people in the Town of Fort Montgomery showed to hikers.

Then it was over the Hudson River by way of the Bear Mountain Bridge. As I walked across the bridge I waved to motorists and was excited about getting back in the woods. I looked down at the river - way, way down to the river. At that moment, if my mother was still alive I would have called her with my answer:

*"No Mom, if my friends jumped off a bridge..."*

Still happy the trail was just a trail, I was back to my normal hiking pace on what could be considered the "deli-blazing" section of the trail. It seemed there was a deli at every road crossing, or at least very close. The first was six miles in, at the intersection of US 9 and NY 403, the Appalachian Market. From the outside, it looked like any other gas station/deli, but inside a hungry hiker could choose from at least three food stations. I went for Italian and got a generous serving of pasta with sausage. To go with it, I bought a nice cold beer, along with a donut, a slice of pizza, and a bagel. My hiker hunger had kicked in, and my body was chanting, *"Eat Brother Blood, Eat."* I obeyed.

The rain was just a drizzle as I was finishing up lunch. I fixed my rain cover over my pack, and at 4:00 p.m., the skies opened up. Rain, glorious rain. It poured, making me soaking wet and happy. The other hikers I saw that day were stopping at the Graymoor Spiritual Life Center, where they could camp for free under a picnic shelter to get out of the rain. I hiked on, thoroughly enjoying getting drenched to the bone, knowing that at least some water sources would be flowing again.

Four miles north I set up camp in the rain atop Canopus Hill. After getting into my hammock, I realized the small tree I hung it on would not hold me all night. Back out into the rain I relocated to more secure trees. Soon I was joined by southbound hiker Bionic Dave. He was just starting a long section with no planned destination, just south. His enthusiasm was contagious. As I sat in hammock enjoying coffee, I was happy. The last sentence in my journal that night was: "Feeling good again."

Life is Good.

**CHAPTER 16: NOT MY BACK**

Life sucks.

After a night of very, very hard rain, I headed out on a wet, cool morning, feeling rejuvenated. Unlike Bionic Dave, I actually stayed dry throughout the downpour. I headed out without a worry on my mind. Within a mile, one of my bootlaces was flapping around, the same way it had a thousand times before. I put my foot on a rock, and like thousand times before, bent down to tie it. I stood up, but like no other time on the journey, my back tightened up in pain and locked up. Still bent over, in pain, I very, very slowly raised upright. *Maybe it will loosen up after a few steps, let's give it a try.* It got worse. I gingerly walked to a large rock, slid my pack off, and sat down.

Was this it? After 1,400 miles is this going to be what ends this journey. Would I be off trail for a day, a week, two weeks, a month? Do I need assistance to get out of the woods? *Breathe, Brother Blood, breathe.*

I hadn't been thinking about my back; we back pain sufferers love the time we spend not thinking about our backs. But after two back surgeries, and numerous episodes of painful spasms, I am too often jolted out of those pleasurable times, and sent to my knees with a painful reminder. I began slowly, and painfully digging in my pack, for the bag containing the ibuprofen. I relaxed and told myself, *"let's take some Vitamin I and see just how bad this really is."* I washed down seven pills, and just sat there. After about 30 minutes, I stood up and tried to loosen up.

What else could I do? I know from episodes in the past, that as my body warms up and gets moving, the pain becomes tolerable. So very slowly I brought the pack up to the rock, sat down and placed the straps over my shoulders, and cautiously stood up. *Alright, I can do this...baby steps.* And with that, I began inching northward again toward Katahdin. My back slowly loosened up, and before long I was making miles again. The hiking actually went well, I was often reminded that when I slowed down and tried to sleep tonight, things would be painful. But I'll worry about that later; for now, I was driving on with Vitamin I.

I took a side trail to the Clarence Fahnestock State Park for a burger with fries and Gatorade. As I hit the trail again, the clouds moved in. It wasn't just rain, it was a deluge that was enveloping the trail. It was awesome. The heat wave had snapped, and water was flowing everywhere. Even though I had some painful nights ahead with my back, I would be hiking on. The rain continued as I reached the RPH Shelter. It's another shelter very close to a road, and both pizza and Chinese delivery is available. But it was Sunday and the Chinese restaurant was closed, making our decision easy.

Cautious and No Worries were there, and soon Slosh and Scavenger came in, drenched to the bone. Despite his use of a rain cover, Slosh's pack was flooded with four or five inches of water, but he too was happy the heat wave was over, and he set up their tent in the driving rain. We placed a pizza order as my back began tightening up, despite the strict ibuprofen regimen I had put myself on. I knew sleep would be difficult, so I took an Ambien with another batch of Advil, hoping against hope to get some good sleep. I didn't. It was a painful night, as a tweaked back is a sleep killer. Even the simple task of rolling over is a painful, arduous task. And getting up is almost worse. A slow and stiff ordeal until about half a mile into the day's hike before the muscles warm up. Today I decided against taking Advil, to see just how bad the pain actually was. Again, it was not bad while hiking, but horrible at night. It was great to see Cautious again. He realized that despite my words to the contrary, my back was really bothering me.

The next day, I stopped at another deli along the way, and enjoyed a true foot-long sub, and chatted with a local man who explained that Lyme Disease was never a problem until the government did some breeding of ticks that made the disease worse for humans, and that I should be very careful because now even mosquitoes were spreading the disease. Because of government experiments, of course. Who doesn't love some "alternative facts."

I feared running out of ibuprofen, and the store/deli only sold it in small packets of two pills. I bought 12 packets. Hiking was the easiest part of the day. I did 16 miles before setting up camp on the second West Mountain in New York. I tried to sleep, but again, the Advil and Ambien were no match for the back pain.

Another tough morning, but I knew it was just pain, not injury, and I'd be fine in a few days. My saving grace was that it didn't hurt much when hiking. So upward and onward I went. Four miles in, I reached a long boardwalk that leads to the lone railroad stop along the A.T., which allows smelly hikers to be dumped into the heart of the Big Apple. It was tempting, but given the money I was spending in small town America, Manhattan might just break the budget.

On the boardwalk I met Hugh, who thru-hiked 40 years earlier. He was with a rescued dog and loved coming back to the trail to help work through his PTSD. I loved talking to him. He was warm, caring, and loved supporting current hikers. He said something that I had thought in my mind, but never heard anyone else express about the hike. He said that no matter what happens, he had thru-hiked the A.T., and no one can take that away from him. It's the same thing athletes say about winning a championship. It was great to be reminded that I was working towards an accomplishment that will be a source of pride throughout my life. Hugh had made my day.

I was surprised to hear the next person I met tell me that the trail has restored her faith in humanity, because she wasn't a hiker. She was working at the Native Landscapes & Garden Center on Route 22, a place known for its kindness and support of hikers. They have a refrigerator full of sodas and ice cream, to help yourself, and pay on the honor system. She spoke of how the gratitude and kindness of hikers truly moved her. Knowing we did that for her, and what so many people like her had done for us along the way, helped me up the next mountain.

Next stop would be the Wiley Shelter, and to my delight, beer! Rolling Rock to be exact. Super Hip had completed two jewels of the "triple crown," the Appalachian Trail and the Pacific Crest Trail, with only the Continental Divide Trail left to conquer. He was out paying it forward with beer and snacks. My back had improved from pain to discomfort, and I was happy to be doing a short 10-mile day. I was just four miles from my destination, Ten Mile River, and after meeting Hugh, enjoying the garden center, and beer with a late lunch, I didn't think the day could get better.

Until it did.

When I moseyed into camp around 7:00 p.m., Slosh and Scavenger had just returned from a dip in the river, and Cautious was relaxing. I began setting up and making my evening coffee. Some say there are no heroes left in the world, but those people never met Super Hip. Walking triumphantly toward our camping area, there he was again, with a fresh, cold supply of beer. We took one down, passed it around. Super Hip was my hero.

*Figure 19 - Enjoying a Rolling Rock, compliments of Superhip*

That night, I slept good! I woke up early, and I was on the trail by 8:30 a.m. like a normal hiker. The heat wave had indeed broken, and my back was feeling pretty good. Anyone that suffers from any type of recurring pain understands the euphoria in the days just after an episode of pain; the joy of remembering what it is like not to be consumed with pain and discomfort. I could stretch my legs out and not feel a twitch in my back, I didn't have to be obsessed with an awkward step seizing my lower back. Freedom!

Freedom... and Connecticut. As I crossed another state border, I thought to myself, *"this shit is getting real."* I couldn't really think of Maine when I was in Georgia, North Carolina, Virginia, or even Pennsylvania. Maine at that time was a far-off place, rumored to have a mountain, atop which a wooden sign sits marking the Northern Terminus of the A.T. But it was so far away, I mean it was up in New England. Way, way into New England.

But now it seemed real. I was well past the Mason/Dixon line, and really up north now. It was August 3rd, and I started to focus on enjoying myself, because now the end was no longer a far off distant place, it was just over 700 miles away. Still a long way, but now it felt like the end was actually coming.

I camped at the Stewart Hollow Brook Shelter and was the only northbound Thru-Hiker there that night. By now I had long stopped hanging my food to protect against the ravenous black bears. I should have thought more about the truly ravenous, vicious mouse that had been prowling around my camp. They say rust never sleeps, and neither do mice.

That night the mouse chewed through my pack, chewed through my food bag, and got into my Ziploc bag of trash. Maybe I should start hanging my "mouse bag."

As the nights became chilly again, my sleep improved, and I was making a point to enjoy the hiking, and not worry about miles. It felt like a mini roller coaster all day, and as always, seemed more up then down. But it was trail, and not rocks and boulders. I started the day 26 miles from Salisbury, CT, and was hoping to do enough miles to make tomorrow a nero (near-zero day). I did over 18 miles, to Falls Village, CT. Unlike the South, many small Northern towns do not have an inexpensive hostel for hikers to spend the night. But that's not to say they are less welcoming; Toymakers, a small café, allows hikers to camp behind their home and business, for free.

The package store in town had just closed, but the owner was still there, and unlocked the door for one last six-pack sale for the day. I proceeded across the street to the Falls Village Inn, a somewhat upscale restaurant and inn. The guide listed lodging at $239 and up; we were definitely not down South anymore. I was one of only two hikers in the bar that evening. Super Tough, a young woman and strong hiker was enjoying a burger when I arrived. I had a few beers and made casual conversation with some locals, when I mentioned to a woman that I had been stung by a bee the previous day, and my foot was a bit swollen. A statement I soon regretted. She pounced on that information to inform me that it is possible to become allergic to bees later in life, and strongly suggested I find a doctor to write a prescription for an EpiPen. Rearing its ugly head again was the culture of fear.

Later I sat in my hammock, sipping my beers, and thinking how normal it felt to be sleeping behind a café. Something unheard of back in the real world, but now home was where the heart, hammock, and backpack were.

Toymakers Café is only open Thursday thru Sunday. It does not accept credit cards; payment can be cash, check, or barter of Triumph Motorcycle parts. I had heard the food was good, but don't be in a hurry. They were right about the speed of the cook, but not so accurate about the food. It wasn't good, it was absolutely amazing! I had the *Big Easy*, a version of Eggs Benedict with country ham and grilled tomato, served over a toasted bagel. Simply amazing. In no hurry to get back on the trail, I enjoyed a wonderful breakfast, coffee, and the company of several very nice locals.

### ###

Salisbury, CT is another town where a cheap motel is seen as often as Bigfoot. So, I reserved a room at the Hitching Post Motel, in Cornwall Bridge, 22 miles south, then booked a $40 shuttle to get there. I needed to be off-trail, because this was the night of the annual fantasy football draft with my brothers. I would have to do it by phone, and it wasn't until the hour of the draft approached that I realized I had booked the only motel in America without cell service. Wi-Fi saved the day, and the draft was a success. But the best thing that happened that evening was another small act of kindness, helping restore my faith in humanity.

After I had tossed my stinky trail clothes in the motel's washing machine, the owner of the Hitching Post took it from there. And just before the draft was to commence, she knocked on my door, with a basket of clean clothes, just out of the dryer. She then asked if I was doing alright, and did I need anything? She was making dinner and asked me to join her if I was hungry. I was touched, not just at the offer, but how sincere she was in making sure I was okay. It was heartwarming, and I really wished I would have had the time that evening to share dinner with her.

After coffee the next morning, I headed to the Cornwall Package Store, where signing their register can be, as the AT Guide states, "refreshing." Refreshing, as in a free beer! I used the opportunity to enjoy my first Genesee Cream Ale since high school, 30-some years ago. I then got a bite at the General Store, trying to figure out how I was going to get back to the trail. But as they say, "the trail provides." A man who I would guess to be in his mid to late 50's struck up a conversation, and soon offered me a ride to Salisbury.

He was a construction worker, currently between places to live, so he had a mattress in the back of his work van. I wouldn't say he was down on his luck, because people like him are never down on their luck. The kind of person that keeps pushing on, despite a few speed bumps. He talked about the difficulty of finding good steady work, mentioning the tough competition from Latinos. Right away I was impressed that did not use the more preferred nomenclature of older white men, "these damn Mexicans." As in, "It's hard to find work because of all *these damn Mexicans.*" Or, "we need a wall to keep out all *these damn Mexicans.*" No, John, spoke with admiration of the Latino work ethic, and the increasingly high quality of work they do.

As we approached my drop-off point, I offered him $20 in gas money, but as expected, he refused. He wanted to help me out, and what is helping someone out if he were to take money for it. I have a feeling, that somewhere, right now, John is making a killing working alongside one or two Latinos.

It's been said that Connecticut people are not always nice to hikers. For me, nothing could have been further from the truth.

I hiked easy that day, just over seven miles to the Massachusetts border. It was Saturday, August 6th, and I was sharing the trail with many weekenders. Some thru-hikers seem to delight in putting down these weekend warriors. But I loved them. They were fun, and excited to be out in the woods. As I approached the Sages Ravine Campsite, a cold stream flowed next to the trail, where a young man was getting water to filter, while his girlfriend sat on a rock. As I dipped my bottle in the stream and brought it directly to my mouth for a nice cold drink, the young lady gasped, her eyes wide open as if a Bigfoot had appeared behind me. I told her that as cold as this water was, it had to be spring fed, so I wasn't going to treat it. The boyfriend mumbled something about not ruining the weekend getting sick on bad water as I continued gulping it down.

A family was just arriving with two young adult women carrying massive packs, while their parents carried little more than day packs. I wasn't sure what was more amazing, that they had talked their daughters into backpacking with them, or they were able to make them their Sherpas as well. The parents set up a little way up from me on a small hill, on what they thought was fairly flat land. The daughters hammocked down by the stream. The next morning, I awoke to see the couple's tent had rolled about five feet down the hill and was upside down and bent out of shape. Soon I heard them laughing as they struggled to get out of the tent door, now directly above them. It was a morning of coffee and laughter. Welcome to Massachusetts.

Water was everywhere. Massachusetts welcomed me with cold and clear flowing streams and lush green woods. Beautiful rock formations jutted out from the waters, and the hiking was not that difficult. I thought of Thoreau and Emerson, and realized that I was in state number 11, just 3 more left.

I wasn't really craving squash, but as I ascended East Mt., along the ridgeline, there on a rock were two large yellow squash and a smaller green one. I guessed that possibly the weight of the gourds was a bit much, and a hiker decided to lighten their pack, and provide a treat for someone else. I grabbed a yellow one and looked forward to bacon and fresh squash for lunch at the Tom Leonard Shelter. At the Shaker Campsite that night the remainder of the squash added a nice twist to my Knorr Rice Side dinner.

It was August 9th, and tomorrow, I would be joined again by the Lawyers. They had decided months ago to meet me on August 10th, wherever I was. The meeting point would be near Lee, MA, along Rt. 20. That meant today would be a leisurely 10 miles to the Upper Goose Pond Cabin, a true hiker resort. No running water, no electricity, no problem. The cabin itself is reminiscent of a well-heeled New Englander's vacation home. Two stories, with large front porch, on the waters of Upper Goose Pond, with a small dock and canoes to use, free of charge. I took a swim, and just before sunset paddled a canoe over its crystal-clear waters.

The cabin's caretakers prepare pancakes at 7:00 a.m. It was tempting, but not tempting enough to get out of my hammock so early. I was told it was a bit of a contest to elbow your way in to get a plate of the hot cakes, and since coffee and Clif Bars have gotten me this far, I'd stay out of that scrum. It's easy to understand why many Thru-Hikers decide to take a zero day at the cabin. I'm sure if beer was available it would become another vortex capturing hikers for a week... or more.

The cabin was owned and operated by the Appalachian Mountain Club (AMC), the largest, and oldest, of the trail clubs. They only took donations at the cabin, and I was more than happy to stuff a twenty in the piggy bank. I had decided early on that I would not pay a fee to stay at any shelter or primitive campsite along the A.T., but they certainly deserved the donation. My first experience with the AMC was a good one, but first impressions can be deceiving.

I had a relaxing morning, knowing the Lawyers would be later than they had hoped, since they didn't get to their hotel rooms until 4:15 a.m. due to flight delays. It was only a mile and a half to where we would meet, and they were coming from Albany, NY, so I had a second cup of coffee, and the rain held off until I hit the trail. I hiked in the rain to Rt. 20, where I had more coffee at the Berkshire Lakeside Lodge, when Reboot came in, and changed from her wet hiking clothes into a dress to hitch into town.

It was 11:00 a.m. when a small car pulled up and Silver Fox, Maverick, and Steve, a new addition to our hiking team, piled out. The rain had stopped, and they took a few minutes to marvel at the amount of weight I had shed on the trail. The band was back together again!

We crossed Rt. 20, and Steve got his first taste of the Appalachian Trail with an 800-foot, fairly steep uphill climb. I was reminded just how strong a hiker Silver Fox is. At 61-years old, he bounded up the hill like so many young hikers who had passed me along my journey. He isn't tall, he doesn't have a hiker's build, but he seems to float like the wind over the trails.

In past hikes, Maverick always seemed to keep one foot firmly planted back in the real world. I've heard him make deals with clients from mountaintops on the A.T. But this time, he seemed to be letting go a bit more, and enjoying the trail without the ball and chain of civilization. As Silver Fox was bounding up the hill, Steve was having a baptism of fire into the world of the A.T.

Six miles later we sat at the October Mountain Shelter, and I remembered how nice it was to hike with Silver Fox, since he made the coffee every evening.

I warned my hiking partners that when I started sensing I was getting close to the town of Dalton, I would likely pick up the pace to get there as soon as possible. Which I did. It was 12 not-too-difficult miles to Dalton, and 6 miles out I was getting the itch. We had called and booked the last four rooms at the Shamrock Village Inn, and then I took off. I was enjoying a draft of Downeast Cider when a text let me know Steve had hitched to town and Maverick and Silver Fox were about two miles out.

We enjoyed a nice dinner at the Dewey Public House, and Steve was thinking about heading home the next morning. The trail was taking its toll. It's a tough thing to do your first section hike with a Thru-Hiker who has ten states and 1,550 miles under his belt. He did head home the next day. After that Steve did buy a better fitting pack, and the following year did enjoy a section hike with myself and the Lawyers.

After dinner, I enjoyed a couple of beers at Jacob's, a local bar popular with hikers. I was enjoying myself until one hiker began a rant about how the government actually recruits people of Indian descent, and provides them $75,000 to buy businesses, which explains why so many small hotels and stores are owned by people from India. He was quite upset that the government didn't do things like that for white people. Yes, racism is not confined to just places like Duncannon, it has many faces, and they are everywhere. My appetite for more beer had vanished.

## CHAPTER 17: THE NIGHT OF THE SNUNK

"The little fucker bit me!" The unwanted visitor had indeed bitten Pacer, but on his boot, not breaking his skin. The visitor was an ornery little skunk that was acting unlike any critter I had ever seen on the trail. Soon the animal had gotten ahold of Pacer's tobacco bag, and Pacer was using a trekking pole to swat at the creature trying to reclaim his tobacco. We all thought the skunk would let out a spray, but it never did. Someone suggested it had used it all up and was "dry." All evening, and throughout the night we were held hostage by this loud, obnoxious, little black and white demon. It was quite disconcerting to hear it under my hammock, wrestling with my water bottles at regular intervals throughout the night.

We woke the next morning and did a head count. We all survived The Night of The Skunk.

The most amusing part of the episode is that we were joined by two women at the shelter, spending their very first night, ever, on the Appalachian Trail. Both named Jessica, they now have the greatest first night story of the A.T.! The skunk seemed to chase people around when they ventured out of the shelter. And every time we thought the skunk was gone, we heard, like nails on a chalkboard, the screeching of that wretched little demon returning.

*Figure 20 – Demon skunk on steps of shelter*

The next day we summited Mt. Greylock. Maverick decided to hit the trail early, and by 5:45 a.m. he was hiking by headlamp. Silver Fox and I enjoyed our coffee, (with no sign of the skunk), and left at 8:30. Maverick had been at the visitors center and restaurant atop Mt. Greylock for at least two hours when we showed up. By then he had talked to just about everybody there, including the two Jessicas. We had a great lunch, and as the protocol usually is with the Lawyers, we'd be spending another night in town.

The shorter days, and frequent stays indoors were just what I needed. My body was feeling less run down, and I was really enjoying my time with them. Motel rooms were booked solid in Williamstown that night, but we lucked out and were able to rent a cottage behind one of them. I cooked a big breakfast the next morning and planned an easy and quick seven-mile day. It wasn't very hard, but it was anything but quick. On the trail at 11:30 a.m., it was up 1,500 feet over the next 4 miles. At times, it felt to me like we were spending more time on breaks than time we spent hiking. I had become so used to hiking at my own pace, that I was getting a little impatient. Then it dawned on me that I was headed for a shelter. Why was I in a hurry to get the Seth Warner Shelter? I then relaxed, and just tried to enjoy the nice, slow hike.

The next day started with a 1700-foot climb, where at the top the Appalachian Trail merged with the Long Trail, I crossed into state number 12, Vermont. Vermont is often called Ver-Mud for obvious reasons, and true to form, the actual state line itself was a huge mud puddle. But the trail wasn't as muddy this year due to a lack of rain. But it was easy to understand what it must be like in a regular year. Despite the lack of rain, it was still muddy enough for me.

The AT Guide recommended that in the muddy areas, hikers should walk through the mud, and not trample the vegetation bordering the trail. I understood the spirit of the suggestion, but also knew it would be as effective as trying to rope the wind.

It was just one night in the woods, then on to Bennington, VT, where the lawyers would leave to re-enter the *real* world, and I would take my first zero day since Wind Gap, PA. I had carried in fresh chicken, capers, pasta, lemons, and butter, and made a chicken picatta dinner my first night in Vermont.

That evening, Silver Fox ventured up to the shelter where an older, grey-haired man was busy building a fire. Silver Fox said the man looked like a trail vagabond; a person that except for the few winter months, spends almost all year on the trail. I walked up to the shelter, and there was Grandpa. The same Grandpa that I had encountered on my first section hike three years earlier.

I was looking forward to being a solo-hiker again, but the love and support the Lawyers had given me, spending their time and money to be part of my journey was quite humbling. They took a shuttle to the airport, and I enjoyed a relaxing night in Bennington.

### 

I returned to the trail just after noon, alone, with 578.5 miles left. I felt as if I was hitting the homestretch, but also knew that "the Whites," New Hampshire's White Mountains, lay ahead. After the summer heat wave, I was happy to be hiking over 3,000-foot summits again, where sleep comes easier with the lower temperatures. Before leaving Bennington, I was told there would be seven dry days ahead. That prediction was off by just a week, as a light rain greeted me that afternoon. I spent the night at the Goddard Shelter with a great bunch of section and first-time hikers.

I was loving Vermont. The hills were not too steep, the nights were cool, and the miles pleasurable. Planning to do 13 miles to the base of Stratton Mountain, I made it by 5:00 p.m. and decided to knock out a good part of the climb now, rather than wake up to a 1,600-foot climb. Low on water, I passed a nice primitive campsite, before coming to a nice spring about a quarter mile up the trail. Not in the mood to do backwards miles, I filled up with water and headed on, determined to stop at the next site I found. Most hikers will tell you that passing a good campsite, with the hope of stopping the "next one," can be a mistake. It seems there are good campsites everywhere along the trail, until you decide to stop at the next one. But tonight, I was lucky. Just after stocking up with water at a spring, there was a nice site about 50 feet off trail, with lots of good wood. After taking a little time to get the wet wood burning, I relaxed. I was home. My only concern was that whenever I felt this good, I am always scared something bad is about to happen.

Nothing bad happened.

I woke up refreshed to a crisp, clear morning, perfect for hiking. The remainder of the hike up Stratton Mountain was not difficult, and on the summit a plaque stated that this was where Benton MacCaye first conceived the idea of the Appalachian Trail. A fire tower stood at the summit, and for the first time I climbed all of the stairs to the top of a fire tower. I am a tad scared of heights, and fire towers made me wobbly-legged at times. I remembered watching Pebbles bound up to the top of the towers in the Smokies, while I would make it over half way and decide that was enough. But today, on Stratton Mountain, I crossed another obstacle and stood atop a fire tower. Small victories.

*Figure 21 - Stratton Mountain fire tower*

From the top of the tower, I realized why Vermont is called the "Green Mountain" state. Evergreen forests as far as the eye could see. I had crossed into a new landscape, and a new climate; I was truly in New England. My only concern was whether to make it to the city of Manchester Center that evening, or just go in for resupply in the morning. After stopping along the shore of Stratton pond and completely pigging out for lunch, my body felt sluggish, and I decided to take it easy and hit town tomorrow.

That day I crossed paths with a southbounder named Splash. We made small talk, and as I turned to continue north, I took two steps, and heard her say, "wait." I turned, and Splash looked at me with caring eyes, and told me not to get down in the Whites. Yes, they are hard, very hard, she said, but they also beautiful. She told me she had seen many northbounders become down, depressed, and demoralized, rather than enjoy the beauty. She assured me that I would get through the Whites, but it would be slow, so just enjoy.

The White Mountains were no longer a faraway section standing as a barrier to Maine. I was 150 miles from Mt. Moosilauke, the gateway to the Whites. Whether talking to hikers, or reading the guide, it was clear the Whites would be the toughest, most challenging section of the entire journey. It was less what Splash had said, than how she said it. I took it to heart and decided I would hit the mountains with an open mind and open heart. After all, at my pace, they couldn't slow me down that much. Could they?

My treat for the day was of a couple cans of blueberry wheat ale. As I passed Prospect Rock, a couple of guys and a young lady were looking out over the countryside and offered me a can from the Vermont Long Trail Brewing Company. I'm normally not a fan of fruit-infused ale, but I wasn't turning down a beer, of course. But this one was good, I mean really good. Just a hint of blackberry, and really, really good. They mentioned that if I was going into Manchester Center, I should have breakfast at the Up For Breakfast café, where a friend of theirs worked. Sounded like good advice.

Despite hearing that there was trail magic with beer just past the road crossing to Manchester Center, I decided to make camp about a half mile south of the trailhead, enjoy a fire, and get a good night's sleep. A flat area next to the trail contained a small pile of bricks, which I used to a make fire ring, and soon a nice hot fire was blazing. The sun was setting when an 18-year old southbounder came hiking by. I offered to share the fire and told her she was more than welcome to set up for the night. It didn't take long before she decided to stay. We talked of the trail, of people, of politics, and life. Once again, my faith in humanity, and her generation, was strengthened.

Despite having her hammock set up, she stretched out her thin sleeping pad next to the fire and cowboy camped right there. The next morning her cell phone alarmed chimed, but it was an exercise in futility. Each time the alarm would sound, the snooze button was promptly hit, and Sphinx was back asleep. My kind of person.

It was a short hike to the road, and as soon as I put my thumb out for a hitch, a man in the adjacent parking lot waved me over for a ride. Liberty was a Thru-Hiker from 2008, vacationing in the area and helping hikers when he could. We spoke of the Whites, and he said that every successful Thru-Hiker in history has made it through the Whites, and I would as well. I was soon in town and headed upstairs to the Up For Breakfast café. Wild Turkey Hash topped with poached eggs. It wasn't the best breakfast of my journey, but a close second, very close.

I picked up two resupply boxes at the local outfitter. One from my wife, and one from my brother's family. My wife had cautioned the family against sending anything too heavy, as it would be left behind, and the family came through with flying colors. Ingredients for about 5 smores, a University of Cincinnati hat, some corn nuts, and a small carton of wine. But even more gratifying were their short notes of encouragement that I carried with me the rest of the journey.

I lounged around town and met Wrong Way, Jack Rabbit and Castaway. I relaxed at the town square and ate lunch at McDonald's before heading back to the woods. It took a few minutes, but soon I had a hitch back to the trail with three generations of women of a family from Connecticut, visiting Manchester Center. They were so wonderful, and it reminded me of the hospitality I had enjoyed in their home state.

Bromley Mountain was next; a little over 1,200-foot climb, to the top of a ski resort. It was Saturday and the summit was packed with day-hikers; some hiked up, others took the ski lift. The skies were dotted with paragliders enjoying the breezy day. I enjoyed the attention a Thru-Hiker receives on weekends. The trail was back to frequent ups and downs, but it was trail, and not rocks, so I was making good time. My goal for the night was the Peru Peak Shelter, the first shelter of my journey in which the local trail club tried to charge a fee for staying.

I had decided a long time ago that I would never pay to stay at a shelter or primitive campsite along the trail. If trail clubs can maintain shelters and campsites for 1,700+ miles of the A.T. it is inconceivable that somehow the Green Mountain, and Appalachian Mountain Clubs can't. So, if the caretaker was present at the Peru Peak Shelter that night, I was going to fill up with water and move forward and sleep in the woods. The guide said the $5 fee applied to camping within a half mile of the shelter. My simple answer to that: no.

The caretaker was not in, so I was able to hang my hammock without hassle. After getting a nice fire going, I sat with four section hikers: an older couple, and two sisters; as well as one other Thru-Hiker. The topic of shelter fees came up. Almost to a person, they didn't feel the $5 was a problem. The older man explaining how if we don't pay for the maintenance of the trail, there won't be anyone to take care of the trail, and soon there would be no Appalachian Trail. I didn't feel like explaining the concept of volunteerism, to him it was all about the money. After all, he had already mentioned he was an accountant.

To me the small fees that these trail clubs try to extort are similar to micro-trash along the trail. Too many hikers think nothing of leaving that tiny piece of paper torn from the corner of a snack wrapper, and one piece is not a problem. But if everyone left just one or two small pieces, the trail would be a mess. My goal on the trail was to clean up at least three piece of discarded micro-trash every day. And it was way too easy to reach that goal. All of those little pieces add up to a lot of unwanted trash on the trail.

The same goes for nickel-and-diming hikers. What if every trail club decided to squeeze a few bucks out of hikers at every shelter and campsite along the trail. A hiker spending 5-6 nights a week in the woods, over a six-month hike would now be spending an extra $700 - $1,000 more to sleep on Forest Service land. Why does there have to be a greedy hand always looking for a buck, even along the Appalachian Trail? I believed this even before I knew how greedy they were.

# CHAPTER 18: MAKING THE TURN

During a coffee break, some day hikers asked me about my favorite places on the trail so far. People love hearing stories about standing atop a mountain and experiencing a spiritual awakening and finding one's place in life. That never happened to me. For me it was about the moments, whether a brief meeting with a wonderful person, having a beer at a former Thru-Hiker's trail magic, and especially the kindness of people up and down the trail. With New Hampshire just around the corner, I was making it a point to stop for more coffee breaks and take in everything the trail had to offer. I told them my favorite place on the trail was sitting in my hammock each evening, proud to have made it another day, enjoying my cup of coffee while living in the woods.

*Figure 22 - Evening coffee in my hammock*

It was getting dark earlier now and with the forecast of rain, the trail was a lonely place tonight. I arrived at the Minerva Hinchey Shelter at 8:15 p.m., but it felt like 3:00 in the morning. Four people were bundled up in the shelter, fast asleep. There was also little movement from the tents and hammocks surrounding the shelter. It had been a while since I night hiked, and it felt good. Cool, with light rain. I was fully set up, and finished dinner, when at 10:00 p.m. the heavy rain came. After 20 miles today, sleep came quick, and deep.

With Killington Mountain ahead, the good night's sleep was welcome. For the first time since Virginia, I would be close to 4,000 feet elevation. The 2,500-foot climb was not too difficult, and upon reaching the Cooper Lodge Shelter, I was tired, but my confidence was soaring. How hard could the Whites really be?

That evening, I met the first of many college orientation groups that I would encounter in the north. This group was incoming freshman at the University of Vermont, led by a few upperclassmen. Wood was too wet to get a fire going, but a Hershey Bar from the students kept my spirits high. For the first time in months I was cold, really cold. As a cold wind sent chills through my body, I sent a message to my wife to send my winter gear to Hanover, NH.

The wind died down as I fell asleep, and the night was not as cold as I had feared. By now I was getting up just after 7:00 a.m., some days I would get up, some days, I'd go back to sleep. Today would be just eight miles to The Long Trail Inn, so I went back to sleep. I faded in and out of sleep, to the sounds of the college kids packing up and hitting the trail. I looked at my phone again, 9:06 a.m., time to get up for good. I was now less than 500 miles from Katahdin.

The night before, I had spoken to a fellow Thru-Hiker who felt he was not getting everything from his journey he had hoped for. He was told the journey would affect him physically, mentally, and spiritually, and while the first two had happened, he hadn't experienced the spiritual effect he had hoped for. I tried to relate, but I couldn't. I didn't set out for the journey to find some deeper meaning or awakening. Like Thoreau, *"I went to the woods because I wished to live deliberately, to front only the essential facts of life, and see if I could not learn what it had to teach."* I entered my journey not with a destination, but a purpose. The purpose was to let go and learn whatever the woods would teach.

And I did learn, I learned how wonderful people can be. I learned to judge less, and judge less quickly. I worked on empathy, to understand people, and see the goodness in them. And if they only showed darkness, accept it, and move on. I learned that happiness comes from experiences and moments, not material possessions, except for beer, of course. I came to appreciate simple moments in the woods, and the therapeutic power of nature.

### ###

The Long Trail Inn is known for its Irish Tavern which boasts having the best pint of Guinness in New England, and among hikers, a bartender named Owen. It is said that he never forgets a trail name, and halfway through my first pint of Guinness, I believed it. The Long Trail Inn loves hikers, because we bring much needed summer business to their ski lodge. From what Owen told me, ski season is hopping at the Inn. "If snow's on the ground, the world goes round." I enjoyed dinner at the bar that evening. Owen had worked the day shift, but now the owner's son was behind the bar.

I continued my habit of not leaving before check-out time, so it was well past 11:00 a.m., when I started on the half mile side trail back to the A.T. After a thirteen-mile day, of steady ups and downs, I settled in to a quiet primitive campsite; alone. By now I was truly enjoying the solitude of camping alone. I wrote in my journal that evening of feeling sorry for those hiking with a group, whose movements are a group decision, and never get to enjoy the peaceful feeling of being all alone in the woods. I hiked when I wanted, I stopped where I wanted, and night hiked if I wanted. I never had to worry about anyone else, and no one had to worry about me.

Not far from Killington is the city of Rutland, and another Twelve Tribes hostel.

### ###

"Cult" is a very nasty word today. And while the Twelve Tribes might technically fit the Webster's definition, I don't think of them as a cult. This is not a group of people we'll read about after a mass suicide, or for believing a UFO awaits them behind a comet. The Tribes live by their own interpretation of the Old Testament, which critics accuse of focusing too heavily on the "spare the rod, spoil the child," philosophy.

The "spiritual community," does provide an interesting subplot to an Appalachian Trail journey. Conversations abound as to whether they are in fact, a cult, as well as speculation about Thru-Hikers who may have left the trail and joined their ranks. Reports say their founder, Gene Spriggs, has amassed millions of dollars and lives a lifestyle very different of that required of his followers.

Rumors will continue to circulate up and down the Trail about the group as long their hostels dot the nearby landscapes. In Harper's Ferry, hikers have the opportunity to do work-for-stay at their farm. I joked with hikers to stay at their hostels, but don't go to the farm, it's where they really try to get you in. But in all seriousness... do not go to the farm.

The next day I kept telling myself that the roller coaster on which I was hiking on had to be a great warm-up for the Whites, I was 33 miles from New Hampshire, and believed I was ready, after all, how hard could the Whites be? I covered 19 miles and was within 13 miles of the state line when I stopped at the Thistle Hill Shelter. While getting a fire going, I debated whether to put my rain fly over my hammock. I did, and it was a good decision, since it rained almost all night.

It was still raining in the morning as I leaned over from my hammock and boiled water on my stove without leaving my sleeping bag, a trail skill I had mastered. By 8:30 a.m., any hopes of the rain stopping were pretty much dashed, so I packed up in the rain and headed north. When the rain stopped, I took a coffee break, and booked a room at the Norwich Inn, in Norwich, VT. I longed for the early days down south where $50 motel rooms were common. Tonight's tab was $109, but did include a "free" beer.

Along the way I was surprised to find a deli open, which the guide had listed as closed. It opened after the deadline to be listed in the guide, so the steak tip sandwich, fried taco, ice cream and soda were an unexpected treat. My hiker hunger was here to stay. By afternoon I descended a small hill then began hiking down Elm Street, Norwich, VT. Norwich is a quaint, upper middle class New England town. After stopping for some cans of hard cider at the package store, I turned off the road (which is part of the A.T.) and headed to the Norwich Inn. The Inn is a beautiful Victorian mansion, where I left behind the smelly proletariat masses of the A.T. and entered the world of the bourgeoisie.

As I stood on the porch of the Inn, near a very well-groomed couple, I could tell by the look on the man's face, my trail stink had wafted in their direction. I apologized, and we shared a good laugh before I went inside to check-in. Upon returning, the gentleman informed me that my pack seemed to stink as bad as I did. I figured it'd be a good idea to shower before getting my 'free' beer. I got cleaned up, headed to the bar for my beer and headed out to the porch. I sat among the well-heeled of New England, sipping my beer, just two blocks, but a million miles away from the Appalachian Trail.

That night I sat at the bar enjoying a lamb shank dinner with grilled asparagus, and a bottle of Pinot Noir. Tomorrow I'd be back to dehydrated meals, Corn Nuts, peanut butter and Clif Bars, but, I'd be eating them in New Hampshire. Before leaving town the next morning, I stopped next door at Dan & Whites General Store, which claims "If we don't have it, you don't need it." I guess I didn't *need* Corn Nuts.

After a mile of road walking I was crossing the Connecticut River, where a concrete plaque on a bridge simply read "VT. | N.H.," I was officially in New Hampshire. I hoped to make a short stop in Hanover, then maybe get in 10 miles for the day. But the town of Hanover had other plans. I picked up my resupply and winter gear from the Post Office, sent back my summer gear, and decided to grab a bite to eat, and a beer, of course. Then stop at the library to download some videos, then head north. After the library, I stopped at Ramunto's Brick Oven Pizza, where Thru-Hikers get their choice of either a free slice of cheese pizza or Pabst Blue Ribbon draft. PBR seemed like the logical choice.

It was a beautiful day, as I sat with Wrong Way, and Twinkle Toes enjoying hard cider drafts and pizza. After just one more and I would head out, but Hanover is hard to leave. Home to Dartmouth College, it's one of the most hiker-friendly towns along the trail. Lodging is prohibitively expensive, but a group called Hanover Friends of the A.T. has volunteers willing to put up hikers for free. College bars, sushi joints, coffee houses, and bookstores line Main St., where outside the telephone poles display painted 2" x 6" white blazes. Ten miles wasn't happening today.

It was 6:30 p.m. before I walked past the football stadium, and back to the woods. Just a few steps inside the tree line a primitive campsite, was already populated with hikers who seemed to have enjoyed Hanover to the fullest. There was a party feel to the crowd, and I wasn't looking for a party. Before I moved on, one hiker who had definitely been enjoying Hanover said we should stay and camp at the site. It was the first time I saw Joyride.

Like all shelters just past a vortex city, the Velvet Rocks Shelter was crowded with several Thru-Hikers, and we were joined by another college group, this time from Dartmouth. We were told that about 90% of incoming students at Dartmouth choose a backpacking trip as part of their orientation. The Dartmouth Outing Club has been around since 1909, and maintains over 50 miles of the A.T. The club displays some of the most fun signs along the trail. Orange with black lettering, their signs sometimes feature moose or stick figure hikers, one even prohibits unicycles on the trail.

*Figure 23 - Dartmouth Outing Club trail sign*

I had packed some wine, and apple-flavored legal, store-bought moonshine, which I passed around the fire. After a day of sipping cider and beer, topped off with apple whiskey, for the only time of my journey, I made a profanity laced statement that earned the ire of some around the fire. Some also laughed their asses off.

My first full day in New Hampshire was a nice fifteen-mile day with a couple climbs, but my mind was focused on the Whites, now just two or three days away. I spent the night at the Trapper John Shelter, named for the M*A*S*H* character, who in the show, had attended Dartmouth Medical School. The views of New Hampshire were becoming spectacular. A 2,400-foot uphill, followed by a 1,400-footer, were reminders that the days of little elevation change were over. At the fire tower atop Smarts Mountain, the views were amazing, but as the wind swirled, I could not repeat my feat at Stratton Mountain, and climbed down before reaching the top of the tower. The air had a chill, and I hadn't seen another northbound hiker all day. At a primitive camp near Brackett Brook, I realized that tomorrow, I would enter the White Mountains, and thought to myself again, how hard can they be?

It was a great night. A nice fire, and just cold enough for a deep sleep. I woke up well rested, and ready for the Whites. The miles were coming at a good pace, when near a makeshift camp with trail magic in 5-gallon buckets suspended in trees with pulleys and rope, there was a slab of wood, with twigs forming the words, "Welcome to the Whites." *This is it.*

It was August 30th, Day 156 of my journey, I was debating whether to summit Mount Moosilauke today, or first thing in the morning. At the NH Rt. 25 road crossing, I walked the third of a mile to the Hikers Welcome Hostel, and pigged out. Two microwave pizzas, chips, pop tarts, ice cream sandwiches, and sodas. As I stuffed my face, it was nearing 2:00 p.m., and I asked the woman working at the hostel if it would be a problem making the summit by nightfall. "No problem," she said. Broken Arrow, who I had seen over the past two weeks was enjoying the hospitality and asked her what's the longest a hiker has ever stayed at the Hostel. She replied, "9 days." Broken Arrow said he might just break the record.

I was sorry I hadn't taken the time to see the sunset at Killington Mountain, so I decided I would summit Mt. Mousilauke, and stay to experience the sunset. The ascent was nearly 3,800 feet, the highest climb since the Smokies. But with the exception of a few rocks, it was pretty smooth hiking. I made the summit well before sunset and began looking for spot in between rocks which would shield the wind enough to boil water for coffee. It was cold, but beautiful. I enjoyed a wonderful sunset, then began heading down the mountain. The Beaver Brook Shelter is 1,000 ft. off the summit, and it was slow going by headlamp.

*Figure 24 - Sunset atop Mt. Mousilauke*

The shelter was full with another group of incoming Dartmouth freshmen, asking an upperclassman about the "Dartmouth Seven," a list of seven sites on campus where amorous students share intimacy, for lack of a better word. The group packed up early and headed out at 4:30 a.m. to catch the sunrise atop Moosilauke. I heard them start to leave and couldn't resist looking out from my hammock and asking if any of them planned to make the summit one of the Dartmouth Seven.

Even with the extended lunch break, I had covered 20 miles my first day in the Whites. I had no problem with the near 4,000-foot climb up Moosilauke, so waking up to a cold and misty morning, I really thought the Whites might not be that bad. The next mile and half completely destroyed that delusion.

The descent down Moosilauke is a steep, very steep, boulder scramble, with the trail running next to, and sometimes through a fast-flowing stream that cascades into a waterfall before reaching the base. As I looked down at each rock and boulder scramble, I realized that one bad move, one slip, could end my hike, and possibly cause serious injury. In my journal, I used one word to describe it: "treacherous." After inching my way down, I crossed NH Rt. 112 at Kinsman Notch, where the trail headed almost straight uphill for 800 feet. I was tired, nearly exhausted, and after three hours I had advanced less than two miles.

The next seven miles were tough. Even the descent to the Elza Brook Shelter, which did not look difficult in the guide, was dotted with rock and boulder obstacles. Upon reaching the shelter, I encountered another group of incoming Dartmouth students. I was at the base of South Kinsman Mountain and had to decide whether to stop for the night, or knock out part of the steep 2,000-foot ascent. It was just past 5:00 p.m., so I hiked on. But nobody had warned me about South Kinsman.

It was not only straight up, but all rocks and boulders. It was during the climb up South Kinsman that I realized the Whites were not going to be as tough as I feared, but much, much tougher.

In the mist, I could not see the summit, which was fine, since it would likely be a false summit anyway. By 7:00 p.m., I was looking for trees to hang my hammock, but having no luck. The small mountain before South Kinsman, Mt. Wolf, had abundant camp sites, and I thought that South Kinsman would as well. But I was wrong, again. As dusk approached, I noticed a tent set up about 20 feet off the trail, and started a conversation with the man inside, as I finally found trees to hang my hammock. I started my evening coffee and asked his name. It was Joyride.

In the morning, he was up with the sun, and while I was still in my sleeping bag, he headed out. We hoped that we were close to the summit, but Joyride took about 30 steps, then yelled back, "it's all straight up again." Time for coffee. I was ready to go at 8:15, and the trail continued to be a steep, rocky, boulder climb. After South Kinsman, the trail was still tough, but some things changed. First was the frequency of white blazes, they were everywhere. Also, on some of the steeper boulders, hand- and foot-holds had been chiseled into the rock, plus there were wooden steps, or blocks that had been secured to some of the rocks on steep sections. If the Whites were this well maintained throughout, it might not be that tough after all.

But the Whites aren't maintained that well everywhere. I had just entered my first "Forest Protection Area" surrounding one of the famed Huts of the White Mountains. The hut system is a series of large cottages that sleep from 36 to 96 people, at $140 per person, per night. They have some running well water and cook dinner and breakfast for their guests. They are staffed by young people referred to as Hut "Croos." The Croos are normally very nice to Thru-Hikers, and each Hut offers a certain amount of "work for stay" spots, where a Thru-Hiker can do a little work, and receive the surplus food from dinner and breakfast, plus the chance to sleep indoors, on the floor of the dining room.

Around each Hut there is a quarter mile radius designated as a "Forest Protection Area." As you enter these areas, a sign greets hikers that reads: "In order to best manage recreation impact in the area, camping and fires are prohibited within ¼ mile of the Hut." It struck me funny that within a so-called "Forest Protection Area," a cottage would be built, propane tanks brought in, and hundreds of people each week would be invited to stay, as long as they can afford it. The protected area around the Huts has nothing to do forest protection at all. It is designed to keep section and Thru-Hikers from camping near the Huts and disturbing the well-heeled patrons.

Many of the Huts' patrons have a wardrobe, hair style, and look found in expensive outdoor catalogs, thus earning the snide nickname, "L.L. Beaners," from many Thru-Hikers. The trails in and around each of the huts are very well-maintained. And while I admire the Appalachian Mountain Club's charade of calling such areas, "forest protection" areas, in reality they are income protection zones. No camping near a Hut, unless you agree to work, and serve the L.L. Beaners that can afford to stay in the Huts.

And not only does the Appalachian Mountain Club do everything in its power to restrict where hikers can camp, it actually charges hikers to stay in shelters, and primitive campsites, $10 a person. So very, very few Thru-Hikers, referred to them as the Appalachian Mountain Club, to us, they were the Appalachian *Money* Club. How can local trail club volunteers for over 2,000 miles, up and down the A.T. provide shelters and maintain the trail, without trying shake down hikers for $10, yet somehow, the Appalachian Money Club cannot?

Therein lies the scam. The scam that all the money the club takes in is needed for conservation, to protect the forest, and care for the A.T. Like so many groups that once held firm to their stated mission, the AMC has become a business, a very big business. The AMC routinely, takes in far more money than it spends, and much of the money it does spend goes to big salaries. In addition to the CEO making $248,000 in 2015, the AMC had 10 more employees making over $100,000, 2 of those in excess of $185,000.

Their fundraising and spending actually make the Appalachian Trail Conservancy look almost respectable. The Potomac Appalachian Trail Club maintains over 1,000 miles of trails in Virginia, West Virginia, Maryland, and Pennsylvania, including 240 miles of the A.T., and manages to do it with their highest salaried person, staff director, making about $75,000 a year. In 2014, the PATC spent just over $400k on all salaries. During the same year, the AMC paid over $1.3 million to just its "key" employees and officers. The CEO and Senior VP of the AMC alone were paid a total of $416,973, which was more than all the employees of the PATC combined.

And what happens to all the money that AMC takes in, but doesn't spend? They hoard it like a wealthy misanthrope. The more I looked into it, the more upset I got about them charging Thru-Hikers, or any hiker, a fee to sleep at a shelter or primitive campsite. They have about $12 million in cash, just sitting in savings and money markets accounts. But that's nothing. Some non-profits love to keep a slush fund known as an "endowment." They like to consider it a rainy-day fund, but for many, it's just their way to hoard cash. And the Appalachian Money Club has their own slash fund endowment. At the end of 2015, it stood at a cool $58 million.

While every shelter south of Vermont is free, maintained by volunteers, these pricks are sitting on over $70 million, and shaking us down for $10 for the privilege to stay in theirs. As I studied the AMC's financials after finishing my journey, I remembered the accountant back at the Peru Peak Shelter, saying that without the $5 shelter fee, before long there would be no Appalachian Trail. I did mention he was an accountant, right?

### 

I hit the first Hut of the Whites, Lonesome Lake Hut, around lunch time. Surrounded by beautiful scenery, sitting on a lake, I can understand why people enjoy these rustic resorts. The common area/dining room consists of picnic table seating, with a table of baked goods, snacks, hot water and instant coffee, with payment on the honor system. One "croo" member was working in the open space kitchen, where soup was available for $2 bowl. (Despite the guide stating it was $2 for all-you-can eat soup.) At one table was Joyride, who did not recognize me, since I was still tucked in my sleeping bag when he left in the morning.

After soup, coffee, and a muffin, we headed out, on one of the few easy sections of the Whites to Franconia Notch, where we were lucky to find Miss Janet for a ride into town. Miss Janet is trail angel known by every Thru-Hiker. She drives an older passenger van and follows the north bound hikers all the way from Springer to Katahdin. Most of what she does is shuttle hikers in and out of town, but to hikers, she is so much more. She is a friend, always looking out for hikers' well-being. Whenever there is a report, or even a rumor of someone needing help, Miss Janet responds. She serves as a vital link in the hiker communication network as well. Often time she's on the lookout for a certain hiker, if there is relevant information needing to get to them.

Between the two front seats on the van, Miss Janet had a small Ziploc bag, which said something like, "this van doesn't run on love alone, donations welcome for gas." As I put some money into the bag, Miss Janet said I didn't need to, because that's Miss Janet. She gives so much to the trail community, yet is still uncomfortable asking for just a little help. That's why she is so loved.

It was my first ride with her. She dropped us off in Lincoln, NH where I needed to buy yet another pair of boots, my fourth of the journey. This time it was Keen's, for just over $120. Miss Janet had offered to come back for us in an hour, but to my chagrin, Joyride demurred. So, with resupply in hand, and wearing my new boots, we set out for North Woodstock, about a mile and a half away, on foot. With about a half mile to go, a man asked if we needed a lift, and we jumped in the bed of his pick-up for a ride to the Carriage Motel.

The next morning, Moose and Sparkles, a thru-hiking couple were leaving and we watched as they put out their thumbs to hitch a ride five miles back to the trail. They were having no luck, so I decided Joyride and I would call a shuttle. When the shuttle arrived, the couple had not yet got a ride, so they jumped in with us. Unlike most shuttles however, this woman charged by the person, not per ride. She made a pretty penny off us four. But soon we were back at the Liberty Springs trailhead, with an easy one-mile hike back to the A.T., Joyride, Moose, Sparkles, and I.

I had now resigned myself to the fact the Whites were going to be the hardest part of the hike. And accepting that, I decided to slow down and enjoy the beauty. Though it wasn't rock climbing, it was a steep and rocky start to the day up Mt. Lafayette. When we reached the top, we learned we had actually climbed Mt. Lincoln, and Lafayette was still a mile and half ahead. It was on Mt. Lincoln that we encountered an older Ridgerunner, probably in his seventies, who was intent on sharing the rules of the Whites with us. "Don't even think about camping above the alpine line," he warned. And as for stealth camping, he called it "bootleg" camping, and frowned on that as well. He went on to tell us about the rules of Baxter State Park and Katahdin, but by this time in the lecture, Joyride and I had pretty much stopped listening.

We were nice, and Joyride even had his picture taken with him. As Joyride handed me his camera, the Ridgerunner made sure to set up the photo just right, making it look as if was explaining something off in the distance to Joyride. As we headed off Mt. Lincoln towards Mt. Lafayette, Joyride and I made a pact that would indeed camp above the alpine line.

Atop Mt. Lafayette, the stunning beauty of the Whites was awe inspiring. Even at the beginning of September, it was cold. We shared the summit with a combination of thru, section, and day-hikers. One was a fellow Buffalo Bills fan, sporting a team winter cap. She was on her first section hike, before heading to M.I.T. to study to physics. I continue to be impressed with the younger generation of women pursing science.

Joyride, Moose, Sparkles, and I headed down and set up camp near Garfield Pond, where we were soon joined by Legs. Despite the policy of no fires, and word that hikers had been fined for violations, Joyride and I soon had a nice warm fire burning as darkness fell over the Whites. Despite the chill, Legs never, *ever* wore long pants. When asked if he even owned a pair of long pants he replied viscerally, "No, do you think I'm a chump!" Legs was aptly named for his pair of long slender hiking legs. He was one of a group of hikers in their early twenties that I would become very fond of on the final segment of my journey.

Joyride was stretched out next to the fire commenting that, prior to starting the journey, this is what he envisioned hiking the A.T. would be like. As we enjoyed the heat from the fire, Joyride and I shared a laugh over the earnest Ridgerunner, repeating the line, "don't even think about camping above the alpine zone," and confirmed our desire that one night in the Whites, we would indeed sleep above the alpine zone. Sparkles came to the man's defense, pleading that he was a "cute old man."

It was a cold morning, and I was up fairly early, but still later than most. Joyride, as usual, was up with the sun and on the trail for quite some time before I was up and enjoying coffee in my hammock. The day started with a climb up Mt. Garfield, steep and rocky, but not as tough as South Kinsman. Despite the trail not being treacherous, the Whites were still humbling. As I passed the Franconia Brook trail, I realized that in two hours, I had covered only 1.3 miles.

My spirits were lifted by another group of incoming college freshmen, this time from Bates College. They were extremely impressed and encouraging about my hike, perhaps believing the entire A.T. is similar to the Whites. My pace quickened after Mt. Garfield, where terrain was less difficult and, sooner than expected, I was at the Galehead Hut enjoying coffee and potato dill soup. Aubrey was the Croo member at the Hut and was extremely nice and helpful.

Regardless of my views of the AMC, and how they hoard cash, the members of the Hut Croos are wonderful people. They treat both their guests and Thru-Hikers great, while working very long, and very hard hours. Every couple of days, they carry all the food for the Hut guests on their backs up the mountains. They basically run million-dollar enterprises through back-breaking labor. And are paid very little.

Next was South Twin Mountain, which I was warned would be quite difficult; it wasn't. By now I had begun to expect the worst to such a degree that most climbs were less difficult than I had imagined. The rest of the day would be downhill, but not smooth and easy, until the end. We made it to Zealand Falls Hut, where Joyride and I sat with Scavenger, as the Croo served dinner. Of all the Huts in the Whites, this one was perhaps the least pleasant. It had nothing to do with the Croo, they were very busy feeding the L.L. Beaners. But the guests themselves looked at us as if we didn't belong. Like we were intruding on their turf. Joyride and I relaxed for a few minutes, but Scavenger quickly left, disgusted with crowd at the Hut.

At Zealand Falls, the trail starts a rare flat and smooth four-mile section in the Whites. We had that to look forward to as we camped with Moose and Sparkles that night. Joyride and I stood by a firm commitment to not pay to camp on the A.T., while Moose and Sparkles thought they'd give the pay campsite a try the following night.

It was strange the next morning, to be on smooth flat trail again. But that would not last long in the Whites, especially today. Today we were entering the Presidential Range, a nearly 20-mile section of 4,000+ foot peaks, with the apex at the summit of Mt. Washington, 6,288 feet. Let the climb begin.

We started at Crawford Notch, at an elevation of 1,261 feet, where the trail became an ascent. We took our first break at Webster Cliffs at 3,288 feet. We enjoyed the breath-taking view, then it was uphill again, and soon we hit the first summit of the "Presidentials," Mt. Webster. I found it ironic that first mountain in the so-called Presidentials was named after a Senator. For today, the heavy lifting was done. The trail to Mt. Jackson wasn't easy, but just 100 feet of elevation, and the first of the 4,000-foot peaks. Mt. Jackson was not named after President Andrew Jackson, but Charles Thomas Jackson, State Geologist of Rhode Island, Maine, and New Hampshire from 1836-1844. So far both mountains of the Presidentials were named for non-Presidents.

We stopped at the Mizpah Spring Hut and made the decision that the next suitable stealth spot is where we would spend the night. The Nauman Campsite was adjacent to the Hut, with a $10 fee to sleep in the woods. No thank you. When I asked about nearby camping to a young man in the Croo, he only mentioned the campsite. When I replied that I wasn't going to pay to sleep along the A.T., a female Croo member said sternly, "I have to advise you it is the only *legal* camping between here and the Lake of the Clouds Hut." I looked back at the young man, and we both grinned as I quietly replied, "good thing I'm not looking for *legal* camping."

For the second Hut in a row, the reception to Thru-Hikers was less than welcoming. The Croo was busy preparing dinner, and the L.L. Beaners didn't seem at all impressed with the fact we had hiked 1850.1 miles from Georgia to get here. There was no Thru-Hiker celebrity status here. The nerve!

Moose and Sparkles decided to ante up the $10 per person for the campsite. Joyride and I headed up Mt. Pierce to find a camping spot. Three peaks in, and finally one named for a President, sort of. Depending on who you ask, some still refer Mt. Pierce as Mt. Clinton, not for Pres. William Jefferson, but 19<sup>th</sup> century New York Governor DeWitt Clinton.

By now Joyride and I were taking pride in our ability to find stealth sites. But at the top of Mt. Pierce, it wasn't that hard. Plenty of flat rock for tents, and a nice small grove of trees, just tall enough for a hammock. We set up, along with Scavenger, and headed up trail about 100 feet for coffee, and a beautiful sunset. A Grey Jay was flying close, looking for any crumbs we might drop, when Scavenger put out his hand, and the bird calmly landed on his outstretched finger.

That night Joyride and I fulfilled our pledge to camp above the alpine line. We were asleep early, tomorrow was Mt. Washington.

I don't remember it, but it was a very weird dream that I was startled from as I heard Joyride saying, "Brother Blood." It was still dark, but I got up, made coffee, and headed back to the spot where we had watched the sunset just hours before. As the sun rose, we were giddy. Like kids on Christmas morning, we were excited for the day. It was Mt. Washington Day! I was on the trail by 6:45 a.m., with just over five miles to the summit of Mt. Washington. The hiking was rocky, and slow. Not difficult rock climbing, but slow, tedious hiking. Watching every step, with a subdued fear that one wrong step could be the end of the journey, after 1,850 miles.

Before long I had crossed every peak along the way and was staring up Mt. Washington. This was it. The mountain is known for having held the planet's wind speed record of 231 mph for decades. Folklore holds that it is one of the most difficult climbs of the entire Appalachian Trail, it is not. But it is amazing, and for most Thru-Hikers, it holds a special significance, present company included.

# CHAPTER 20: THE FRENCH LOVE MT. WASHINGTON

It was Labor Day, and the summit of Mt. Washington was a packed. Between traffic from the Mt. Washington Auto Road, and the "Cog" passenger railroad, tourists were standing in line to get a picture at the sign reading: "MT WASHINGTON SUMMIT 6,288 FT 1,917 M." I doubt that many knew why, on the sign post, there was a mysterious 2" x 6" painted white stripe. I spent two hours charging devices, while visiting the visitor center and museum, and enjoying food from the snack bar. There is even a post office, for outgoing mail only, to send a post card with the Mount Washington postmark. During that time, I was surprised at the number of French speaking people there and thought this must be a popular destination for tourists from France.

Joyride and I headed off the mountain together, doing our best to figure out which of the downhill trails was actually the A.T. We managed to not stray off the trail, and set our sites for Mt. Madison, and, hopefully, enough trees where I could hang my hammock. The trail remained slow and tedious, but populated with day hikers. While talking to one trio of young men, they commented that they had driven down for the day. When asked from where, they replied, "Quebec." I realized then it was not Air France bringing the French speaking tourists to the mountain.

For most of the day, we remained at over 5,000 ft. elevation, and there was no sign of trees capable of supporting a hammock. In fact, there were no trees at all, just rocks, miles and miles of rocks. Anyone who thinks Pennsylvania is rocky never hiked the Whites. As we skirted the summits of the mountains named after the Adams Family, (Sam, John, and John Quincy), I began to worry that the area around Madison Spring Hut, at 4,800 ft., might not be low enough in elevation to find trees for hanging my hammock. Joyride reminded me of the skills we had displayed in stealth camping up to this point and assured me that if anyone could find a spot, it was us. He was right.

We arrived at the hut as the sun was starting to set, and noticed a very small patch of trees no more than 100 feet up the trail. One way or another, we'd have to find a flat enough patch for his tent, and two trees for me. After crawling into several openings along the trail into the trees, we found a place that would work. It was without a doubt not *legal* camping, but we laughed at the thought of a young Croo member coming to tell us we had to leave.

We woke with no plans for the day, other than me picking up a resupply box at the Joe Dodge Lodge at Pinkham Notch. But after finding out the Twelve Tribes shuttled hikers from Pinkham Notch to their hiker hostel in Lancaster, NH, Joyride put on the full court press. He said the experience of spending at least one night with the Tribes should be part of anyone's thru-hike. After hearing there was Irish Pub not far from the hostel, I decided I would go with Joyride to the Twelve Tribes hostel.

But first, the Whites would give us one more kick in the gut. The ascent of Mt. Madison was rocky and cold, with a misty rain. Not horrible, but again, tedious and slow. After the summit, the descent was a series of short, rocky, slow sections, punctuated with short uphills. This continued for a few hours until we were quite sure we had covered at least five miles and had about three remaining. Then came the kick in the gut when we saw the sign for the Osgood Tent Site. We had covered only three miles.

We hiked on, and soon met SoJo, a 75-year old hiking with his dog, which he wisely had his doctor register as a service dog, enabling him to take him anywhere, even the Smokies. I liked SoJo immediately. He told us that a day earlier he showed up at the Madison Spring Hut and inquired about work for stay, but was told it was only available for hikers who show up after dark. He said he would come back after dark, but was told that wouldn't work, and the Hut Croo sent a 75-year old man packing.

Joyride liked to hike early, then take an extended lunch break. I liked to start later, but take shorter breaks. When Joyride was ready for his break that day, I just kept moving on. The miles came faster now, and soon I was crossing the Mt. Washington Auto Road, and ready for a break myself. Before long Joyride came bounding across the road, happy to be done for the day. I hated breaking it to him that that this was not Pinkham Notch, and we still had two miles to go. A few minutes later, SoJo showed up and exclaimed, "Yeessss." For the second time in fifteen minutes, I was the bearer of bad news.

*Figure 25 - 75-year-old Soren West, "Sojo"*

But the two miles to Pinkham Notch were a breeze, and in less than an hour we were on the porch of the Joe Dodge Lodge laughing with a group of hikers, all waiting to be shuttled to the Twelve Tribes hostel. It was a full van headed to Lancaster. I wasn't as enthusiastic as Joyride to be sleeping in a hostel, but the thought of a shower and cold beer kept my spirits up. Soon we were piling out of the van and the rush to claim a bunk was on. The hostel was divided into men's and women's sections, and the wife of the van driver was telling some hikers to let me have a bottom bunk because I was older. I assured her I would be okay climbing to the top bunk, and asked if they offered an AARP discount. *(I didn't really.)*

As I settled in with my gear, the woman was, in a very polite way, reading the riot act to two hikers that had stayed at the hostel a couple of nights before, and enjoyed the tavern, and almost certainly some less than legal substances a bit much before returning for the night. Already one of them was more than half in the bag, and they were told that if they left, under no circumstances, could they return that night. It was the nicest, and most polite, dressing down I ever heard.

I managed to be one of the first to shower, then on to the bar. I walked through Lancaster, and finally settled into the bar around 8:30 p.m. I was sure that last call was going to be well before midnight, so I quickened my drinking pace to make up for lost time. There I was, 50-years old and drinking fast to get a buzz like I was 18 again.

Soon the bar was well populated with hikers, along with three men touring the area on motorcycles. Joyride and SoJo were there, and as fate would have it, one of the motorcyclists, like SoJo, was from Lancaster, PA. So, two men from Lancaster, PA met each other in a bar in Lancaster, NH. By now my attempt at getting a buzz had succeeded, and a local patron sat next to me. I hate to say he was kind of strange, but, he was really kind of strange. Just my luck, I rush to get a buzz, then end up next to someone that makes me want to drink even more.

He talked about the Twelve Tribes and what good people they were. I was curious about the Tribes, so I began a series of questions, which made Joyride a bit uncomfortable. Next to me, Joyride would lean in to warn me that people like the Tribes, and I should be careful. On the other side was the strange one extolling the virtues of his communal neighbors. I was stuck in the middle. I ordered another shot and a beer.

Before long I was able to get a conversation going with the motorcyclists, and escape from the push and pull of the Tribes talk. It was a good night overall. The young woman working the bar told me that she believed the Tribes was indeed a cult, and they had tried to recruit her. She also agreed the man previously sitting next to me was strange. We got back to the hostel after the 10:00 p.m. curfew but were let in by a female hiker. I climbed up to my bunk, thinking that drinking water would have been a good idea. But I was too tired, and too lazy to get back down for water, so I put my head down for a restless night of sleep.

The Tribes prepared breakfast, featuring something that was maybe egg-based, maybe not. It wasn't traditional, and not very appealing to me, so after a few bites, I covertly threw it away, like I had the mate tea back in Georgia. I was on the first shuttle at 8:30 a.m., Joyride stayed behind in hopes of procuring a new pair of hiking shoes. Instead of a smooth ride back to the trailhead, the driver took a shortcut over a dirt road through the woods. My stomach bumped along with van, making me fear an expulsion of last night's dinner, beer, and Grand Mariner. As I looked around the van, I was obviously not the only one feeling that way.

We finally made it back to the Joe Dodge Lodge, and upon getting my pack, I gave the driver the "suggested donation" of $20 for a night at the Tribes hiker hostel. I might have been the only one to make the donation, and the driver was a bit surprised. I think they were more interested in recruiting than collecting the "suggested donation."

I was in no hurry to get hiking, my stomach was still rumbling, and the hike would start with the Wildcats, a series of peaks that represent the last real difficult test of the Whites. I charged some electronics, and after coffee and a Clif Bar, was almost ready to move on. A young man stopped briefly in the downstairs lounge, discussing an overnight hike he had been on, and it "only" costs a few dollars for the shelter where he slept. I mentioned my disdain for paying for primitive camping, but he explained he didn't mind, because, "it all goes to conservation." I'm sure he believed it. I'm also sure he didn't know of the nearly $2 million in executive salaries they pay, or the $70 million the AMC is sitting on.

It was 11:30 a.m. before I headed out to take on the first, and steepest climb of the Wildcats, Peak E. Once again, my habit of preparing for the worst served me well. As tough as the Wildcats were, they were neither as tough as South Kinsman Mountain, nor as tough as I had imagined. Wildcat Mountain serves as a ski resort in the winter, but they run a gondola up the ski lift during the summer for tourists, as well as Thru-Hikers who decide to skip the climb up Peak E. The two hikers who had been lectured the night before by our Twelve Tribes hostess, along with their female hiking partner, had chosen to take the gondola.

I did just six miles, before finding a great campsite just outside of the last of the AMC Huts, the Carter Notch Hut.

I hadn't had a zero day since Bennington, VT, and really hadn't planned for one, but after the steep 1,000 ft. climb out of Carter Notch, the miles started coming easier, and instead of making it close to Gorham for a nero tomorrow, I decided to push the extra miles to earn a zero day. The final four miles were one of the rare smooth downhill sections of the Whites, and I hit Rt. 2 at 7:30 p.m. and there at the trailhead was the Twelve Tribes van, this time driven by the hostess who two nights ago had delivered the stern words to the two hikers... and called me an "older" hiker. She agreed to drop me off at the Royalty Inn in Gorham.

I figured Joyride was about half a day behind me, so I texted him that I had a room, and he was welcome to crash on the floor if he made it the next day. After walking to get some hard cider, then a shower, I headed off to Mr. Pizza for dinner. I really didn't expect much from place called "Mr. Pizza." It sounded like a place that specialized in cheap delivery, with a few hard-plastic seats for dine-in service. But I was wrong. Mr. Pizza was a really nice tavern and restaurant, with great atmosphere, and great service. I was going to enjoy my zero day in Gorham.

The Royalty Inn was also much more than I expected, at a hiker rate of $79 a night ($89 on weekends), I didn't expect much. But I got a nice room, and a pass to the Royalty Athletic Club next door. When

Joyride showed up the next day, we headed over to the health club, which for a couple of grungy Thru-Hikers, was pure luxury. A great indoor pool, hot tub, and a sauna for a nice "schwitz." After that we enjoyed French Gewurztraminer wine with cheese by the pool. I think we made a very cute couple.

It was Friday night, and Gorman was coming to life. Bikers, antique cars, and pick-up trucks with trailers carrying ATV's began populating the small town. As we enjoyed the wine, a couple pulled up and began unloading their ATV's. It took us a minute or two to figure out why the woman asked if the trail was very dusty. After some confusion, we explained we were on the hiking trail, the Appalachian Trail, not the ATV trails. And yes, we explained, we hiked all the way from Georgia. I then enjoyed a prime rib steak and wine at Mr. Pizza. It was the last zero day of my journey

The next morning, we had donuts, then lunch at Mr. Pizza, before getting a ride from a section hiker, also staying at the Royalty Inn. We were dropped off at the Rt. 2 and headed north, toward Maine.

## CHAPTER 21: WRONG WAY TO MAINE

The worst of the Whites were behind us and the last major test of the A.T. lay ahead, Southern Maine. Mt. Hayes was "only" 1,800 ft. uphill to start the day. Of course, we didn't leave until after check-out time, and made it a short seven-mile day before settling in to camp at the Trident Col Campsite. We hiked in a liter of wine plus a fifth of Bailey's Irish Crème. I imagined I would enjoy the Bailey's in my evening coffee the next few nights. We drank it all within an hour.

I heard Joyride heading out just after 7:00 a.m., and I hoped to get going around 9:00, but a thunderstorm convinced me it would be a good day to stay in the hammock and get caught up with my journal writing. I was in no hurry, and once the rain slowed, I was on the trail just before 10:00 a.m. Hiking conditions were wonderful when I headed out toward Maine.

Maine! The fourteenth and final state of the journey. Maine! Mahoosuc Notch, the 100-mile wilderness, and Katahdin! Tonight, I would be sleeping in Maine! It was misty and chilly as I headed out, and soon I was at the shores of Page Pond, searching for the next white blaze and the way north. After a few minutes of back and forth, I finally saw the trail and was again following white blazes. I really thought I was making decent time, until I turned a corner and saw it. A wooden sign marking the side trail to the Trident Col Campsite.

For the first time in almost 1,900 miles, I had accidentally hiked south, the wrong way, on my northbound journey. I had hiked for an hour and half, covered two miles, and was standing in the exact spot where I started the day. I stared for a moment in disbelief; how did I not realize I had been on the same trail? But what could I do? There was only one thing to do, turn around and hike. Maine would still be there when I got there.

I think almost every Thru-Hiker does that at least once, whether it's a wrong turn over a boulder field, like Cautious in Pennsylvania, or Tater racing to make Erwin, TN. Today was my turn. Before long I was back at Page Pond, taking a little extra care to make sure I was really heading the right way, and then set my sights on Maine. Mt. Success would be the final climb in New Hampshire. The climb wasn't tough, but crossing the summit was another story.

The peak is mired in deep mud bogs, lined with narrow wooden planks for hikers to navigate. Today the wind was making the crossing resemble a carnival ride. Fortunately, the boards were not slippery, and I kept my balance, barely. After crossing the windy summit, at 6:27 p.m., after a day of rain, and wrong way hiking, I stood and took a selfie next to a white sign marking the New Hampshire/Maine border. I was in state number 14 out of 14. Maine!

*Figure 26 - MAINE !!*

Joyride had talked about doing 15 miles, but when I arrived at the surprisingly crowded Carlo Col Shelter, after 10 miles, there he was. His early start resulted in him being soaked to the bone, and cold. He was still working on warming himself up when I arrived. Fortunately for him, the Carlo Col Shelter has four walls and provided a fair amount of protection from the high winds that night. My hammock did not, but the chilly evening allowed me to bundle up and get a good night sleep in preparation for the famed Mahoosuc Notch.

The Mahoosuc Notch is described as the "most difficult or fun mile" of the A.T. The 1.1-mile section consists of huge boulders that hikers traverse by going over, under, and around the rock monoliths. Some hikers take the Notch as a challenge, and try to speed through, then brag about their time. Those hikers that know the price of everything, but... While others spend days fearing the crossing. Joyride and I decided to make it fun. We knew there was a campsite right at the north end, so we were in no hurry when we hit the south end of the Notch at 3:00 p.m.

The Notch lived up to the hype, as Joyride and I spent two and half hours negotiating the boulders. Much of the time is spent plotting the proper course through the boulders. At one point, we came across one rock formation I had gone around, but Joyride had gone under. I looked down and saw a white arrow pointing to the crevice Joyride had just passed through. At that point, due to as much to the kid in me as the purist in me, I stripped off my pack and climbed through the opening and past the arrow. We were having a great time.

About two-thirds of the way through, we came across the coldest, freshest spring water I encountered on the entire A.T. The water was cold enough to make my hands uncomfortable as I filled my bottle, but it tasted wonderful. We filled up with water, and I asked Joyride if he thought we should make some popcorn in the Notch. He loved the idea! I found a crevice protected from the wind and soon we were enjoying fresh hot popcorn in the Mahoosuc Notch.

*Figure 27 - Joyride navigates a boulder Mahoosuc Notch*

We still had plenty of daylight when we made the campsite at Bull Branch. The first thing I noticed was the "no fires" sign. Just below that was the fire ring. We collected wood and had a nice blaze going by the time we were joined by three other Thru-Hikers: Pookie, Tetris, and Willow. Their arrival signaled that it would not be a quiet evening, as they played jokes and took verbal jabs at each other as darkness fell.

When Joyride and I talked about how wonderful and cold the spring water was in the Notch, Pookie explained why he felt the need to filter it, after all, *you never know what's in it.* After 1,914 miles, the culture of fear remains ingrained in some. It was an early night for me, and thankfully things quieted down as I got in my hammock.

The campsite was bustling early, way too early for me. Joyride was stoking up the fire, while Pookie was explaining to Willow he wanted to get going, "it's *already* seven o'clock," he pressed. I relaxed and enjoyed my morning coffee in my hammock. I was wondering how hard the climb would be up Mahoosuc Arm, and how close to the town of Andover I could get. I had read in an online trail journal that the Arm was a steep frightful climb fraught with danger, but to my relief, it wasn't exactly that. Also to my relief, the downhill side was fairly smooth trail.

We were making pretty good time when Joyride suggested a half hour break at Grafton Notch, before making another two miles plus to the Baldplate Lean-to for the night. In Maine, the shelters are no different than anywhere else on the trail, but are now called "lean-tos." The Baldplate Lean-to would leave us eight miles from town and would mean crossing over the west and east peaks of Baldplate Mt. first thing in the morning. I decided to push on. I passed the lean-to by 4:30 p.m., and began my climb up Baldplate Mt. Both peaks were rocky tops, with the second resembling a huge slab of concrete. Steep, but great traction. My frequent stops to record video were the only things that slowed me down.

I started down from the east peak at 6:00 p.m., realizing that traveling both east and north, with autumn coming, the days were becoming much shorter. The descent was rocky and steep to start, then smoothed out, and I remembered how it felt to push for extra miles. It felt good hiking again in the quiet hours of dusk and into the evening. By the time I made Frye Notch Lean-to, it was dark, but some southbounders had a nice fire going. I was only four and a half miles from East B Hill Rd., leading to Andover, and most of that would be downhill. Tomorrow would be a nero day.

### 

"I ran away from home when I was fifty."

Ilene Trainor and her husband were both on second marriages when they fell in love with Andover, Maine. They opened Pine Ellis Lodging, a hostel which was also their home. Ilene doesn't like calling it a hostel, because she sees it as welcoming hikers into her home. When her husband passed away in 2007, she hoped she'd be able to keep her home open to hikers. Now in 2016, nearly 80 years old, she has succeeded

I showered and did laundry by 12:30 p.m. and then walked to South Main St. to the heart of tiny Andover. After lunch at the Little Red Hen Diner, I headed back to Pine Ellis with some Hard Cider to relax. Joyride arrived and I offered him a spot in my room. There were two stores with food service in town, but since the hostel had a kitchen available for guests, I decided to cook my own dinner. I hit the General Store for ribeye steak, onion, green pepper, rice and teriyaki sauce, along with a bottle of red wine. Steak stir-fry!

As I uncorked the wine and began prepping my feast, Ilene came in and sat down and we chatted as hikers began calling it an early night, most filled with beer and booze, but well-behaved. As I ate my dinner and chatted with Ilene, I realized, that if her goal was make hikers feel welcome in her home, at least with Brother Blood, she succeeded.

It was back to the Little Red Hen the next morning for breakfast. Today's special was raspberry and white chocolate chip pancakes, with pure Maine maple syrup, for an additional charge. I was back on the trail by 11:00 a.m. Other than a steep uphill out of Sawyer Notch, the hiking was not too difficult, and at 5:30 p.m., after 10 miles, I came across a campsite just before South Arm Rd, which also goes into Andover. I passed the campsite with the goal of getting up at least some of Old Blue Mt. before calling it a day. I started heading up the mountain, and in less than half a mile, from off the trail I heard, "Hey Brother Blood." It was Joyride.

He had everything set up for the night, camped about 50 feet off the trail. Even a full bottle of Jim Beam. Everything but a fire, a situation I quickly remedied. As Joyride stretched out by the fire, I sipped some bourbon, and realized he must have really enjoyed himself in Andover that day.

He had gotten a ride from a former Thru-Hiker, who convinced him that it was a good idea to get a ride to South Arm Rd., then hike south the next day back to East B Hill Rd., where the former Thru-Hiker would shuttle him back to where we were now. It made no damn sense, but the conversation that night around the fire wasn't exactly intellectually inspiring. Thank goodness for the bourbon. Soon after dark, Joyride staggered his way to his tent, telling me to drink all the Beam I desired.

That was last time I saw Joyride.

I expected Joyride to be just a little slower getting up the next morning, but I was mistaken. As I emerged from hammock around 8:30 a.m., there was no movement coming from his tent at all. After packing up, and having coffee and a Clif bar, I hit the trail at 9:30, Joyride still hadn't budged.

It was September 14th, and after almost six months on the A.T., it was time to start planning the finish. My wife would be flying up, one-way, and we'd rent a car and drive home. We talked about which day she would fly up, and settled on either October 4th or 5th. She had checked flight prices for each day, and the 4th was $129, the 5th was $169. "I'm guessing you want the cheaper flight?" I asked. She responded, "well, it is $40 bucks." My summit date was set for the fourth.

It would be less than two days to my next town stop, Rangely, ME. I was 26 miles out, so as usual I decided on extra miles today, to enjoy a nero tomorrow. The hiking was pleasantly non-eventful, and for the first time in over a week, I covered 15 miles in a day, Rangeley was just over 11 not-too-difficult miles. The trail was not as flat as the elevation profile suggested, but it was still relaxing hiking on the way to Rangely, when at the Little Swift River Campsite, I met "Lard Ass."

He introduced himself as a Thru-Hiker, "I did the trail in 1983, my name on the trail was Lad Ass."

"Lad Ass?" I replied

No, "Lad Ass."

"Lad Ass?"

No "Laaadddd Ass."

*What the fuck? Is this guy crazy? I know what I'm hearing.*

"Lad Ass?"

"Laaadddd Ass. I lost 75 pounds on the trail."

"Ohh, Lard Ass!"

*Welcome to Maine, Brother Blood!*

He was just months shy of 70, but younger than most 45-year-olds I know. He was wielding a chain saw and cutting down dead trees that posed a danger of falling on a tent or hammock. I had a snack as we chatted and he took a break. From there it was mostly downhill and I made fairly good time, making it to Route 4 by 2:30 p.m.

Route 4 is quite narrow, so the guide suggests walking a third of a mile to the end of a guardrail before getting a hitch. I figured why not stick my thumb out while walking. My effort was rewarded as the driver of the third passing car beeped, and pointed ahead to the pick-up point. After tossing my pack in hatchback and getting in the car, I was treated to some fresh pears and grapes she had just picked.

She had left a high-paying job in the corporate world. The kind of job that made most people believe she was "successful." But Looney Laura explained that even with all the money she was making, she was not successful, because she wasn't happy. She admitted that a simpler life didn't magically turn her life into a state of blissful euphoria, but she was finding more clarity and purpose not equating money with success. She talked about writing about the hikers she has met, and I gladly gave her my email address. I still hope to hear from her someday.

She dropped me off at the Town & Lake Motel, and as I checked in I asked Joey, the owner, if it would be hard to find a ride to the IGA grocery store. "No," he smiled, "just take my truck." I was a bit taken back, and offered to show my driver's license if he had any concerns, but he wasn't interested in seeing my license. He simply told me where he kept the truck, the let him know when I was ready. After a quick shower, I was behind the wheel heading into town. Right away I saw Legs and El Jefe, so I stopped to offer them a ride. It took a second for it to register that it was a fellow Thru-Hiker at the wheel. They jumped in and asked how I managed to get a truck, so I told them, "I started walking to town and saw someone left their keys in their truck, so I jumped in." They believed me for a about 1¼ seconds.

We ran into Butcher and Two Plates at the IGA, and soon I was driving four hikers around Rangeley in Joey's old pick-up. After getting Butcher and Two Plates back the trail, and El Jefe and Legs, back to the laundromat, I headed to the motel to relax for a while. I realized how long I had been on the trail as I sat watching college football highlights. Fall had arrived.

I was falling in love with Maine; the people were nice, and it was beautiful. At the Town & Lake Motel I looked out my window at Rangely Lake, and saw a combination of small boats, and planes. Airplanes! I realize that floating bi-planes are pretty commonplace in Maine. Where I live nobody's taking off or landing planes on water.

There are some places along the A.T. that are unique, and cannot be mistaken for any other location on the trail. And the state of Maine is the most unique. Minnesota has nothing on Maine when it comes to lakes. The A.T. twists and turns around lakes and ponds, and through rivers and streams. The overlooks are breathtaking. Where the southern landscape was dotted with small villages and towns, the views across Maine were forests, and nothing but wilderness.

Not doing 20 miles a day for months, or pushing to finish my journey at an arbitrary date were now paying huge dividends. The leaves were starting to change colors, and I would experience the changing of seasons in Maine. I remembered a line Kyle Rohrig wrote, "last one to Katahdin wins."

It was September 17th, and I felt sorry for those who had already finished their journey.

Perhaps the nicest part of thru-hiking is enjoying whatever junk food I wanted, plus no amount of beer would lead to gaining even one ounce. It was Saturday night and I learned the place to be in Rangeley was Sarge's Pub on Main Street. The sun was starting to set as I walked to the Pub just after 6:00 p.m., another sign fall had arrived. After a steak and cheese sandwich and a few beers, it was Karaoke Night.

For just the second time on my journey, I was in a bar near the trail and was the only Thru-Hiker in the place. Given the price of lodging in town, most hikers opted for The Hiker Hut hostel, or the bunkhouse at the Farmhouse Inn, both a couple miles from town. Sarge's was indeed the place to be in Rangeley. It was Karaoke Night, and not until almost midnight before I had enough liquid encouragement to belt out Engelbert Humperdinck's *"After The Lovin.'"* Before long a class reunion finished up at the Rangeley Inn across the street, and well-dressed revelers joined the jeans and t-shirt crowd. I stayed and closed the place down.

Understandably, I was in no hurry to get moving the next morning. It was 10:00 a.m. before I headed to breakfast at Moosely Bagels, then checked out of the Town & Lake Motel, precisely at check-out time. Walking back through town, I saw Joey from the motel, and thanked him for the use of his truck and giving me some hiker-cred when I shuttled the others. I bought a new fuel canister, and was thinking about sticking out my thumb, when I saw Moose and Sparkles. We were across the street from Sarge's, so I told them I'd join them for a beer.

Several of the people that had also closed down Sarge's the night before were there again today. None of us were moving with the same gusto we had mere hours earlier. I ordered a Bloody Mary and talked trail with Moose and Sparkles. Outside, it looked like rain, so I ordered a beer. I was enjoying talking to Moose and Sparkles again, when I mentioned that despite the older Ridgerunner's warning, Joyride and I did indeed camp above the alpine zone. Sparkles didn't miss a beat as she responded, "Brother Blood, you're a cute old man."

One Bloody Mary, three pints of Sam Adams Octoberfest, a shot of Grand Marnier, and I was ready to head back to the woods, much later than I had planned. It didn't take long to get a ride with a man who spent his summers in Maine, and his winters in Florida. Maine was his home, but his official residence was Florida, "taxes, you know."

The miles came slow, and after less than four miles in three hours, I decided to stop for the night, I'll hike up Saddleback Mountain tomorrow. Along with my resupply, I was carrying a liter of red wine, but after last night, and the drinks over lunch, I needed sleep, not wine. I was just past Eddy Pond when I set up for the evening.

Saddleback Mt. the next day wasn't hard. Fairly smooth, thankfully not a rock scramble to the summit. But right after Saddleback was the Horn. Again, the climb up wasn't all that bad, but coming down reminded me, that before I reached Katahdin, Southern Maine would get its pound of flesh. My journal entry that evening summed it up: "Going down the Horn was hell." On the Horn I bumped my knee on a boulder, which seemed mild enough, at the time that I didn't even blurt out a four-letter word. But while sitting down at lunch, it had started to tighten up.

By now my knees had stopped playing the game they had in the Whites, taking turns each day hurting. Now they both hurt, all the time. Nothing serious, just nagging.

After the Horn I traversed Little Saddleback Mountain, again reduced to hiking one mile per hour. At the bottom of the Saddlebacks, at the base of Lone Mountain, I came upon another of the features that makes Maine unique, fording rivers and streams. For almost 2,000 miles, I had crossed tiny brooks and streams, but most real water crossings were done over footbridges. Not since leaving Damascus had I done anything that would be considered a "ford." And that was nothing, but Maine is different.

The first southbounder I ever met, back on my third section hike in September 2013, told me that in just one day in Maine he forded 14 rivers or streams. The larger fords have a steel cable stretched across to hold on to for balance. But the real challenge is not that a strong current might pull you down river, but that the rocks on the river bottom are slippery as if covered with a fine slime. Again, I kept thinking, one wrong step could end my journey.

For all the grief a dry year caused in Pennsylvania and New Jersey, it was somewhat of a blessing in Maine. In a normal year, the water can come up well over the knees, and in places, to the waist, making the fords a bit more challenging. But with the lack of rain this year, the water was rarely up to my knees. In some cases, rocks that had not been exposed in years could be used to cross the water without getting wet at all. That wasn't my style. After making it to Maine, I was not about to end my journey by breaking an ankle or foot by jumping on to a slippery rock. So, at each crossing I would change into my flip flops, strap my boots to my pack, and slosh through the water. Plus, the cold water always made my feet feel better.

After fording the Orbeton Stream, I hoped to get up half of Lone Mt. before calling it a night. At the halfway point, the trail hits a flat section for about half a mile, where it crosses what the guide listed as a private gravel road. Upon reaching the road, I came across several hikers from a young group with whom I'd been leapfrogging. The young ladies admitted they actually "road walked," skipping the Saddlebacks and the Horn. It was clear the gravel road had not been used for a quite a while, and some hikers were already setting their tents up on it.

Just a few dozen feet away a stream cascaded down a large boulder, where I filled my water bottles and decided to stop at the next good spot I found, which didn't take long. In about a quarter mile, where the trail paralleled a small stream, I looked down and saw a perfect place just across the water. It was easy to cross, and soon I had a fire going and a cup of coffee in my hands. A couple of the male hikers I had seen at the gravel road hiked by and I let them know they were welcome to camp. They declined and hiked on, like I hoped they would.

I spent that night with three wonderful companions: fire, red wine, and solitude. It felt poetic sitting in my hammock drinking what tasted like the greatest red wine ever fermented, while the babbling brook and the woods played nature's symphony. Those three companions, and the woods, had me in a very reflective mood. I was realizing that the journey was going to end soon. Tomorrow was day 177 of my journey, and I would pass the 2,000-mile mark.

I had only had two remaining town stops, Stratton and Monson. As I prepared to leave my wonderful campsite, I wondered if the terrain would allow me to cover the nearly 19 miles to the Stratton trailhead at Maine Route 27. Again, I had to negotiate some one-mile-an-hour topography, and starting down Sugarloaf Mt., I really doubted I'd be in town that night. However, at times the trail taketh, but sometimes it giveth as well. The descent of Sugarloaf got much easier, and soon I was moving along at almost three miles an hour.

Summiting South Crocker Mt. was no joke, but then after the short ascent of North Crocker Mt. it was downhill, and smooth. I sped down the trail and reached Rt. 27 at 7:00 p.m., and before I could stick out a thumb, someone stopped, asking if I needed a ride. I did.

I was headed to the White Wolf Inn, where I had made reservations earlier in the day. It was Wednesday, and the motel was closed, but luckily the owner happened to be there when I called, took my credit card info, told me to go to room 6 where the key would be inside. One problem averted, but another still lay unsolved; the on-site bar was closed on Wednesday as well. My ride, Matthew let me know that was not a problem, since right across the street was the Stratton Plaza Hotel, with a restaurant and full bar. It was where he was headed, so the least I could do was buy him a beer. I went to the Inn and dropped my pack in room 6, grabbed my key, and headed to the bar.

I don't like sitting in bars still stinking from the trail, so after one beer, I went and cleaned up. Once clean, I picked up a six-pack of hard cider for later, then headed back to the bar. But not before stopping next door at the Stratton Motel and Hostel where some of the young hikers were outside drinking beer. Wrong Way was there, with Cheddar, a young lady I had met in Andover. The Stratton Motel was full, but the owner had a couch that Cheddar had booked for ten bucks, but didn't seem that excited about it. Since I had two beds, I told her she was welcome to one of them, and I'd be at the bar if anyone wanted to join me.

Miss Janet showed up at the restaurant with some hikers, while I enjoyed a nice quiet night at the bar. The highlight of the evening came when I ordered a shot of Grand Mariner, and the bartender filled a small rocks glass to the rim. There had to be at least four ounces of luscious French orange cognac in that glass. Soon, Cheddar arrived to take me up on my offer. That night, we sat outside the motel room as she smoked and told of the divorce that led to her thru-hike, in addition to a trail romance that went bad over a thousand miles back. My hard ciders went down like water.

The next morning, I was told that the motel property map in my room was wrong, and the Inn did not have a guest laundry room. I was also informed by the housekeepers, not so subtly, that check out time was 11:00 a.m., and my ass better be out of the room by then. I had spent three of the past seven nights in town, but now I would be back to longer stretches between towns. My next town stop would be Monson, over 70 miles away, at the edge of the famed, 100-Mile Wilderness.

I took my time leaving town: laundry, lunch, and generally being lazy. At the Flagstaff General Store, I drank a Downeast Hard Cider, then packed one 16-ounce can for the trail, before hitching a ride. I felt sluggish when I hit the trail; thankfully the first two miles were flat, or slightly downhill. Following that, it was the Bigelows, starting with South Horn. The first shelter was Horns Pond Lean-to, after a 2,000-foot climb. I decided that would be my stopping point. I enjoyed the can of cider, watched a beautiful sunset, and was in bed early. Days in town seemed tougher on my body than days on the trail.

With just one more town stop, it was really sinking in that the journey was coming to its end. I was torn between wanting and not wanting it to end. But after climbs up South Horn, Bigelow Mt., and Avery Peak, the scales tilted toward looking forward to being done. I was tired of one-mile-an-hour terrain. It was then that the A.T. showed some mercy, and flattened out for the final two and a half miles to East Flagstaff Lake.

The trail meanders around the shores of East Flagstaff Lake. I heard voices and laughter in the distance, and figured it was a group of young locals enjoying some beers. But as I approached, I realized it was fellow Thru-Hikers. Just about every hiker I had been leapfrogging was camped on the shore of the lake. Robin Hood, Legs, Wrong Way, Golden Boy, Two Plates, El Jefe, Jack Rabbit, Cheddar, Keg Legs, Calamity Jane (the same cursing Brit I met in Maryland), and more.

A fire was raging as I set up my hammock and settled in for one of the nicest nights of my entire journey. Cheddar kept busy cooking and sharing her stash of dehydrated mashed potatoes, which seemed endless. The night was filled with laughter and talk about how it didn't seem real that we were within two weeks of Katahdin. The more I got to know these young people the more I liked them. They were caring, supportive, generous, and fun. I was beginning to realize that what they had learned about life in under 30 years, took me almost 50.

As I sat in my hammock, taking it all in, Wrong Way walked over and sat next to me in my hammock to chat. It was impossible not to like Wrong Way. She always had a smile and a kind word for everyone. It didn't matter how hard the miles were, or how hard the rain might be falling, I always felt better when I was around her. She was another who restored my faith in humanity. She is a young Latina, and I remain both sad, and angry that any American would vote for a bigot who thinks this country would better off by deporting her.

They didn't buy into the "hiker midnight" notion, that once the sun sets, it's bedtime. Laughter continued well into the night. We finally went to sleep to a beautiful quiet night by a lake, and as we slept, the winds came.

The morning was chilly, and the calm lake of the previous night was swirling with whitecaps as gusts pounded the tents on the beach. At one point the final stake struggling to keep Two Plates' tent anchored on the beach gave way, and his ultralight tent went tumbling toward the water. Luckily, Golden Boy, who stood at least 6'2" was between the careening tent and the water. He positioned himself like a hockey goalie and averted a wet, soggy disaster for Two Plates.

I was more than 100 miles into Maine, and the trail was getting easier, I had conquered Southern Maine. (*Perhaps conquered is the wrong word.*) Rain was coming, and the only thing that would keep me from a big mile day was the Kennebec River. The official way to cross the Kennebec is not by fording, but taking a canoe ferry provided by the ATC. In 1985, Alice Farange, hiking with her husband George is said to have panicked while fording the Kennebec, and was soon swept under by a strong current, and drowned. Since then the ATC has contracted local outfitters to operate the ferry. Given my feeling toward the ATC, I feared the crossing would be a true shit-show. But all I could do today was get as close to the river as possible to camp, and hope for the best.

### 

Every Thru-Hiker seems to have at least one story about some unexpected encounter that added a twist to the journey. Joyride seemed to have more than anyone on the trail. I, on the other hand, had none, until tonight. While almost every hiker had stopped at the Pierce Pond Lean-to, I hoped to get a little closer to the Kennebec, which was four miles up trail. A side trail near the shelter led to Harrison's Pierce Pond Camps, where the guide listed "bed, shower, and 12-pancake breakfast, $40." Plus, "Okay to get water at camp and dispose of trash." My plan was to at least get water, and dump trash. If available and nice, maybe pony up $40 bucks for a bed.

After negotiating a walkway of wooden pallets, falling down only once, I approached a mountain lodge, where a man was working in the kitchen. I waved and decided to take a look around. Soon I saw a group of non-hikers enjoying a tailgate party in the woods. Among the male revelers stood Cheddar, holding a beer. As I said hi, I was quickly brought in to the group and not just offered, but given a beer. Halfway through the first beer they gave to me another. I was then told, not asked, that I'd be enjoying a "red" hot dog in just a minute. I liked these guys.

Soon another hiker, Fremont, arrived and enjoyed the same treatment. From what I could figure out, the group were friends who work in the excavating, irrigation, and construction trades, and this was their annual weekend trip up from Massachusetts. It seemed like an outing the owners of the companies used to thank their employees, in a very unofficial capacity. This was *not* a company function! They agreed with my describing them as a hunt club, without the guns.

Thankfully, no other hikers showed up, and we blended in with the group without it becoming a hiker bash, or trail magic. And the beers kept coming, as they refused all offers of cash. One of the elder statesmen of the group, Tim, began telling stories, that were a bit off-color, but not at all offensive. I hadn't laughed that hard the entire journey. Beer, hot dogs, and laughter would have been enough to make a great night. But then the leader of the group, came and announced to the group that dinner was ready, and he made arrangements that the hikers were joining them. The guys around seemed happy that we were joining them, but my heart told me it was really because of Cheddar.

It was steak and lobster night! Not steak or lobster, but steak *and* lobster.

The food was cooked using only an antique fire stove, and was amazing. I got a steak, a really good steak, and passed on lobster, unless there would be some left over. There wasn't. We drank and ate and laughed, and headed back to the fire to drink and laugh some more. Surprisingly, Cheddar was told, "I love you," only once that night... that I heard.

I offered the propitiator the $40 bed fee to sleep in my hammock, but he didn't want his place to be one where hikers tented or hammocked. I understood. It was pretty late and I strapped up my pack as the last of the revelers were about to call it a night. I smiled as I walked past the lodge and filled up with the water I had come for hours earlier. I headed out across the pallet obstacle course and back to the trail. I camped about a mile down the trail, and laughed as I drank the beer they gave me, "for the road," or was it two?

Any hopes of getting up early to avoid delays at the river ferry had been gloriously dashed. So I headed to the river bank, expecting the worst, hoping for anything better. There were 10 or 12 hikers already in line, which was fine with me, I had time for a cup of coffee. I cranked up my stove and prepared to wait. But to my surprise, and delight, the ferry operation was fast and smooth. A clipboard was passed around with release waivers, and the round-trip across the river only took a few minutes. It would be a short wait.

I enjoyed my coffee as hikers paired up for their turn across the river. I was happy to be paired up with Jane. On the shore hikers were talking about heading to Caratunk, on the other side of the river, where there was a brewpub, with a hot tub. It was tempting, but I had to make miles, I planned to be in Monson in three days. After all, October 4th is approaching.

Then Keg Legs spoke up. "Brother Blood, this is all going to be over soon; you have to enjoy it while you can." At that moment, I knew I was wrong. I was wrong that these young people had learned as much about life in their 20's as I had at 50; they had learned more. And now, they were teaching me. It was on to the brewpub and hot tub! At Rt. 201, we quickly got a ride in the back of a pick-up to Northern Outdoors.

Everybody was there. The whole group from East Falstaff Lake, plus Moose and Sparkles. I figured I'd sit at the bar and have a few, then hit the trail. Good luck with that. Soon I was showering in the men's locker room, putting on my camp shorts, and jumping in the hot tub. All along my journey, I had been posting pictures of me with a beer, and a shot of Grand Marnier, with a caption, "I hiked x miles for this shot and beer." The picture of me with two plastic cups in the hot tub after 2037.9 miles, was my favorite.

*Figure 28 - Brother Blood and Keg Legs in the hot tub at Caratunk.*

Now when people ask me the moment I remember most from my journey, I simply say, "the hot tub."

As they look bewildered, I explain the closeness and love I felt with the people with whom I was sharing my journey. The laughter, and the struggles, but mostly the laughter. The intense camaraderie I felt with those who had passed through the same 13 states to get to Maine to be sitting with me in this hot tub. I'll never forget the caring and sincerity in her voice when Keg Legs said I should join them that day.

I sometimes wondered if this journey might lead to good things in these young people's careers, but I hope not. I hope this journey isn't reduced to just another resume building rung on a ladder. I hope the journey will always remind them, as it reminds me, that life is about experiences, and joy in the pursuit of happiness. I hope they don't surrender their lives to materialism.

Jack Rabbit, El Jefe, and Two Plates took on the "Exterminator," a burger loaded with a pound of meat, fried chicken, a fried egg, fried pickles, fried mac & cheese, and more, surrounded by a shitload of fries. Eat it all in 30 minutes, it's free; if not, $30. One completed the challenge, but word leaked that the other two helped him to avoid them going zero for three. Even hiker hunger has its limits. As the day went on, and the beer flowed, I realized I'd have to do extra miles tomorrow to make Monson in two days, but I had already hiked over 2,000 miles So doing a few extra shouldn't be that tough.

The Kennebec River's dangerous currents are created when water is released upriver at the Harris Station Dam. The releases are scheduled and people raft down the rapids that are created. By late afternoon, we were joined by the those who had ridden the rapids that day.

One of the hikers had indulged a bit too heartily, and was kindly cut off by the bartender. A little while later he was in trouble for trying to climb up the side of the building, using the chimney. Some hikers were able talk him out of it and put him on a shuttle to Monson, 38 miles north.

It was well past dark when many of the hikers were planning to head out to get more beer and stay at the Sterling Inn down the road for $25 in the bunkroom. I knew that if I stayed in town, I wouldn't get on the trail until after noon, and would really have to push it to make Monson in two days. Luckily, a woman at the bar mentioned she had attended Kent State. I told her of my two nieces attending Kent, and showed my Kent State cap which I had carried from Georgia. Soon I had yogied a ride back to the trail.

It didn't matter that I only hiked a half mile before setting up camp, the goal was to be on the trail somewhat early, to make up the miles I didn't do today. After spending the day drinking beer in the hot tub, I wasn't exactly up with the sun the next day, but I was on the trail early enough for me. Making up miles didn't bother me, and I decided to hike well past dark. At 10:00 p.m. I noticed a small nook to the side of the trail, and after 23+ miles, decided that was home for the night.

Moose scat looks like a pile of large acorns in the summer, and along the trail near my camp there was a fairly fresh pile. My one moose sighting was a few days back, across a pond. As I got a fire going and prepared for late cup of coffee, I heard something sloshing around Marble Brook about 100 yards north on the trail. That night I learned moose are not stealthy creatures. As I sat in my hammock with my coffee, as my dinner was rehydrating, the sloshing got closer, then stopped. The sloshing was replaced with the sounds of hoofs on a trail, getting closer. Not knowing much about moose, I really didn't want one strolling in to my camp, so I put on my headlamp and headed down the trail. I walked about 20 yards, when the sound stopped, and there on the Appalachian Trail was a moose cow. The look on her face seemed to say, "oh well, guess you were here first," and then it slowly turned around on the trail, and back to sloshing through the brook.

I then looked around my campsite. There was moose scat everywhere, especially where my hammock was strung. As I scanned the area with my headlamp, it looked like a game trail coming off the A.T., and the last thing I wanted in the middle of the night, was a startled moose stumbling in to my hammock. I found trees closer to my fire to hang my hammock. If it was indeed a game trail, I wasn't going to block it.

## CHAPTER 23: THE LAST SHOT & BEER

I woke up and thought to myself: *tonight, I'd be sleeping at Shaw's Hiker Hostel!* It dawned on me how far I'd traveled since meeting the owners, Poet and Hippie Chick, back in Damascus at Trail Days in May. It was almost surreal that I would be there today. With Southern Maine behind me, it was a relatively flat, not too difficult hike. Just after 4:30 p.m., I made it to Maine Rt. 15, where Moose and I were lucky to have a day hiker offer us a ride to the hostel. After cleaning up, and walking to get a snack and hard cider, a local alerted me to a moose that was swimming across Lake Hebron. I love Maine!

Shaw's is another iconic landmark along the A.T. Founded in 1977 by Keith Shaw, it quickly became a favorite stop for weary hikers. After their 2013 thru-hike, Poet and Hippie Chick saw the hostel was up for sale, and took on their new role of part trail businesspeople, part trail angels. No one gets rich running a hiker hostel. Despite the long hours, they remained upbeat and were always there to help a hiker, any way they can.

The hiker who had been drunk and attempting to climb up the chimney in Caratunk was still at Shaw's, camped on the lawn. I learned that Poet had been like a big brother and had a good heart-to-heart conversation with him. It seemed to me to be just what the hiker needed. He was feeling good and ready to go on.

It was a quiet night in Monson. Being my final town stop, I would have liked to belly up to a bar one last time before my journey ended, but it was Monday, and the only bar in town, The Lakeshore House, was closed. I settled into a private room at Shaw's, and returned to the gas station/pizza joint/deli for a pizza. After hiking until 10:00 p.m. the previous night, I was beat, and in bed early. Tomorrow, I would enter the 100-mile Wilderness.

I was up early for the famous Shaw's hiker breakfast, and after thoroughly stuffing myself, I walked into Monson for my final resupply of the journey. It was foggy, and chilly, and I was in a somewhat melancholy mood, part from the big breakfast, but mostly because the end was now very near. In less than ten days I would summit, then descend Kathadin, and become a sojourner in society again.

I lollygagged and took my time getting ready to return to the woods. My food bag was heavier than any time of the journey, except possibly leaving Neel Gap, and at 11:00 a.m., with my total pack weight at 44 pounds, Poet gave me a ride back to the trail. My entrance into the Wilderness was briefly delayed when I realized I left my jacket at Shaw's. Fifteen minutes later, Poet and Hippie Chick dropped it off, and I was on my way. Upon entering the woods, a sign read:

THERE ARE NO PLACES TO OBTAIN SUPPLIES OR GET HELP UNTIL ABOL BRIDGE 100 MILES NORTH. DO NOT ATTEMPT THIS SECTION UNLESS YOU HAVE A MINIMUM OF 10 DAYS SUPPLIES AND ARE FULLY EQUIPPED. THIS IS THE LONGEST WILDERNESS SECTION OF THE ENTIRE A.T. AND ITS DIFFICULTY SHOULD NOT BE UNDERESTIMATED.

GOOD HIKING!

M.A.T.C.

I stepped north and entered the home stretch of my voyage.

Despite the dire warning from the MATC (Maine Appalachian trail Club), the 100-mile Wilderness isn't exactly as advertised. It's true there are no resupply stores, but recently, hostels and outfitters have offered to place resupply caches within the Wilderness, for a fee. It was a very popular service, but I wanted to experience the wilderness as it once was, void of resupply.

The trail wasn't as easy as the elevation profile suggested. What appeared as blips in the guide were often steep up and downs. Just enough rocks, roots and small ups and downs to keep me at less than an optimal pace, plus, I was carrying 44 pounds. But I did manage to make it 10 miles to Big Wilson Stream before nightfall, where I caught up with three section hikers who had been at Shaw's, one kindly pulling down the steel cable strung up across the water to assist hikers with their ford, to where I could reach it.

They stopped at the Wilson Valley Lean-to after another mile, I didn't want to put myself in a position where I'd have to really push miles at the end, so I decided to hike on. Just after the shelter, what looked like an easy, small downhill in the guide, was actually a steep boulder climb. It was only 100-150 feet of descent, but again, I was watching every step, inching my way down big rocks at a snail's pace. It was a real pain in the ass, and that night I wrote: *The Wilderness is no joke.*

I was happy that I wouldn't be starting my hike with that rock scramble in the morning. It was past dark when I found a nice quiet place camp near Wilbur Brook, with no people, and no moose. I was savoring my evening coffee even more these days, not taking for granted any of the things I'll miss when I get home.

The first part of the Wilderness continued with steep terrain, especially down Chairback Mountain. I hiked until just past nightfall, which was coming earlier each night. After passing four hikers camped off-trail, I got as close to the West Branch Pleasant River as possible. I would ford it first thing in the morning, not wanting to push my luck fording a waterway in the dark. At an established primitive campsite, I found a perfect spot to sling my hammock, and built a fire, which soon brought light to the yellow "Kindle no fires" sign. As I relaxed, a hiker arrived who would test my resolve to be less judgmental, and more open-minded.

Rifiki, named after the Lion King character, was a veteran of the second Gulf War in Iraq, and like the A.T.'s first ever thru-hiker Earl Shaffer, was out to, "walk the war out of my system." Rifiki was outspoken with a deep, but well-earned, distrust of the government. He battled PTSD, and already survived one bout with cancer that he believed, and I agree, was likely caused by exposure to depleted uranium the U.S. used in the first Gulf War. Any bitterness Rifiki harbored, I understood.

He believed that one of the main goals of our government was disarming the public. And to Rifiki, it didn't matter which candidate or party won the Presidential election, since they were not the ones in charge anyway. For me, there were enough reasons to keep my distance, and do my best not to engage him. But the more I did talk to him, the more I liked him. He wasn't afraid of drinking water on the trail, and rarely filtered it. But he understood where noroviruses were prevalent, so he "never slept in shelters, nor pooped in privies."

He didn't wake up with the sun, and advised hikers that if they didn't feel like getting up, go back to sleep, it's your body telling you it needs more rest. He liked night hiking, and hiking alone. And while he believed he was right in a conversation, he didn't feel the *need* to be right. He could let a subject go without needing the last word. And as I got to know him better over the next few days, I realized he'd help any hiker in need.

Later that night, Bad Penny joined our camp. She also didn't mind night hiking, and was happy we had a warm fire going. I was first to bed, and the next morning, for the first time of my journey, I was the first one out of camp. The four people I had passed camping near the trail last night were at the river getting ready to ford. The water was low enough that they were able to hop from rock to rock and get across without getting wet. As I watched them, my mind raced with visions of hopping onto a wet slippery rock and cascading into the drink with a sprained ankle, or worse. I changed into my flip flops, tied my boots to my pack, and sloshed across the river like a moose in the night.

From there it was gradually uphill until traversing a series of peaks ending with White Cap Mountain. the last mountain on the A.T. until Katahdin. As I neared the summit of White Cap, heading south was Wild Horse and her dog Milo, the same Wild Horse that I shared the bottle of French Burgundy with in Tennessee, before the Smokies. She had come up to do a section hike and see some of the Thru-Hikers she met down south. The trail is a small world. As I began my descent down the north side of the mountain, I saw Foxy, who I hadn't seen since leaving Harpers Ferry. A small world indeed.

Days ago, atop Avery Peak, we were told that a barely visible, far away mountain on the horizon was actually Katahdin. I looked and thought, maybe...maybe not. But as I rounded White Cap Mountain and reached the north slope, there was no mistaking it, I was looking at Katahdin! There it was, a lone, large mountain in a strangely flat area of the Maine wilderness. After six months, the end was in sight.

At the East Branch Lean-to, I gathered wood and had nice blaze going before Rifiki, and then Bad Penny, showed up, in the dark. The chilly nights of Maine had now turned downright cold. It had been a sixteen-mile day, and the trail was flattening out for the home stretch. I laid warm in my hammock and fell to sleep to the now familiar sound of a moose sloshing through a nearby stream.

With the exception of 400-foot Boardman Mountain, the trail was pretty flat, and I didn't mind it one bit. I was enjoying the change of colors in Maine, happy to have the strenuousness of the southern part of the state behind me. The main obstacle hiking this section was the roots. They protruded from the ground in all directions. At times I hiked on roots, without touching the trail at all. On one such stretch my foot caught a root and tripped me up. I heard my hiking stick crack as I was falling. I had carried this walking stick from just north of Pearisburg, VA, and had grown quite attached to it. We'd been through a lot together. I laid on the trail for a minute or two, realized I wasn't hurt, and got up to retrieve the stick. It was split, but still felt strong enough to continue the journey.

It was day 187 and I did another sixteen-mile day, but it was easy. I took pictures, video, and several coffee breaks. I knew I was on pace to make Katahdin on October 4th, so I was in no hurry. I made it to the Antlers primitive campsite well before dark. The campsite sat on Jo-Mary Lake, which even by Maine standards was not a small lake. Rifiki was already there with a fire going. About a hundred yards from the fire pit, a small peninsula jetted out where I found two trees to sling my hammock. I enjoyed my evening coffee with the lake on both sides. That night also confirmed what I had been sensing as I moved north, that the tougher the elements became, the tougher became the mice. I shared the site that night with a true ninja mouse who, even after I had hung my "mouse bag" on a nail on a tree, forced me to get up and hang it between two trees with a cord to keep the rodent away. Maine mice seemed a different, tougher breed.

I wanted to wake up before dawn, and somehow did, in time take a time-lapse video of the sunrise. It was a little cloudy, not the greatest morning to video the rising sun, but I was happy with the effort. And since I was already awake, why not get started early? It would be the last long hiking day of the journey, 23 miles. I was on the trail by 8:00 a.m.

Before the journey, I told friends that I would probably hike the whole A.T. in five to five and half months and would likely finish in mid-September. Today was October 1st.

This was the last night I would spend in the woods. I'd arrive at the Abol Bridge Campground tomorrow night, the next at the Birches campground in Baxter State Park. I made up my mind that tonight, I would stealth camp, alone. My last night of true solitude on the journey. Throughout the journey it was always the same, places to set up camp were easy to find in the daylight, but after dark, searching by headlamp for a spot was never easy. And tonight was no exception.

I stepped off-trail several times where it looked ideal to camp, just to be disappointed and continue heading north. It was almost 10:00 p.m. when I detoured up what looked to be a game trail to a nice secluded spot for the night. One thing was for sure, I was going to break Maine law one last time and build a fire. I understand why forest rangers discourage fires. For every person like me, who makes sure their fire is completely extinguished of all coals before leaving, there's always an idiot who leaves behind glowing embers. And it only takes one idiot to start a forest fire. And Maine's peat moss-like soil needs extra precautions.

With late night coffee in hand, I sat in my hammock and savored the peacefulness of the forest. My time living in the woods would be over in three days. I wasn't sad, nor reflective, I just sat and enjoyed how comfortable I had become in the woods, sleeping all alone. It's not that I was ever uncomfortable, but bumps in the night, which once had me reach for my headlamp to look for the cause, were now just peaceful reminders of the joy of being in nature. That night, for the final time of my journey, I slept all alone in the wilderness.

Katahdin was no longer a mountain in the distance. It loomed large, and got larger with each sighting. I marveled at how the forested green base turned to a rocky grey summit. And one thing was becoming clear, the climb up would be steep. Some say it is the hardest climb of the whole hike, but I never heard of anyone making it 2,188 miles just to turn away before the summit. It wasn't quite sinking in that just the day after tomorrow I would be standing atop the majestic mountain as a successful Thru-Hiker. What was sinking in was that I would like a cold beer when I get to Abol Bridge.

*Figure 29 – Kahtadin*

The AT Guide rarely fails to mention whether or not a camp store sells beer. The guide did list a restaurant with a full bar that was open from June 1st to September 30th. I was two days late. "Breakfast sandwiches & subs, sodas, ice cream, long-term resupply," was all that was listed for the camp store. The trail was flat and easy as I hiked, trying not to get my hopes up for a beer. I crossed Abol Bridge just after 4:00 p.m., with an incredible view of Katahdin, now just 10 miles away. I walked into the camp store, and in the cooler was a large selection of sodas - and beer!

I bought pasta, a bottle of Alfredo sauce, some trail food, a 6-pack of Long Trail Ale, and a bottle of Chardonnay. The store was sold out of firewood, but the clerk said I would have no trouble finding enough wood to burn. He was right. I booked a cabin with four bunks with cheap mattresses, and a battery-operated light. If Rifiki and Bad Penny showed up late, they could grab a bunk. I drank the beer, collected firewood, and as night fell, prepared my pasta, and opened the wine, I enjoyed dinner by the fire, with the Alfredo sauce from the bottle tasting as bad as I had feared.

After dinner Miss Janet pulled up to say hi and joined me by the fire for a few minutes, getting me updated on all the trail gossip, as well as asking about a few hikers she hadn't seen for a while. Rifiki and Bad Penny didn't hike in after dark, so I had the cabin to myself. I fell asleep thinking that maybe finishing the whole bottle of wine was a bit much. When I woke up the next morning, that was confirmed. A bit hungover, I was in no hurry to get on the trail for the 10 miles to the base of Katahdin.

The camp store had coffee, and a group of hunters were filling their mugs as I thought about packing up. Soon Rifiki came hiking across the bridge and he and a couple others bought some beer. They got started on the path that would have them feeling like I felt now - tomorrow morning. The campground had a magnificent view of Katahdin, so while sipping my second cup of coffee, I strolled over for one more look before packing up.

I'd heard a lot about Baxter State Park over the past year. Fear of overcrowding due to the increase in Thru-Hikers, combined with breaking rules like having alcohol on Katahdin and summiting in large groups had officials publicly threatening to move the Northern Terminus of the A.T. away from Katahdin. The controversy peaked when officials seemed to have led ultra-runner Scott Jurek into believing it would be okay to take champagne and a large group to the summit as he finished traversing the A.T. in record time, only to publicly issue a summons of his violations when he came down.

I can't say for certain that the Baxter Park Rangers set Jurek up for their own public relations, or he felt privileged. But if they did, it was brilliant. The citations were covered by every paper or magazine that hikers read, and swept through the hiker community on social media like wildfire. And it seemed to have worked. After the flurry of press regarding hiker behavior in 2015, there were little if any problems in 2016. I didn't talk to a single Thru-Hiker who was planning a celebration with alcohol atop Katahdin.

As much as I enjoy my beer, wine, and Grand Mariner, I also know that it has its time and place. And the summit of Katahdin is not the place. For one, it's a tough descent and could be downright dangerous, or even deadly with a buzz. Plus, the last things I wanted to see at the summit were broken champagne or beer bottles, and as long as people drag alcohol up there, some will leave the litter of cans and bottles. And finally, not every place or circumstances improves with the addition of alcohol. In 50 years of life I have never heard:

*"Things began to settle down after people drank more liquor;" or*

*"Things were better at home once Dad started drinking again."*

Between the press, the flyers posted at every shelter about the rules of the park, and word that you needed to register and get a permit at the park, I feared that the rangers at Baxter State Park were operating it as a police state. I was expecting the entrance to the park to resemble passing through TSA security to board a plane. This could be worse than the Smokies.

But I was not greeted by a ranger, nor was there an application for a permit, just a simple kiosk with a register to sign in. Hiking through the park was no different than any other part of Maine, so far. Perhaps the Rangers were just waiting for me at the campground. But when I got there, the ranger station was empty; word was they were on the mountain for a search and rescue. A small sign said they would come to the camp site later to collect the $10 camping fee.

The Birches Lean-to, for Thru-Hikers only, was up the road from the ranger station and away the campground, almost like they were trying to keep us away from other campers. For the last time of the journey I set up my hammock. For the last time, I had my evening coffee and dinner. And for the last time, I climbed into my sleeping bag.

Then, for the first time during my journey, I set my alarm to wake up early.

I knew the climb up Katahdin was one of the toughest of the entire A.T. and didn't want to be coming down in the dark. My alarm was set for 4:30 a.m., yet before it sounded I was getting restless. It was just after 4:00 a.m., when I woke and checked the time, and though I put my head back down, this time, I didn't fall asleep. I laid awake until the alarm sounded, then prepared coffee, and packed up for the final time of my journey.

The rangers did not show up to collect the $10 camping fee, so I succeeded in never paying to sleep in a primitive site along the trail. In the dark I walked down to the empty ranger station and stashed everything except what I needed for the day, plus two extra shirts my wife had included in my resupply sent to Monson, for pictures at the famous Katahdin sign: my REI "Team Fairfax" employee t-shirt, and a replica of a bowling shirt worn in "The Big Lebowski." After 2183.9 miles with a full-pack, this purist was slack-packing the final 5.2 miles.

It was day 191 and I headed out in the dark with my headlamp lighting the way to start the final day of my journey. The base of the big mountain is a smooth, gradual, uphill hike through the woods, paralleling Katahdin Stream. I could hear Katahdin Stream Falls, which is where the trail turns steep. It became steep with rocks, and finally steep with boulder climbing. This was it, the final climb. The final couple of miles to the wooden sign with the magical words *Northern Terminus of the Appalachian Trail.*

The trees got smaller as I approached the treeline. The climbing was tough, but the beauty of both the mountain and the Maine wilderness were awesome. Unlike most mountains on the A.T., Katahdin is not part of a series of mountains, nor does it overlook farms and towns. Just wilderness as far as the eyes can see. The day was at times misty, at times sunny, and after passing "The Gateway," where the tough climbing comes to an end, clouds hovered and passed beneath me. At this point the rocky landscape looked like an alien planet from the B movies of the 1970's.

My last stop before the summit would be to drink from the Thoreau Spring. To dip my cup into the same water source as Henry did in 1846. But unfortunately, the spring was dry. I sat down for the last break of my journey, just one mile from the finish. The last mile was uphill, but not difficult hiking, and it wasn't long before I first saw the wooden sign; the end was in sight.

At 11:34 a.m., October 4, 2016, I walked the final steps to the Northern Terminus of the Appalachian Trail. I wasn't sure how I would react to actually completing my journey. Would I be overwhelmed with emotion, and for the first time of the hike actually cry? Would I be filled with adrenaline and shout with joy that I had done it! The answer was neither. I reached the sign and placed one hand on it and raised my split hiking stick above me with the other, and just stood there. I knew what I had accomplished wouldn't sink in for a while, and I was tired.

I had my picture taken at the sign, with both shirts I had carried up, and chatted with day hikers who had come to the summit on other trails. I was certainly happy, and definitely thinking about what I had accomplished, but at that moment I was also thinking, *"Damn, now I gotta hike DOWN this mountain."*

I passed some Thru-Hikers on my descent and we shared congratulations. I traversed the boulders and rocks and again heard the sounds of the Katahdin Stream Falls, and upon seeing the falls to my right, the trail smoothed out. Within a couple hundred yards of the campground, my wife met me on the trail. I loaded up my gear form the ranger station, chatted with some hikers, then left the Appalachian Trail.

Now was the time for a celebratory drink, and in the town of Millinocket at a small tavern on the town's main drag, with me and my wife the only patrons in the place, I posted a picture of me holding a beer and a shot of Grand Marnier, with the simple caption:

*For this shot and beer, I hiked every inch, every foot, every yard, every mile of the Appalachian Trail, 2189.1 miles*

*Figure 30 - Atop Katahdin*

# EPILOUGUE

April 2018

I had a pretty damn good year as a 50-year old. In addition to hiking the A.T., just two days before turning 51, I bowled my first perfect 300 game; wearing the same Big Lebowski shirt that I wore on Katahdin.

On the journey I took 15 zero days, and filtered water 13 times.

It's been two years since I took the first steps of my journey, and not a day goes by that I don't think about the trail and wonderful people I met.

Pebbles hit her stride and passed me somewhere in Virginia, and summited Katahdin almost a month ahead of me on September 8th. After her hike, she accelerated her studies to graduate high school early. I believe by the time she is 30 she will have taken over the world.

On our drive home, my wife and I stopped for a night at Northern Outdoors in Caratunk. And in the same hot tub that I had enjoyed just days before, there was Taylor. She made it! Her summit date was October 19th.

The twenty-somethings I had grown so fond of summited Katahdin one day after me.

Frisbee and Stubbs, did start again at Springer in 2017, and completed well over 3,000 miles of the A.T. in two years, and now have pictures of themselves together at Springer, Harpers Ferry, and Katahdin.

And Cautious remains the same wonderful, and loving person we all grew so fond of.

In early April 2018 I took my wife to Franklin, NC to share with her some of the places that I loved early in my journey. At our first stop, as we walked in to the Lazy Hiker Brewing Co. I was greeted with a massive bear hug that lifted me off the ground; my wife had just met Wok Man. Wok Man hadn't changed a bit, and as you read this Wok Man, please don't ever change!

Strider was in Franklin as well, and hiked the PCT in 2017, and was hiking the A.T. again in 2018.

Kim was still bartending at the Lazy Hiker and was even more wonderful than I remembered. Robbie is still the manager at the Root & Barrel and treated me and my wife with same warmth and generosity as he did me on my journey.

I've run into Miss Janet a couple times since my hike, and we are planning to do some trail magic together this summer...with beer.

Mrs. Moulder now teaches second grade, and I had the chance to speak to many of the students at her school. I even received a wonderful note from one of her second graders.

I am often asked if I'm planning another long hiking journey, and at this point, I just can't see myself leaving for another 6 months. I still hike sections with the Lawyers, and even convinced my brother and a niece to do an overnight hike with me in Shenandoah. I think a hike of a month or so might be possible, maybe the John Muir Trail in California.

The weight came back pretty quick since we have a machine at our house that keeps beer cold for anytime I wanted one.

And although she's not a backpacker, my wife has enjoyed helping hikers whenever we have the chance, and the more trail people she meets, the more she wants to do more for the trail community.

A Thru-Hiker leaves the trail, but the trail never leaves us.

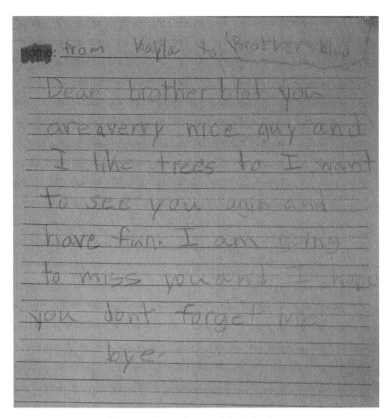

Figure 31 - Letter from 2nd Grade Student

# Endnotes

[i] Jennifer Pharr Davis, Becoming Odyssa, (Beaufort Books, 2010) Kindle Edition, Location 2349

[ii] University of Calgary, Beware of predatory male American black bears: Attack rates are rising with human population growth. ScienceDaily www.sciencedaily.com/releases/2011/05/110511074807.htm May, 11, 2011.

[iii] Lisa Provence 2/25/2015 http://www.c-ville.com/ruins-afton-mountain-eyesores-along-scenic-byway/

[iv] Patrick Doyle, "Meet Trail Life USA, Conservatism's Answer to the Boy Scouts," *Backpacker Magazine*, July 28, 2016

[v] https://cindyrosstraveler.com/2016/10/28/poor-mans-country-club-frank-russo-the-port-clinton-barber-shows-us-how-to-live/

[vi] Ethan & Joel Coen, *The Big Lebowski*, Polygram Filmed Entertainment, 1998

[vii] Georigie Pauff, The Morning Call, Allentown, PA, September 02, 1999 http://articles.mcall.com/1999-09-02/news/3261300_1_lehigh-river-coal-new-ballgame